READ THE REVIEWS

"Oh, how I wish I had the resources in this book when I struck out to form my own company. This book is a treasure. But don't think you need to have your own consultancy to gain insights from this valuable work; many chapters are beneficial even when one is working inside an organization, especially at the senior levels. Whether you are an independent business analyst, project manager, or other type of IT consultant, Karl's book is for you."

—Kathleen B. (Kitty) Hass,
Co-founder of Business Analysis Leadership Consortium,
Principal Consultant, Kathleen Hass and Associates

"I've looked to Karl Wiegers for business guidance for many years and I'm thrilled to see him share these ideas in this interesting, practical, and to-the-point book. I'm not an independent consultant, but this book's breadth of topics reaches well beyond that audience. Whether you are a consultant, business owner, aspiring leader inside a professional services organization, or budding author, you will find value here."

—Joy Beatty, CBAP, PMI-PBA,
Vice President of R&D at Seilevel

i

"*Successful Business Analysis Consulting* provides fantastic practical guidance and insights. Although I have been consulting for many years, I found it loaded with relevant advice that helped validate my own practices. This book truly is the next best thing short of calling up Karl Wiegers personally for career advice as a consultant. You will find this book highly valuable, whether you are a seasoned consultant or just starting to think about taking the plunge into running your own consulting practice."

—**Laura Paton**, CBAP, PMP, PMI-PBA,
Founder of BA Academy, Inc.

"*Successful Business Analysis Consulting* is full of powerful advice. Even now, 20 years after first going independent, I learned a few things from this valuable resource. If you are a newly independent consultant or are contemplating it, this book has the advice you need to succeed."

—**Mike Cohn**, CST,
Co-founder of the Scrum Alliance and the Agile Alliance,
Owner, Mountain Goat Software

"Simply put, this is the book I wish I'd had available to me when I started consulting. It provides valuable advice on pretty well everything that touches on the consultant's life. It almost seems unfair: Karl Wiegers lets the reader in on the secrets that took the rest of us a lot of pain to learn. It took me years to figure out how to leverage my work through passive income; Karl devotes a large section to it. If you're starting out on your own, you couldn't do yourself a better favor than reading this book."

—**Howard Podeswa**,
Author of *The Business Analyst's Handbook*,
Chief Executive Officer, Noble Inc.

"I have been in the IT business for over 50 years now, spending the last 20 or so as an independent consultant. The mark of a successful self-help book is that it prompts the readers to immediately help themselves. I have put a number of the author's suggestions into practice, some as soon as I read them in the book. *Successful Business Analysis Consulting* proves that there is always a lot more to be learned."

—Steve Blais,
Author of *Business Analysis: Best Practices for Success,*
Solutions Architect, Parkson International

"There are two things that make this book stand out from all the other consulting books I've read. First, it easily covers the broadest landscape of issues that you may encounter as a BA consultant with practical, down-to-earth advice to navigate these issues. And second, the action-provoking *Next Steps* at the end of each chapter compel you to behave differently based on that sage advice. Even after consulting for 15 years, I picked up a handful of valuable tips, and I have already applied a few!"

—Jim Brosseau,
Principal at Clarrus Consulting Group

"*Successful Business Analysis Consulting* is a singularly lucid and entertaining guide to the full life cycle of working as an indie consultant. No one considering leaving the dark side of corporate employment should make the jump until they have read this book—twice. It will save you unimaginable grief."

—Gary K. Evans,
Agile Coach, Trainer, and Use Case Expert,
Founder & Principal, Evanetics, Inc.

"This book provides a wide range of advice on topics that will help make you a successful speaker, advisor, and consultant. It also captures a collection of lessons learned from the author's years of experience that you won't have to learn the hard way. I found two techniques described here to be especially helpful to me: the use of checklists, a simple but very effective way to avoid mistakes; and the collection of business rules or policies."

—Dr. Joyce Statz, Principal Business Analysis
and Process Improvement Consultant,
Statz Consulting

Successful Business Analysis Consulting

Strategies and Tips for Going It Alone

Karl Wiegers, PhD

J.ROSS

PUBLISHING

Copyright © 2019 by Karl Wiegers

ISBN-13: 978-1-60427-168-3

Printed and bound in the U.S.A. Printed on acid-free paper.

10 9 8 7 6 5 4 3 2 1

Library of Congress Cataloging-in-Publication Data
Names: Wiegers, Karl Eugene, 1953– author.
Title: Successful business analysis consulting : strategies and tips for
  going it alone / By Karl Wiegers.
Description: Plantation, FL : J. Ross Publishing, [2019] | Includes index.
Identifiers: LCCN 2019010605 (print) | LCCN 2019013328 (ebook) | ISBN
  9781604278118 (e-book) | ISBN 9781604271683 (pbk. : alk. paper)
Subjects: LCSH: Business analysts. | Business consultants.
Classification: LCC HD69.C6 (ebook) | LCC HD69.C6 W535 2019 (print) | DDC
  001--dc23
LC record available at https://lccn.loc.gov/2019010605

Phone: (954) 727-9333
Fax: (561) 892-0700
Web: www.jrosspub.com

For Chris, who ate countless dinners alone
during all those years when I was a road warrior.

CONTENTS

FOREWORD

One thing I've learned from creating my own training business and helping talented mid-career professionals launch business analysis careers is that there is always more to be, to do, and to have. It is a natural human state to want more from life, to want more from our careers, and to seek an expansion of our work and contributions.

For many of us, this path to more achievement leads us to working on our own, starting a business, and truly making our mark on the world by creating the organization we most want to work in from the ground up. And one way to do this is through consulting.

Consultants can enjoy more freedom, higher salaries, and a bigger impact than those who work within a larger organization. They also get to expand their knowledge by learning from several different companies, not merely one source. Consultants often even have the opportunity to travel the world—and to get paid for it! But they can also end up sacrificing what matters most if they build a practice that doesn't serve them.

When I started down the path to consulting back in 2008, I held a big limiting belief—that to be successful as a consultant, I had to sacrifice my schedule, my personal time, and even where and when I showed up to work. So I pivoted before I even really got started, and instead I went down the path of creating a more flexible, freedom-based online training company. While the success of this company has exceeded my wildest dreams, this pivot was based on a false belief and a lack of knowledge.

If I'd had *Successful Business Analysis Consulting: Strategies and Tips for Going It Alone* then, I might have learned how to build a consulting practice around my talents and strengths, and how to set healthy boundaries with clients. It would have saved me a lot of time and headache in building my online training business too.

Luckily for you, you have this book. You get to peer inside the mind of a successful business analyst consultant in Karl Wiegers as he walks you through the key decisions he made to start and grow his business. Read it. Learn from it. Apply it.

Karl outlines exactly what you need to do—and what decisions you need to make—to create a thriving consulting practice. He shows you the insider keys to his success, from how to draw in your first client, to the nuts and bolts of running a practice, to handling challenging clients, pricing your services, and even the more advanced ways of marketing yourself and your consulting.

Getting a peek inside successful consulting like this reveals a true gold mine. Enjoy!

Laura Brandenburg, CBAP
Founder and Creator, Bridging the Gap
www.bridging-the-gap.com

ACKNOWLEDGMENTS

Consulting by its nature often is a solitary activity. Unless you're working in an actual consulting company, you rarely have a chance to learn by observing other consultants as they perform their daily work. I'm grateful to the many other consultants who have shared their wisdom with me over the years through discussions or observation. Some of these were people we brought in to help when I worked at Kodak, highly experienced consultants and trainers like Dr. John Alden and Dr. Joyce Statz. Others from whom I learned much were professional peers too numerous to mention. Insights from Larry Constantine, Norm Kerth, and Steve McConnell were especially helpful. If you know me, and if you and I have had such conversations, I thank you!

I'm grateful to the other consultants who generously contributed original chapters to share their wisdom: Adriana Beal, Claudia Dencker, Gary K. Evans, Vicki James, Margaret Meloni, and Jeanette Pigeon. I received many helpful comments from Joy Beatty, Tanya Charbury, Joan Davis, Barbara Hanscome, Richard Hatheway, Linda Lewis, Dr. Scott Meyers, Laura Paton, Betsy Stockdale, Megan Stowe, Stefan Sturm, and especially Gary K. Evans. Joy Beatty also made valuable contributions to the description of professional certifications for business analysts and project managers. Thanks also to Mike Cohn for sharing several of his checklists.

Thanks to Drew Gierman, Vice President of Sales and Publisher, for his insights and guidance, as well as to Steve Buda and the J. Ross Publishing production staff.

A very special, heartfelt thank you goes out to my exceptionally patient wife, Chris. Like the partner of any consultant, she ate a lot of meals by herself and spent hundreds of quiet evenings alone in the house while I was who-knows-where, teaching who-knows-what class. I sent her a postcard from each destination. It always said the same thing: "Having a wonderful time in <wherever>. Weather is great, sunny and 80s every day. I spend most of my time at the beach. Wish you were here!" The first card came from Peoria, Illinois, one January. It wasn't sunny and 80s. Chris has quite a collection of postcards now. Without her love, encouragement, and patient support for my crackpot schemes, none of the events that led to this book would have been possible. Thanks a million, hon!

ABOUT THE AUTHOR

Since 1997, Karl Wiegers has been Principal Consultant with Process Impact, a software development consulting and training company in Happy Valley, Oregon. Previously, he spent eighteen years at Eastman Kodak Company, where he held positions as a photographic research scientist, software developer, software manager, and software process and quality improvement leader. Karl received a PhD in organic chemistry from the University of Illinois.

Karl is the author of the books *Software Requirements, More About Software Requirements, Practical Project Initiation, Peer Reviews in Software*, and *Creating a Software Engineering Culture*. He has written some 200 articles on many aspects of software development and management, chemistry, and military history. Karl also is the author of a forensic mystery novel, *The Reconstruction*, and a memoir of life lessons titled *Pearls from Sand: How Small Encounters Lead to Powerful Lessons*. He has served on the Editorial Board for *IEEE Software* magazine and as a contributing editor for *Software Development* magazine.

Several of Karl's publications have won awards, including *Software Development* magazine's Productivity Award (*Creating a Software Engineering Culture* and *Software Requirements, 1st Edition*) and the Society for Technical Communication's Award of Excellence (*Software Requirements, 3rd Edition*).

You can reach Karl through www.processimpact.com or www.karlwiegers .com, provided he isn't playing one of his guitars, out delivering Meals on Wheels, or volunteering at the library.

CONTRIBUTING AUTHOR BIOGRAPHIES

ADRIANA BEAL

Born and raised in Brazil, Adriana Beal (www.adrianabeal.com) has been working in the United States since 2004, helping Fortune 100 companies, innovation companies, and startups build better software that solves the right problem and aligns with business strategy. She has two IT strategy books published in her native country and work published internationally by IEEE and IGI Global. Her educational background includes a B.Sc. in electronic engineering, an MBA in strategic management of information systems, and a specialization in Big Data Analytics.

JOY BEATTY

Joy Beatty is a Vice President at Seilevel, www.seilevel.com. She has provided software requirements training to thousands and is PMI-PBA and CBAP certified. Joy is a contributing author to *The PMI Guide to Business Analysis*. She was part of the core team that developed version 3 of the IIBA's Business Analysis Body of Knowledge, as well as PMI's *Business Analysis for Practitioners: A Practice Guide*. Joy co-authored *Visual Models for Software Requirements* with Anthony Chen and *Software Requirements, 3rd Edition* with Karl Wiegers.

CLAUDIA DENCKER

Claudia Dencker is a software business executive with over 35 years of team, project, and business management experience in the IT/software service sector. Most recently, she was employed at Stanford University as Director of Special Projects, Business Analysis, and Communications. She is a long-standing member of ASQ and IEEE.

GARY K. EVANS

Gary K. Evans is an independent agile consultant. He has spent two decades helping Fortune 500 companies incorporate agile methods and object-oriented techniques. He is a Certified Scrum Master, an Agile Coach, and a SAFe 4 Program Consultant.

VICKI JAMES

Vicki James is a certified Project Management Professional (PMP), a Certified Business Analysis Professional (CBAP), a certified PMI Professional in Business Analysis (PMI-PBA), and a Certified Scrum Master (CSM). Vicki has consulted with several Seattle-area companies. Most recently, she has found her ideal match as a permanent employee of Capital One and looks forward to a long career at the company.

MARGARET MELONI

Margaret Meloni, MBA, PMP, is the community leader at pmStudent.com, a website devoted to helping you successfully navigate the art and science of project management. Her background in IT project management and PMO leadership enables Margaret to understand the challenges you face in managing projects. A recipient of the UCLA Extension Distinguished Instructors award, her wish is to see her students take on tough projects and emerge as strong and sought-after project managers.

JEANETTE PIGEON

Jeanette Pigeon, President and CEO at aBetterBA IT Solutions, Inc., is a Certified Business Analyst Professional who has worked in government, health care, higher education, and marketing industries and is a business analyst leadership subject matter expert. She can be contacted at abetterba@gmail.com.

 Web
Added
Value™

This book has free material available for download from the
Web Added Value™ resource center at *www.jrosspub.com*

At J. Ross Publishing we are committed to providing today's professional with practical, hands-on tools that enhance the learning experience and give readers an opportunity to apply what they have learned. That is why we offer free ancillary materials available for download on this book and all participating Web Added Value™ publications. These online resources may include interactive versions of the material that appears in the book or supplemental templates, worksheets, models, plans, case studies, proposals, spreadsheets and assessment tools, among other things. Whenever you see the WAV™ symbol in any of our publications, it means bonus materials accompany the book and are available from the Web Added Value Download Resource Center at www.jrosspub.com.

Downloads for *Successful Business Analysis Consulting: Strategies and Tips for Going It Alone* consist of:

- Editable templates for writing consulting, speaking, and licensing agreements
- Sample book proposals and outlines
- An Excel spreadsheet for tracking the status of a book you're writing
- Numerous checklists and forms for helping to plan and manage consulting engagements

Part I

Setting Up Shop

1

THE JOURNEY FROM PRACTITIONER TO CONSULTANT

Practitioners in the fields of business analysis and project management follow a common career path. You begin, of course, as an entry-level novice. As you gradually accumulate knowledge and skills through both work experience and professional development activities, you move to an experienced intermediate, or journeyman, level of proficiency. Ultimately, you might become an advanced, expert-level business analyst (BA) or project manager (PM).

Senior BAs are recognized by their colleagues as experts in numerous analysis techniques. Their peers look to them for advice and assistance. Advanced BAs often are selected by management to spearhead changes in processes or methodologies on the organization's projects. It's an important—and valued—position to achieve.

But then what? To where do you steer your career from being a respected internal expert? Some people take their unique skill sets, organizational knowledge, business acumen, and technical knowledge and become successful business analysis consultants, trainers, and entrepreneurs. The path to consultant is paved with expertise in business analysis, product management, project management, process improvement, leadership, software development, and other areas of information technology (IT). Whether working as an employee of an established consulting firm in this industry or going it alone in a company of one, consulting offers the highly talented BA a fulfilling—and challenging—career opportunity.

WHY THIS BOOK?

There are many books on consulting written by business people who successfully climbed the corporate ladder to a senior management level and were among the fortunate few to achieve success in consulting. However, I noticed a significant void in the current consulting literature geared toward practitioners in technical fields, most noticeably in business analysis and project management. You don't need to become a corporate executive before launching a career as an IT consultant. But you do need deep knowledge, broad experience, good observational abilities, and excellent communication skills.

I have been self-employed full-time as a software consultant since early 1998. Without necessarily planning to, I wound up specializing in software requirements and business analysis, project management, software quality, and process improvement. I began doing this sort of work even before going independent, while I was still working for a large corporation. This let me wade into the pool instead of diving straight into the deep end.

I wrote this book to share the many insights I have accumulated over the years, sometimes through the painful experience of making mistakes. This is the kind of book I wish was available before I decided to give consulting a try. Several other seasoned consultants with IT backgrounds also contributed chapters to this book to share their own experiences and perspectives. The information we present will reduce both your learning curve and the fear factor when you decide to test the waters as an independent consultant.

The examples and stories in this book come from my personal experience and those of my contributing authors working in the worlds of both traditional and agile business analysis, project management, and software development. The strategies and tips provided apply both to the practicing consultant and to those planning to make the transition to independent consultant in nearly any field. Even if independent consulting isn't in your immediate future, you'll discover many useful suggestions here about giving presentations, writing for publication, and working with others.

CONSULTING IN THE IT INDUSTRY

The IT industry has an abundance of consultants who perform many types of work. Some become well known in their domain, publish popular books, become featured speakers at conferences worldwide, and earn impressive incomes. Others find that they just don't get enough business to stay afloat and have to go back to regular employment. Many independent consultants relish the diversity of the work, with its many opportunities to collect and leverage insights from their clients and to influence both practitioners in their field and the field in general. Others discover that the travel is grueling, frequent absences are hard on family life, and having an unpredictable income is unsettling. Consulting is not for everyone, but it can be a fun, rewarding, and lucrative career for those who learn how to make it work for them.

Perhaps you've heard this rather disparaging saying: "Those who can, do; those who can't, teach." I extend this by adding, "Those who did, consult." The effective consultant has a breadth and depth of experience in his or her field, the skill to assess a situation quickly and diagnose the root causes of problems, and the ability to convey new ways of working to clients so they achieve better business outcomes. Consultants must be adaptable, able to choose the right techniques from their tool kits to suit each client's needs and culture. By working with diverse clients, effective consultants soon recognize patterns of common problems and solutions that span organizations and business domains.

Having a wide range of project experience helps prepare you for a consulting career. But there's more to it than that—simply being very good at what you do doesn't necessarily make you a great consultant. You must be familiar with a rich suite of techniques in your field, so you can help people tackle many different kinds of problems effectively. You need to keep up with the literature in your domain, so you know about important topics and trends and can advise organizations based on the best available wisdom.

An effective consultant can distinguish practical techniques that we know are effective from the latest buzzword-laden fad. As a skilled observer, a good consultant notices what works and what doesn't work in various situations and synthesizes that knowledge into practical solutions. On top of all this, a consultant must be a credible and talented communicator who can pass along frank observations about an organization's shortcomings and gently persuade clients to try new methods.

People in IT use the term *consultant* in various ways. I have a friend who is a true software development consultant. He's one of the world's leading experts in a particular programming language. He doesn't build software for clients, but he is highly respected as an authority who can come into an organization and convey deep insights that help developers solve leading-edge problems in that language. On the other hand, many software development *consultants* are really independent contractors who are self-employed and find their own jobs writing code for one client after another.

Some BAs also work as independent contractors, coming into an organization for a period of time and performing BA services on development projects, either on their own or as part of a BA team. Business analysis naturally lends itself to this form of consulting since the team role is not necessarily full-time throughout the entire duration of the project and BAs are accustomed to moving from project to project. True expert consultants, though, might lead and coach a team of BAs. They could deliver training, or they may assess and then advise organizations about how to tune up their current BA practices and address performance shortcomings. Consultants will sometimes help develop and instill new techniques into organizations and steer them to a more sophisticated business analysis culture.

Similarly, project management consultants can either work on contract, leading one project after another, or they can train and coach the organization's own PMs to enhance their effectiveness. Some PM consultants specialize in project recovery—coming in to get a struggling project back on track.

Still other kinds of IT consultants focus on process improvement or change leadership, helping organizations evolve. Or, they might specialize in particular areas of software development, such as architecture, software design, database development, or testing. Some experts help their clients learn to use specific languages, methodologies, or development tools. The varieties of IT consulting match the varieties of IT work.

Both business analyst and project manager are project roles. Someone must perform these essential tasks on every project. They might have the corresponding job title (or an equivalent, such as requirements engineer, requirements analyst, or systems analyst), or they might do it along with other project responsibilities, such as coding or quality assurance. Traditional software teams often are accustomed to having these roles staffed by specialists, whereas BA and PM responsibilities may be distributed across multiple individuals on agile development teams. As projects become larger and more complex, the need for team members who are very good at business analysis and project management increases. Organizations that lack BA or PM expertise can benefit from bringing in consultants in those areas to educate and advise. That's where you come in.

The diversity of independent consulting experiences is practically boundless. You can guide your career in whatever direction you like, taking best advantage of the kinds of work you find most satisfying—so long as the phone rings enough to keep you in business.

HOW I GOT HERE

By way of background, let me describe how I got started in the consulting business. After obtaining a PhD in organic chemistry from the University of Illinois, I began my professional career in 1979 as a research scientist at Kodak in Rochester, New York. Computer programming was my second interest after chemistry; one-third of my PhD thesis was code. For several reasons, I moved into software development full-time at Kodak in 1984. Six years later, I took over as the manager of my small software group.

I began learning as much as I could about software process improvement through books, periodicals, and conferences. Soon I found myself helping other groups inside Kodak with various aspects of software development, thus serving as an internal consultant and trainer. This ultimately led to a position guiding software process improvement efforts in one of Kodak's digital imaging technology areas. Shortly before I left the company, I was leading process improvements in Kodak's web development group, the people who bring you kodak.com.

In 1991, I began speaking at conferences, while continuing to write magazine articles about various aspects of software engineering. Three years later I received my first invitation to speak at another company on some of the work I'd been writing about. More of these types of opportunities arose, thanks to my increasing visibility as an author and speaker. Before long I was delivering training and consulting services for other companies on my vacation time, while still working full-time at Kodak. This was all done with my management's knowledge and approval. It was a comfortable way to ease into a consulting career.

My first book, *Creating a Software Engineering Culture*, was published in 1996, while I was still at Kodak. Shortly thereafter, a well-known software consultant asked when I was going to leave the corporate world and hang out a shingle as an independent consultant. My initial reaction was that this seemed pretty risky, considering that I like to eat every day. But after reflection, I decided to give it a shot.

I officially launched my one-person consulting company—Process Impact—in December of 1997. A few months later I left Kodak to see how things might go on my own. I figured I could always get a real job again if consulting didn't work out for whatever reason. As it happened, being an independent consultant, trainer, and author has worked out just fine.

BEING SELF-EMPLOYED

Some consultants find work through agencies. Others are employed by a company that contracts their consulting services out to clients. However, with one six-month exception very early on, I've always worked entirely on my own through Process Impact. (Incidentally, I have found that, even in a one-person company, management is uninformed and unreasonable, and the staff is lazy and has a bad attitude.) When I started out, I knew little about this new mode of employment, yet I had few resources from which to learn.

I did learn several things about consulting early on. First, I was fortunate to get plenty of work. That was a relief, as many new consultants struggle to stay afloat. Second, I found that I really enjoyed the flexibility of being self-employed. While at Kodak, I concluded that I do not need to be managed and I do not enjoy being a manager, so self-employment in a one-person shop suits me well. And third, I discovered that there's a *lot* to learn about being a self-employed, self-managed independent consultant.

Many of the strategies and tips in this book will also be useful to practitioners—sometimes called consultants—who are engaged in staff-augmentation contracting relationships as temporary corporate or government employees. Certain topics covered here might not be as important to consultants who work for larger companies rather than being self-employed. But even if you aren't on your own at the moment, someday you might be.

CASTING A LARGE NET FOR KNOWLEDGE

When I told my Kodak colleagues I was going to give consulting a shot, someone asked how I'd be able to keep up with what was happening in the software industry if I didn't work on projects anymore. That was an interesting question I hadn't considered. However, I quickly realized that, as a consultant, I could see how *many* projects and organizations operated, instead of just observing a few projects in one company for a prolonged period. Instead of making every mistake and climbing every learning curve myself, I could learn by looking over other people's shoulders. Everyone I met at a client site, conference, or professional society meeting was a potential source of knowledge.

Visiting a wide variety of companies was far more informative than working inside a single microcosm with people steeped in the same corporate culture. It let me collect a breadth of information that I could then share with others, for a very reasonable price. I'm pretty good at synthesizing knowledge from multiple sources, packaging it, and delivering it in a practical and accessible way. That's the essence of being a consultant.

There was a second unobvious aspect regarding the knowledge you can—and cannot—acquire through consulting. I've done a lot of work in the field of software requirements over the years. People occasionally ask me, "Karl, what do the companies that are really good at requirements do?"

My reply is, "I don't know; they don't call me." That is, my clients are always people who know they want to improve how their teams perform certain aspects of their work. They invite me in to help assess those opportunities, provide knowledge through training or coaching, and assist them in migrating toward better ways of working. Companies that are already confident in their business analysis capabilities don't ask me to work with them. Hence, I have no way to learn what's working well for them unless they publish their experiences for all to see.

The other people who never call me are those who either aren't even aware that they have problems or don't opt to address them. It's hard to sell a better mousetrap to people who don't realize they have mice.

HOW THIS BOOK IS ORGANIZED

This book contains 35 chapters that are grouped into six parts. Part I (*Setting Up Shop*) addresses laying the foundation for your consulting business, including letting the world know you're open for business, several different modes of consulting engagements, and the impacts that being a self-employed consultant can have on your life and your family. Another chapter offers some comments on participating in professional organizations, both as a way to find possible clients and to pursue relevant professional certifications.

Part II (*On the Job*) covers many realities that I had to learn through trial and error; the errors weren't that much fun. Chapters address using checklists to keep all the activities you're juggling under control, techniques for engaging with clients in various situations, descriptions of some ideal clients, and some warnings about clients who can cause headaches for you and how to deal with them.

In Part III (*Practicalities*) you'll find valuable tips for such essentials as setting rates, managing your finances, and negotiating and crafting written agreements with your clients. Other chapters discuss establishing business policies and the important topic of purchasing appropriate insurance coverages. You might have the opportunity someday to partner with another consultant on a larger project, so I'll share some tips about how to make such arrangements work well.

Your business will probably start out a bit slow, leading you to look for ways to create growth. Part IV (*Building the Business*) suggests ways to do this. I will describe how I established multiple revenue streams, so I could hear the *ka-ching* of incoming cash even when I wasn't doing anything related to the company. Other chapters in this section provide suggestions for landing both new and repeat business, as well as many tips for consulting from a distance.

Although I've always called myself a consultant, most of my independent work has involved training. Teaching classes and making presentations are common consultant activities, so Part V (*Media Matters*) offers many tips for delivering effective presentations with confidence. It also describes ways to leverage your intellectual property (IP) repeatedly through different media formats, as well as addressing some important issues of copyright, fair use, and managing your valuable IP.

This book closes with Part VI (*Writing Your Way to Success*). Written communication is a core skill for any consultant, BA, or PM. Publishing lets you simultaneously share your knowledge with the world and market your expertise to prospective clients. This final set of chapters provides a wealth of information about writing for publication, including magazines, websites, blogs, and books. A prolific author once said that you can't consider yourself a good writer until you've written at least one hundred thousand words. My books alone total well over one million words. It's not for me to say if I'm a *good* writer, but I've learned a few useful things along the way, which I share in Part VI.

Each chapter in the book ends with a list of next steps, actions you can take immediately to begin applying the guidance and tips presented. If you are just starting out or early in your career as an independent consultant, I suggest you try the activities in these next steps as you finish each chapter. They can save you time and pain in the future.

Several chapters refer to items you might find useful, such as sample forms, checklists, and other reference items. You may download these from the Web Added Value™ Download Resource Center at www.jrosspub.com.

SOME CAVEATS

Let me emphasize that nothing in this book should be construed as legal advice. I am neither an attorney nor an accountant. Consult appropriate professionals with questions regarding legal matters, including finances, taxes, insurance, contracting, and how to structure your company.

You might conclude that certain approaches my colleagues and I have found to be valuable are a poor fit for your situation. In that case, it would be silly to take our advice. Instead, look for the idea behind each recommendation here, and then see if there is some thoughtful way to adapt that to your situation. As with all such writings, your mileage may vary from mine.

WHY KEEP READING?

I wish I had had a mentor to rely on for assistance, to answer the countless questions I had when starting out as an independent consultant. One seasoned colleague warned me, "You'll be making a lot of trips to your local office supplies store." True, but there's so much more I needed to learn, from essential matters like how to find clients and how much to charge, down to minor practicalities such as how to uniquely identify invoices. (I use a code with an abbreviation for the client's name, the current year, and a sequence number within the year, such as IC1904 for the fourth invoice I submitted to client InfoCorp in 2019.)

Perhaps this book can serve as a useful resource for you if you're pursuing a career path similar to the one I chose. Even if you're not aiming to be an independent consultant just now, you'll find plenty of information here to enhance your own professional capabilities.

Next Steps

- List your professional goals as a BA or PM. In what ways do you feel that your current position would make it difficult to achieve these goals? How might becoming an independent consultant help you achieve those goals?
- Identify the reasons why you want to be an independent consultant. Consider why you think being a consultant would be better than your current position, and balance that against the advantages of your

current position. Does the comparison give you confidence that independent consulting makes sense for you?

- If you're aiming to become a business analysis consultant, take an inventory of your suite of BA knowledge, skills, and resources. What are your great strengths as a BA, what are your competencies, and what gaps in your knowledge should you close to be able to help clients most effectively?
- If you've worked with consultants before from the client side, which ones impressed you the most? Why? Did they have particular knowledge, abilities, or behaviors that you found especially effective and beneficial to your organization? List those attributes that you could try to emulate in your own consulting career.
- Think of any experienced consultants you know who might be able to mentor you in this new way of working.

2

HANGING OUT THE SHINGLE

I've known several knowledgeable and talented people who declared themselves to be consultants but never got enough work to make a living at it. The message I got from these experiences was that:

It doesn't matter how good you are if nobody knows you're there.

One man's experience particularly sticks in my mind. I'll call him Kevin here.

Kevin was very bright and had considerable experience in the broad domain of software process improvement. One day he decided to leave his corporate job and become a consultant. However, Kevin made some mistakes getting started.

To begin, he didn't do enough to let prospective clients know that he was available and had something to contribute. Kevin never selected an official company name and never developed a website to market his services. He published just a few articles in software magazines and on websites. These are good ways to establish some name recognition. Blogging is another useful technique, as is being an active contributor to blogs and discussion forums, such as those on LinkedIn. If people realize you have good ideas and useful information to share, they might want to learn more about you and possibly hire you. Kevin didn't do any of those things.

Kevin did give several presentations at software conferences. Unfortunately, he didn't understand that the types of presentations and tutorials one typically delivers at conferences might not have much of a market in the corporate world. Even if you do get invited into a company to give a short talk, it won't pay much, and there's only a small chance that it will lead to longer engagements.

Kevin also positioned himself in too narrow a specialty, just a couple of software engineering subdomains. In my experience, few organizations bring in consultants to help in those particular areas, important though they are. You're better off targeting the large market, not a small niche.

The net result of all this was that Kevin never gained much traction as an independent consultant. Eventually, he had to go back into corporate employment in order to have a reliable income.

You can learn from Kevin's experiences as you chart your own path for independent consulting in any field. Somehow, I was very fortunate. I always had as much work as I wanted to do when I was an active consultant. Maybe I just hit the sweet spot in terms of developing expertise, training materials, and other resources in areas that were in demand, such as requirements engineering, project management, and software quality. But I think I took some of the right actions too, as I describe in the following paragraphs.

CHOOSE A GOOD NAME

I thought long and hard about what to name my company. Some consultants don't use a company name at all, just their own name: *J. Fred McGillicutty, Independent Consultant*. It was important to me to look like a real company though. I didn't want to call myself something like: Wiegers Consulting Group or Wiegers & Associates. You might be surprised at how many such-named companies have but a single employee—no group, no associates.

After considerable contemplation, I realized that my business goal was to have an impact on the processes that software organizations use to build their products, and for those processes to have an impact on the organization's business success. Hence the name I chose for my one-person company: Process Impact.

Incidentally, Process Impact has a company slogan: "Our employee is our greatest asset." And we really believe that.

There are various ways you can set up a consulting company, ranging from sole proprietor, to limited liability company (LLC), to S corporation. In Chapter 15 (*Money Matters for the New Consultant*) Gary K. Evans describes these various options.

I have always been a sole proprietor, just myself with no employees. I registered my business name as a sole proprietorship in each state in which I have lived. I am officially: *Karl Wiegers dba Process Impact*. DBA means *doing business as*, although in the state of Oregon where I now live, it's also referred to as *doing business under an assumed name*. That sounds a bit shady, but it's just the phrasing the state uses.

GO ONLINE

When I launched the company I immediately created a website named www.ProcessImpact.com. This site is simple in design, but it offers a lot of useful content. I've always favored substance over glitz, function over form. Big, meaningless stock images of people smiling at work take up screen space and don't do much for me. I now have several other websites, including my personal site, www.KarlWiegers.com, and individual sites for each of my nontechnical books. A good website isn't just an online business card; ideally it replaces the sort of interaction that once might have required a phone call or e-mail.

DRAW A CROWD

Building a website is a good starting point, but you still need to attract people to that site. As time went by, I posted increasing quantities of material there, including articles and white papers I had written, document templates and other useful work aids, and so forth. This kind of bait clearly draws visitors who are searching for specific items. The most popular item on my website, my software requirements specification template, has been downloaded many thousands of times. It's gratifying to create materials that others find useful. (However, see the cautionary tales in Chapter 26 (*On Intellectual Property*) regarding misappropriation of your creations.) When people know your website offers valuable resources, they will bookmark it and come back for more later on, thereby giving you further opportunities to sell them something at the right time.

One of the kinds of resources you can post consists of supplemental content associated with any books you write, such as document templates, spreadsheet tools, checklists, and forms. A book buyer who visits your site can then easily learn about your other products and services. You might invite your website visitors to join a mailing list so you can notify them about new goodies or books, presentations you have coming up, and new training courses you offer. That lets you easily reach out and touch people who have already indicated interest in your work. It helps increase your impact in your field, as well as potentially increasing your revenue. Be sure to include an "unsubscribe" or "opt-out" link in any promotional emails you send to your mailing list members. It's the law, per the CAN-SPAM Act of 2003.

SHARE WHAT YOU KNOW

Way back in 1984, I wrote the first of some 180 articles for numerous information technology (IT) magazines and websites on a wide range of subjects: software engineering, requirements, project management, people management, quality, metrics, and process improvement. I published up to ten articles per year with an average length of about three thousand words. Well-written, substantive articles generate good visibility and establish the author's credentials in certain areas of expertise. See Part VI of this book— *Writing Your Way to Success*—for many tips on writing for publication.

I began writing books even before I launched Process Impact. As of now, I have published seven books on software development and management, a memoir of life lessons titled *Pearls from Sand: How Small Encounters Lead to Powerful Lessons*, and a novel, *The Reconstruction*—oh, and this book too, of course. Having your name on a book gives you both visibility and credibility. The research I did while writing each book also greatly broadened my knowledge. This is not to say that I am the world's expert on any particular topic. You only have to know a little more than the next guy to be helpful, though.

GET ON STAGE

Early in my career I spoke at as many as six or eight conferences per year, often delivering multiple presentations at each event. This is a way to directly reach hundreds of people a year with your message. You become a real person to them, not just a name in an article's byline. You know your career is progressing nicely when conference producers invite you to submit papers, to sit on panels, and ultimately to deliver keynote presentations. As you gain recognition, you can get paid increasing amounts for your presentations. The conference fee is virtually always waived for speakers. Conferences provide great networking opportunities. Plus, it's always a treat to meet people who are familiar with your work.

I've lined up a lot of consulting work with clients who first heard me speak at a conference or a professional organization meeting. For example, I once gave a one-hour presentation at a SPIN (software process improvement network) meeting in Olympia, Washington. One of the attendees coordinated the IT and project management training programs for many Washington State government agencies. She must have liked my presentation: she hired me to teach more than thirty classes in Olympia, just a two-hour drive from my home, over the next several years.

Many cities around the world have chapters of the International Institute of Business Analysis (IIBA), Project Management Institute (PMI), and similar professional organizations. If you can speak at such chapters close to home, that raises your profile in your own community and presents opportunities for generating local work. Local professional society meetings also are good places to polish a new presentation before you take your show on the road.

Look for chances to partner with tool vendors in your domain for joint presentations. I have collaborated with numerous vendors of requirements management tools to give both live and online presentations. These have ranged from half-hour webinars to a two-week European seminar tour. These vendors understand that I do not publicly endorse any specific tools. They invite me to participate because of my expertise and visibility in the domain of software requirements. Attendees might come to the presentation to hear me talk about the requirements process, thereby providing a ready-made audience for the vendor to describe their tools and services. Everybody wins.

Be sure to announce any upcoming presentations, webinars, interviews, or podcasts on your website and through social media channels such as LinkedIn and Twitter. Every pair of eyes (or ears) you draw represents a potential future source of income. Whoever is sponsoring the presentation forum will appreciate your additional marketing efforts for the event. When you become recognized as a speaker who draws more than the usual number of attendees, more invitations will appear.

IT ALL ADDS UP

There are nice synergies and positive feedback loops among the various self-promotional activities previously described. Figure 2.1 illustrates some of these connections. For instance, giving a presentation may lead to writing an article on the same topic. Conversely, if you write an article on a topic in your field, you might well be able to give a short talk on that sometime.

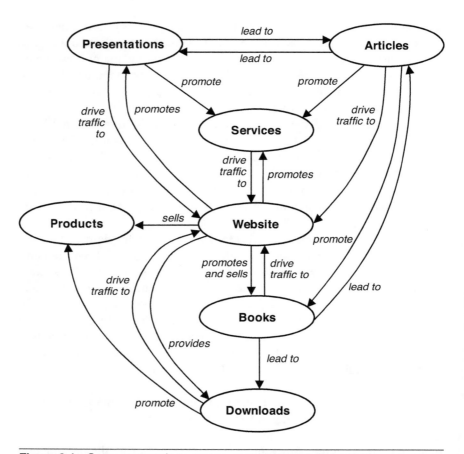

Figure 2.1   Some connections among consultant visibility activities

Both articles and presentations are ways to make potential clients aware of the services you have to offer, and they drive traffic to your website so visitors can learn about your products and books. Someone who reads one of your books might visit your website to learn more about what you have to offer. In fact, this is how I've gotten most of my consulting work. Study Figure 2.1 and consider how you could interlace the various assets and services you have available to inform the world about your existence and talents. It just might pay off.

Doubtless it was the combination of all these activities that presented the software world the opportunity to learn about me and what I could do for them. As a result, I was fortunate to make a decent living as a consultant and trainer. I never had to think about going back to work in a larger company. At this point, I don't think I could.

Next Steps

- Think of several possible names for your consulting company. Run them past some of your colleagues to see what they think. What name best represents your company's mission?
- Mock up a business card or logo for your company that you think would convey your value to a potential client.
- List at least four actions you could take to increase your visibility as a consultant. Think of possible speaking venues, conferences in your field, and periodicals or websites you could write for.
- List five topics about which you could write articles of 1,000 to 3,000 words each. Do you have an idea of where you could submit each article for publication or posting?
- Identify several topics you could speak about at a conference or professional society meeting. Look at the past proceedings of some conferences in your field to see what the hot topics are, and then consider how you could both fit in with them and go beyond.

3

HEY, WORLD, HERE I AM!

By GARY K. EVANS

So you've decided to leave the corporate world and start out on your own. Congratulations! It's a big step. It can be kind of scary, leaving the comfortable security of a corporate womb with its reliable salary, decent benefits, advancement opportunities, and network of coworkers. Not everyone has the self-discipline to treat their home as their workplace. If you have small children you will have special adjustments to make so that your home life continues smoothly. The abrupt shift to working in isolation can be jarring if you've always been used to having a lot of people around for both professional and social interactions. Before you make the leap, think carefully about how you might react to those sorts of changes.

When you're independent, you have full responsibility for everything that happens in the company. Those who take best to self-employment are the self-starters who can chart their own career paths and work independently. Being able to work alone and to switch easily between work contexts is a definite advantage. You'll need to find your own employment opportunities, which means showing initiative, patience, and creativity in how you present yourself to potential clients. In addition to your own professional skills, you'll have to become a little bit of a marketer, accountant, writer, presentation designer, and office administrator. Whether you're out of notepads, coffee, or jobs, it's your problem. So let's see how you might start lining up those all-important clients to get the ball rolling.

MARKETING YOU!

Finding work isn't the same as waiting for work to find you. A business plan of *make lots of money* isn't a plan—it's a wish, not unlike *win the lottery and retire*. To become a successful consultant, you must have a plan. Think hard about what you do best, and build on your strengths. If you're uncomfortable around strangers or can't articulate in fifteen seconds the value you will bring to the client, attempting to go it alone might be unrealistic for you. If you're not interested in marketing, bookkeeping, or the myriad other nontechnical tasks required to run even a one-person business, plan on hiring—that means paying—someone to do these for you.

To find work, you must actively seek it out. This means marketing yourself. But don't limit yourself always to the same channels; your options will change over time. Technologies evolve quickly. These days you can exploit professional networking mechanisms such as LinkedIn, direct marketing through email campaigns, and the like. Think about where your prospective clients congregate and what communication mechanisms would be most effective for reaching them.

When I started out, my first client fell right into my lap. I had invested fifteen years working for a well-known computer company until I, along with one-third of the other employees in my facility, received a severance notice. I hit the ground running, looking for a full-time job, but I was overqualified for every position I interviewed for. Then a New York company heard about the layoff and contacted me because I had the skills they needed.

For my next three or four engagements, I found work primarily through third-party groups who marketed me. On every engagement, I met people and cultivated relationships. In a short time, those relationships became a marketing channel as I began obtaining work from word-of-mouth recommendations. By expanding my base from just design and programming to teaching object-oriented (OO) technology, I aligned myself with several large OO software companies. When consulting positions were sparse, my training work served as a safety net. And, after teaching various OO courses (of varying quality) marketed by these companies, my dissatisfaction with them led me to start writing and marketing my own training courses.

Next, I attempted cold-call marketing, with limited success. At the end of 1998, I made a conscious decision to try a more aggressive marketing plan, so I created a website. Then I started speaking at professional conferences. In 1999, I began writing magazine articles on object technology and OO software development and modeling tools. I soon had the privilege of being asked to serve as a judge for the prestigious Jolt Awards for software productivity—a position that I held for eleven years. And a few years ago I started a second business to produce a commercial software product for people who want to manage their nutrition and health.

My point is this: *you must continually step out of your comfort zone.* I'm really not kidding when I say that now I'm comfortable only when I'm out of my comfort zone.

DEALING WITH THIRD-PARTY PLACEMENT

If you're an independent consultant, this doesn't mean you'll always have to find your own clients. Especially in the beginning of your independent career, you might find ready-made contracting opportunities through third-party placement agencies or system integration groups. Some of my best work experiences have come in this way. They handle the marketing, cold calls, payroll, and other details; I do the technology. The only downside is that they get paid from my pay.

Don't fall into the trap of whining about this, however. Recognize that the third party through which you're working has to make money too. After all, they're taking care of sales, bookkeeping, contracting, and so on. Should you care what margin they're making from you?

My position is simple: I have no right to know the margin, and I don't care what it is. If I decide to work through a placement agency for $75 per hour and then discover that they are charging the client $125 per hour for me, so what? If $75 per hour meets my goals, I'm satisfied. Grousing over someone else's margin is bad public relations, earning you the label of malcontent. Then you won't get any more work through that group.

Negotiate, never demand. Keep your eyes and ears open, and if you learn what the third party is charging for you, just sit on that information until the next contract renewal or project. Concentrate on what you must do to make yourself worth $100 per hour, and let the placement group worry about how to pass the increase on to the client. That's what they're getting paid to do.

CUTTING THE CORD

As you gain industry visibility and respect, you'll likely find that more prospective clients begin to contact you directly about providing services to them. Maybe they liked an article you wrote or got a lot out of one of your conference presentations. When this happens, you'll rely less on third-party companies and contractors to locate work for you. The margin that a contracting company made from your work will then go right into your own pocket. Just remember that when you're on your own, you'll have to take responsibility for all of the services they used to provide for you. Everything has a trade-off.

Independent consulting is a way of working that has become common in many industries. It seems destined to increase as our economy continues to mutate into integrated, electronic cottage-industry services. It has tremendous reward potential, along with its downsides. You can slice and dice your independence almost any way you wish, but you must also take care of business. If you really think you want to be independent, carefully count the costs, get prepared, and charge ahead. It could well change your life forever.

Next Steps

- List the marketing techniques you have tried in the past. Which ones worked? Why? Which ones didn't work so well? Why not?
- Identify three new methods you could try to market your services. Think of specific organizations or people you could contact or any actions you could take to exploit these methods.
- Think of any companies you might approach to assist you in finding employment opportunities as a consultant.

4

PARTICIPATING IN PROFESSIONAL ORGANIZATIONS

With JOY BEATTY

Perhaps it's because I began my career as a research scientist, but I've always believed it was important to join and participate in the activities of professional societies. At one time or another, I have belonged to the American Chemical Society, Association for Computing Machinery, Institute of Electrical and Electronics Engineers (IEEE), IEEE Computer Society, American Society for Quality (ASQ), and others.

Participating in such organizations promotes professionalism and disseminates knowledge among the members. Some professional societies publish journals. Reading those helps you keep up with the latest thinking in your field; contributing articles to them enhances your reputation as an accomplished practitioner and insightful thinker. Society meetings and conferences provide valuable opportunities for networking, which can lead to employment possibilities both for independent consultants and for those seeking regular jobs. You can also make new friends.

PRESENTATION OPPORTUNITIES

Since I became an author and speaker in the software arena I have received many invitations to speak at local, national, and international meetings of various professional organizations. One came in just as I was writing this chapter, in fact. I've had invitations from local chapters of the International Institute of Business Analysis (IIBA), Project Management Institute (PMI), IEEE, and others around the country.

Speaking at local meetings of organizations like these is a great way to practice a new keynote presentation in a friendly environment before I have to deliver it to hundreds of people at a conference. I've also delivered webinars for some organizations from my home office, which extends my visibility and impact beyond those who can attend a particular event. It's nice when I don't have to travel to give a talk.

These presentations serve as a marketing tool for my books and services as well. Earlier in my career, presentations at local professional meetings generated numerous training and consulting opportunities, although that is no longer the case. I still give talks from time to time, but no one calls for follow-up training. I'm not sure why. Be aware that the people who attend local professional groups are more likely to be dedicated practitioners than the kind of people who could sign a purchase order to bring you in for some consulting or training work. But, each contact you make is a potential open door.

I don't charge a fee to speak at local meetings of professional organizations, although I do request an honorarium for conference presentations. As I explain in Chapter 19 (*It's a Matter of Policy*), I view giving such talks as a way to contribute to my profession. Some people who invite me to speak at their local chapter seem surprised when I explain that it's not feasible for me to fly across the country to give a short talk, without compensation, even if they reimburse my travel expenses. The argument that "it will be great visibility for you and might lead to some work" is not persuasive at this stage of my career. That might be different if you're just starting out as an independent consultant and seeking all the exposure you can get.

When travel is involved, I try to arrange these presentations to piggyback on some work I'm already doing in the vicinity. Sometimes, the professional group has contacts with a local training company that can arrange for me to deliver an open-enrollment public seminar. This generates some revenue so I can be in town to speak at the professional meeting. Since I'm not being paid for that presentation, I'm not shy—but neither am I flagrant—about promoting my books, e-learning courses, and other products and services. I might give the attendees a secret discount code for, say, 30 percent off the Process Impact Goodies Collection, to draw them to my company's website. Hey, if you're self-employed, you have to do all your own marketing.

PROFESSIONAL CERTIFICATIONS

Numerous organizations have established professional certification programs for people working in information technology (IT). If you work in a field other than IT, you doubtless have your own suite of certifications to consider. This section summarizes the certifications available from three major professional organizations for business analysts (BAs) and project managers (PMs). The IIBA and PMI also offer agile-related accreditations, which might be appropriate for some BAs to pursue.

Practitioners typically earn these certifications through some combination of work experience, professional development education, and passing an examination based on a body of knowledge established for the discipline. The IIBA maintains the Business Analysis Body of Knowledge (BABOK®), and PMI's Project Management Body of Knowledge (PMBOK®) has been available for many years. The PMBOK® principally is for PMs who seek the Project Management Professional (PMP®) certification, but PMI now also publishes *The PMI Guide to Business Analysis*, targeted specifically at the BA profession. These resources are rich collections of knowledge that are assembled and maintained by teams of practitioners. Each describes an accepted set of terminology, practices, and skills with which professionals should become familiar, whether or not they choose to pursue certification.

International Institute of Business Analysis (IIBA)

The three IIBA certifications reflect a wide range of business analysis experience levels. Each level's evaluated competencies build upon those of the previous levels. All IIBA certifications are based on the current version of the BABOK, as published in *A Guide to the Business Analysis Body of Knowledge (BABOK® Guide)*.

The extent of your BA work experience indicates the level of IIBA certification for which you might apply. The work experience must involve actual business analysis activities and must be spread across a variety of knowledge areas, as defined by the IIBA. Each level of certification requires you to pass a separate exam. You must also have a certain minimum number of professional development hours for each level to demonstrate your continued growth in the BA field. In addition, the IIBA requires you to provide two professional references for the two advanced levels of certification.

The Entry Certificate in Business Analysis™ (ECBA™) is for individuals who have no experience in business analysis but who believe they are ready to perform BA activities and wish to enter the profession. You must have acquired a basic knowledge and understanding of business analysis, typically through self-study or coursework. While you can certainly pick up a lot of BA information on the job, there's no substitute for some structured training to close the gaps in your knowledge. If you're interested in going for the ECBA, build yourself a solid foundation of knowledge before applying.

If you have at least 3,750 hours of BA work experience, consider the Certificate of Capability in Business Analysis™ (CCBA®). Individuals who apply for the CCBA should be able to apply foundational knowledge to their work, make recommendations to others about techniques to use, and perhaps modify how business analysis is applied in practice in their organization.

Practitioners possessing a minimum of 7,500 hours of experience performing BA activities may apply for the Certified Business Analysis Professional™ (CBAP®). Professionals at this level often establish the BA disciplines within their own organizations or project teams, applying their extensive work experience and advanced knowledge. Other team members come to them for insights about the business analysis problems they confront.

To summarize, ECBA is about foundational awareness and understanding, CCBA is about being skilled at applying BA techniques, and CBAP is for the advanced practitioner who guides others to apply business analysis. Becoming an independent consultant is a logical next step for a BA who has mastered these three levels of education and experience and seeks new challenges.

Project Management Institute (PMI)

PMI traditionally has focused on project management through their long-standing PMP certification. In addition, PMI offers several related certifications in portfolio management, program management, risk management, scheduling, and agile practice. Their core body of knowledge for PMs appears in the publication *A Guide to the Project Management Body of Knowledge (PMBOK® Guide)*, which is updated periodically. Each of the other certifications has its own corresponding published standard.

More recently, PMI has developed the Professional in Business Analysis (PMI-PBA®) certification. This credential is designed for people who work on product-focused—rather than project-focused—activities, such as eliciting and managing requirements and driving business outcomes over the life of a product. Most relevant for those who perform business analysis—under any job title—this certification also is appropriate for project or program managers who perform mainly BA activities in their daily work.

The PMI-PBA certification and PMI's definition of what qualifies as business analysis activities are based on *The PMI Guide to Business Analysis* and

Business Analysis for Practitioners: A Practice Guide. To become certified, you must pass an exam that focuses on the application of BA concepts as described in those publications. PMI requires you to have a specified minimum number of hours of work experience on BA activities, which depends on the level of formal education you've completed. As with the IIBA certifications, the PMI-PBA also specifies a minimum number of professional development hours as a prerequisite.

International Requirements Engineering Board (IREB)

Founded in Germany in 2006, IREB offers the Certified Professional for Requirements Engineering (CPRE) credential at three levels. Requirements engineering constitutes the largest fraction of the work for many BAs. Other common activities that BAs might perform lie outside the scope of the CPRE.

To achieve the Foundational Level of CPRE certification, you must pass a multiple-choice exam that evaluates your basic knowledge about requirements engineering. Although no work experience is required, IREB assumes that you have studied or taken training to prepare for the exam.

The CPRE is not based on a prescribed body of knowledge. However, IREB has developed a detailed syllabus of key practices in requirements engineering on which training providers can base their course materials. Candidates pursuing the CPRE will find the syllabus helpful to identify areas where they need to enhance their knowledge. IREB also recommends several books that encompass the concepts and practices tested. These certifications do not specify any required professional development criteria.

Advanced Level certificates require you to demonstrate mastery of the concepts and techniques in four modules: elicitation and consolidation, modeling, management, and agile. One certificate is awarded per module, and you may apply for one or more of the modules. You must complete the Foundational Level before you may apply for an Advanced Level certificate. Achieving an Advanced Level entails passing an exam and also completing a written assignment that demonstrates your application of concepts on a real project. There's no stated threshold for previous years of work experience, but you'll likely need multiple years of experience to demonstrate mastery in any one topic. The IREB provides an individual syllabus and handbook for each of the four advanced modules.

Not surprisingly, the Expert Level builds upon the Advanced Level. Prerequisites include holding at least three Advanced Level certificates (alternatively, one certificate plus other relevant degrees or certifications, such as CBAP), at least three years of work experience, and demonstrated capability as a trainer or coach in the field. Instead of taking a written exam, candidates submit an application to demonstrate how they met the prerequisites, complete a written assignment to demonstrate deep understanding and application of concepts, and undergo an oral examination to discuss how to handle a case scenario.

Is Certification for You?

Employers increasingly expect the professionals they hire to be proficient in the bodies of knowledge established for their domain. Holding a certification from an organization like the IIBA, PMI, or IREB can provide a competitive advantage when you are seeking employment. It's not enough simply to be able to recite the contents of the body of knowledge on demand though. You must be able to apply the practices in real project situations, knowing which tool to pull from the tool kit to solve a given problem.

Numerous companies now provide exam-preparation training for certification candidates. I fear this sometimes results in teaching to the test as opposed to necessarily helping the candidate acquire the right set of practical knowledge and skills to enhance her job performance. Ideally, these objectives are congruent, but I'm not sure that's always the case.

You might consider whether having one or more of those abbreviations following your name would enhance your professional standing and make you more attractive to prospective consulting clients or employers. As one of my consultant colleagues put it:

> These professional credentials have brought forth a lot of work for me, leading me to develop and augment my course content to align with the standards so I can teach exam-prep classes. They are my personal signage to say, "consultant for hire who has first-hand experience with a particular credential and who can help you prepare to do the same."

I've always had great respect for adults who went back to school or committed to focused self-study to obtain advanced degrees or professional certifications. This shows a serious commitment to continuous learning and growth of one's knowledge, skills, and capabilities.

I don't hold any professional certifications myself. The only letters I can put after my name are MS and PhD, and those were in organic chemistry. Some people appear to collect certifications, appending a long string of abbreviations to their name. The following are some of the most extreme examples I've encountered:

- ACS, ALMI, CSM, FIII, IPGDRM, MIB, AHM, SAFe
- MBA, PMP, RMP, SIPM, PRINCE2, CABA, CAT
- MSc, PhD, PMP, CSM, CSP, PMI-ACP
- PMP, MIET, MQSi, MCIOB, MRICS
- PMI (PBA, ACP), PROSCI, ITILv3, PSM, PSPO

I don't know what most of those abbreviations stand for. A long list of credentials looks impressive—and maybe it really is—but spending significant time studying to get certified isn't necessarily the same thing as gaining a lot of practical, hands-on experience. Organizations and hiring managers must conduct skillful interviews to distinguish between candidates having only credentials and those having true experience. I wonder if the objective for some of those collectors is merely procurement of the credential and the appearance of expertise, not the effective application of all that hard-learned knowledge. Do you think anyone would notice if I were to recast my professional identity as Karl Wiegers, MS, PhD, MIC, KEY, MO-USE?

CERTIFIED TRAINERS

Professional organizations such as the IIBA, PMI, and IREB recognize that continuous education is a vital part of professional development. People who obtain their professional certifications must accumulate a certain number of continuing development units (IIBA) or professional development units (PMI) to maintain those certifications. To help control the quality of the available training, both IIBA and PMI established programs to certify companies that provide training services in their fields. The IIBA maintains a registry of Endorsed Education Providers (EEPs); PMI certifies Registered Education Providers (REPs). Similarly, IREB maintains a list of recognized CPRE training providers.

As a consultant, you might deliver training courses in your domain, and some of your potential clients might wonder if you are an EEP or REP. Even if you aren't, students can still apply to the IIBA or PMI to receive development credits for courses they take from you, but the process is more automatic if the student takes a course from someone on the magic list.

To become an EEP or REP, you have to submit your courseware and information about your company for evaluation to verify they are consistent with the organization's standards and its pertinent body of knowledge. Each of your courses might have to be evaluated and approved separately, so the process really is a combination of certifying both the provider and the courseware itself. The instructors themselves may be required to hold specific credentials, such as IREB's CPRE. You can get specifics about applying for these training certification programs from each organization's website (www.iiba.org, www.pmi.org, and www.ireb.org).

If you have licensed your courseware to other providers, they might need to go through their own certification process, even if they are using the same material you developed. Also, if you deliver material in multiple forms, such as with live instructors and also through self-paced e-learning, you might need to get those different representations of the material approved separately. Check with the pertinent organization's current policies to be certain.

The cost of obtaining such approval for your company and its courseware is substantial, but it does provide some advantages. People seeking training often turn to the IIBA and PMI websites to find prospective instructors they feel they can trust because of their EEP or REP status. If they specifically want training that is aligned with a particular established body of knowledge, the certifying organizations are a good place to look.

I have elected not to go through this courseware certification process myself for several reasons. I'm sure this has cost me some business, but I'm okay with that. You might decide that the benefits outweigh the cost for you and your company.

PROFESSIONAL ORGANIZATIONS AND YOU

If you are—or hope to become—an independent consultant, I encourage you to join relevant professional organizations and participate in their local activities. I enjoy meeting the people who attend these sessions. Sometimes there's pizza or cookies. I have occasionally established relationships that have continued for years. The networking opportunities might indeed help you to generate some visibility and possibly some consulting leads.

If you are already established in your field, appearing at such events is a goodwill gesture that helps to enhance your reputation as a constructive contributor to the community and all-around nice person. That's not a bad image to cultivate.

Next Steps

- Identify the major professional organizations in your field and consider joining them. Look for local chapters you could join and whose meetings you could attend.
- Look into the various professional certifications that are relevant for your work and judge whether it would be to your advantage to procure any. List the reasons why you would want each certification and what you hope it would do for you, both in terms of your own knowledge expansion and your consulting opportunities.
- If you have developed business analysis or project management training materials, look into what's involved with becoming an endorsed or registered provider of training with the IIBA or PMI, respectively. Assess whether the cost and time involved with the certification process is likely to pay off for you.

5

MODES OF CONSULTING: WHAT'S YOUR PREFERENCE?

In his classic book *Flawless Consulting*, Peter Block described three types of roles that consultants might take on: expert, pair-of-hands, and collaborator. Each of these represents a different kind of interaction when working with clients and a different source of satisfaction for the consultant. This chapter describes some of my experiences with these three modes of consulting engagements.

OUTSIDE LOOKING IN: THE EXPERT MODE

As an expert, you're working with a client who has a problem and wants you to fix it. You're working in the expert role when a client brings you in to deliver some training, perform a process assessment, or review some project deliverables or process documentation. They might also seek an outside perspective when their internal improvement efforts have stalled out.

More than one client has told me, "You're here because the pain has become too great." The organization was suffering from problems resulting from ineffective practices and processes in some domain, and they hired me to help them rectify those problems. That is, they sought help from an outside expert.

Unfortunately, I cannot actually fix the problems in an organization. I can evaluate the current reality, suggest root causes that lead to the pain, and identify areas ripe for improvement. I can provide the clients with knowledge and resources that can help, and I can propose a roadmap for applying that knowledge on their projects. However, it's up to the managers and practitioners in the client organization to implement those actions effectively themselves. Sustained improvement actions also demand culture changes. Those take time and must be driven from within, not by outsiders. So, part of my job as a consultant is to encourage key members of the client organization to aspire to higher standards of performance and show them ways to get there.

I've found that when I perform a process assessment—whether formal and structured with a written report or simply by providing feedback based on informal discussions—I rarely tell clients things they don't already know. My clients generally are aware of their pain points. However, they might not be able to get senior management to take the matter seriously or to provide the necessary resources to address the issues.

When a manager brings me in, it's not unusual for him to say, "Please tell these other people what I've been trying unsuccessfully to tell them for six months. They'll listen to you." For reasons I've never understood, it's more acceptable to have an outsider make the same observations and recommendations that in-house employees have already made. It helps that the consultant is independent of the local organizational politics and isn't caught up in the history of "the way we've always done things around here." The outside expert has the perspective of having worked with numerous other organizations and noted patterns of both effective and ineffective industry practices.

Some of the most fun I've had in the expert consulting mode involved sitting in a room at a client site for a day while a procession of people came in to discuss various random problems they were facing. I never knew what question was going to come up next. It might be about getting customers engaged in requirements discussions, dealing with configuration management problems, or generating better estimates for project planning. I found these all-too-infrequent types of engagements stimulating and challenging. I really had to think on my feet to understand the situation quickly and try to come up with suggestions that were likely to be effective.

I've done a great deal of consulting that involved reviewing process or project deliverables—most commonly requirements documents—to point out errors and provide improvement recommendations. I'm functioning as an outside expert in this sort of engagement too. After having reviewed a lot of requirements for clients over the years, I have an idea of what constitutes a good set and some of the common problems to look for. This body of experience allows me to examine a set of requirements efficiently and to spot many improvement opportunities. Of course, I can't confirm that the document contains the *correct* requirements for the project because I wasn't involved with setting the business objectives, defining the needs, or interviewing customers. But I'm very good at finding other kinds of problems that someone who has less experience working with requirements might overlook.

One more way in which you might work in the expert consulting mode is as an expert witness in a lawsuit. I had this experience just once. The project involved an organization that had purchased a packaged software solution and then hired the package's vendor to perform some customizations and data migrations. The project failed abysmally. One of the parties in the resulting lawsuit between the organization and the vendor hired me to determine why.

After studying numerous project documents, I concluded that the party whose attorney had hired me caused most of the problems. The attorney read my report, said thank you, paid me, and that was the end of that. I heard much later that the parties had reached a settlement, so I never had to testify. This engagement led to an article titled *See You in Court*, in which I shared some advice about making such outsourcing projects more successful. Some consultants earn a very good living working as expert witnesses, applying what they've learned through years of industry experience. One told me about twenty years ago that he charged $500 per hour when he was in court, $300 per hour otherwise. That sounds like good money to me.

The Idea Generator

When I'm working as an expert consultant, I view my key responsibility as supplying ideas that will help a client solve a problem or build software faster and better. Some solution ideas are better than others, so I try to come up with a lot of them. For every 10 ideas, I figure that two will be ridiculous, two others might not be very effective or won't suit the culture, three more will be obvious, two of the remainder will be clever and novel to the client, and the final one will be brilliant. I need to produce enough ideas to get a nice handful of solid hits in those last two categories.

I use a mental test as a reality check on any advice I propose in consulting discussions or when I write a formal recommendation report. First, I consider whether the actions I'm suggesting have a high probability of actually solving the client's problem. That is, my proposal must be effective. And second, I ask myself if the client actually *could* implement my suggestions if he chooses to do so.

In other words, what I'm proposing must be both practical and appropriate for the client's culture and situation. Each practice that I have in mind must pass both of these checks before I deliver it to the client. The last thing I want to do is give clients advice that wouldn't help them, isn't realistically feasible in their world, or might do them more harm than good.

The Coach

Another way to function as an expert consultant is in a coaching role. You could work with individual business analysts or project managers to assess their current ways of working and recommend more effective practices. On a larger scale, you might help an organization establish a business analysis center of excellence (BACoE) or a project management office (PMO). These are groups that establish, maintain, and monitor standards of practice within an organization.

An organization that sets up a BACoE or PMO is demonstrating a serious commitment to enhancing the professionalism of business analysis or project management practice and its practitioners. As an expert consultant, you could help the client organization define the composition, structure, and responsibilities of such a group. Your expertise could help a budding professional group develop methodologies, training materials, templates for project deliverables, process and guidance documents, spreadsheet tools, and other resources. You might help define career paths and professional development sequences for practitioners.

Providing such leadership lets you leverage the effective techniques you've observed from previous clients to help new clients work in better ways. It also presents a business opportunity to possibly license your own training materials or other assets to the client company and perhaps to customize them to best suit the client's needs. This could yield revenue that goes well beyond the consulting services themselves.

The Informal Expert

Once you become recognized as an authority in your field, you'll probably receive random emails and phone calls from people who wish to tap into your expertise. As few of these people will ever become paying clients, it's your choice whether you want to spend the time answering their questions. I try to be a nice guy and respond to each inquiry I receive, but obviously we all have limited time to devote to such pro bono consulting. These inquiries are a risk of becoming well known.

There's an upside to such informal consulting activities though. For instance, someone once asked if I had any resources to help his team assess the impact of a proposed requirement change on a project. At that time, I did not. However, I saw that others might have this same question and that I might be able to come up with something quite easily. I devised a couple of checklists and sent them off to the requester, who found them helpful. Those checklists then became part of the process assets I could provide to paying clients and make available for download on my website, something to include in my books and articles, and material I could add to future presentations on requirements management. All because someone I didn't know asked me for a favor.

On occasion, someone presents a question through these informal channels that I haven't encountered before and haven't really thought about. If it seems like something I ought to know, I'll try to concoct a substantive and useful response. I save those answers and have often incorporated them into some publication later on.

I can't anticipate all the information and resources that might be useful to future clients on my own. When I take the time to understand these informal "consulting" inquiries I receive, I can often develop knowledge and materials that I know will provide value to the clients I serve. And sometimes I just have an interesting conversation with a person who's passionate about the same topics that I care about. That's okay too.

Roadblocks

Perhaps the biggest sources of resistance to input from an outside expert are NIH and NAH syndromes.

NIH means *not invented here*. The solution proposed by an outside expert might be rejected because the affected practitioners didn't create the solution themselves, so they don't necessarily buy into it or trust it.

NAH means *not applicable here*. I've often heard the claim "we're different" from clients who weren't interested in trying my recommendations. They thought whatever I was suggesting might work in other places but certainly not in their environment.

Organizations and cultures do come in many flavors, but there are also many similarities between them. For instance, I think nearly all software-developing organizations can follow basically the same change-control process. Citing NIH or NAH as a reason not to accept the consultant's recommendations often signals resistance against change in general. If you detect either NIH or NAH symptoms, your challenge shifts from proposing solutions to considering how best to have those solutions reach a receptive audience.

And Then What Happened?

One of the frustrating aspects of working with a client as an expert consultant or trainer is that I rarely learn what happens after I leave the client site. Unless the client has engaged me for some ongoing work, it's totally up to the organization to decide how to apply my training or recommendations. Of course, I hope they will maximize their return on the investment they made in the engagement. But if they just keep on doing whatever it was they did before I came along, they'll get a return on investment of zero. There's no way to find out what happened afterward unless the client opts to share that information with me.

Occasionally, I have received feedback about the outcome some time after I taught a class. I once had a student in a public seminar who had taken a requirements class from me about a year earlier. He told me that his company now had product champions serving as key user representatives for all of their projects, a practice I strongly advocate. He said this approach was really helping their projects be more successful.

Such anecdotes validate that I am presenting ideas and practices that are practical and can lead to better results in companies that learn how to make them work. Because my professional goal is to help organizations do a better job with my help than they could otherwise, it's always great to hear that someone has found my advice to be valuable.

MANY HANDS MAKE LIGHT WORK: THE PAIR-OF-HANDS MODE

When working in the pair-of-hands mode, the consultant is providing a service that the client company might be able to perform themselves but for which they lack sufficient staff or time. The client defines the need and sets the project boundaries and expectations. The consultant then performs the work largely on his own, with the client contact assessing the deliverables to ensure they are satisfactory.

Some companies, for instance, hire an experienced BA on a contract basis for a specific software development project. The consultant comes into the organization and performs the traditional BA tasks of identifying users, eliciting requirements, writing specifications, and so forth. Such short-term staff augmentation for a specific project is a pair-of-hands engagement mode.

I have done a great deal of work for one client (I'll call him Jack) over more than fifteen years. Jack leads the software center of excellence in a large product-development company. Much of my work for Jack has involved off-site consulting (that is, in my home office) in either the pair-of-hands or collaborative mode. Most of the pair-of-hands work has involved developing process descriptions, templates, and other work aids. Jack knows how to perform this sort of work, but he doesn't have the time or the internal staff available to do it in a timely fashion. Therefore, he outsources it to me.

Jack carefully reviews each deliverable I create and we iterate, working back and forth, until he finds the final product acceptable. For the most part, though, Jack simply delegates the work to me. He relies on my domain knowledge and our previous agreement on the form and structure for such documents to feel confident that he'll get a product that makes him happy.

Frankly, I haven't always been totally comfortable producing process-related deliverables in this pair-of-hands fashion. I trust my experience and my ability to prepare sensible process documents, so that's not the issue. Rather, I am sometimes concerned about how readily the people in the client organization will accept process materials—or any other artifacts—created by an outside third party (remember NIH and NAH?).

I saw evidence of this issue when I worked at Kodak years ago. Certain departments would hire consulting companies to create templates or other process documents for them, but some practitioners would resist using those items. The artifacts were created by people who didn't know the organization well. Sometimes they weren't a great fit for what the client teams needed or expected, often being more elaborate and fancy (lots of colored text) than necessary.

I've worried about encountering this reaction when performing similar work for Jack's company. It hasn't turned out to be a problem in practice, partly because of Jack's credibility and reputation in the company, and partly because of mine. Nonetheless, I believe that process-related deliverables are best created in a collaborative mode between a highly experienced consultant and members of the client organization. This helps the client staff buy into the new artifacts as their own.

My consulting agreements with Jack always include a general description of the type of services I will be performing and a list of deliverables. Such an agreement is called a statement of work, or SOW. Most of the time this works fine. We generally have a good mind meld and need little planning or scoping documentation. I understand what Jack is asking for and I can accomplish the objective independently without demanding a lot of his time.

Sometimes, though, Jack asks me to do something novel. Neither of us has a clear idea at the outset of exactly what the desired outcome is. In those cases, I ask him to write a short vision statement using the following keyword template, which is described in Chapter 5 of my book *Software Requirements*:

For	[target customer]
Who	[statement of the need or opportunity]
The	[deliverable name]
Is A	[type of deliverable]
That	[major capabilities or key benefits]
Unlike	[current reality or process]
This Deliverable	[primary differentiation and advantages of new deliverable]

Jack usually grumbles a bit about having to write this vision statement because I'm asking him to think carefully about just what he wants out of the project. That's hard! But then he works through the keyword template, and he always comes up with a clear, one-paragraph, structured statement that keeps us wonderfully focused on our mutual objective. I highly recommend asking your client to write such a vision statement anytime the nature or goals of the consulting engagement are too fuzzy at the outset.

WORKING SIDE-BY-SIDE: THE COLLABORATOR MODE

In the third type of consulting engagement—the collaborator mode—the outside consultant joins forces with members of the client organization to work on the project or solve the problem together. In contrast to the more independent work that characterizes the pair-of-hands mode, the collaborator mode involves frequent interactions between consultant and client to identify solutions, set priorities, make decisions, and create deliverables. As an analogy, you could think of co-authoring a book as being a collaborative project, whereas hiring a ghostwriter to craft your memoirs would be a pair-of-hands type of engagement.

A client hired me a few years ago for an extended off-site collaborative engagement. This financial services company wished to implement peer reviews as part of its architectural governance process. A manager at the company was familiar with my book *Peer Reviews in Software*, so he engaged me to help. The clients relied on my experience to advise them on how to make peer reviews effective in their environment for a specific set of work products and review objectives.

One member of the client's staff worked closely with me on this project to define their review process. We then developed several hours of e-learning presentations to train their staff in the new approach. The client drafted the slides and key talking points for the presentations, and then I fleshed out a script for each slide with a more detailed narrative. I have considerable experience giving presentations and developing e-learning training, so I could improve his initial slides for a richer presentation. I also recorded the audio from the scripts and generated the e-learning courseware, as I was already set up to do all that.

This was a fine example of collaboration, with a consultant and a client employee working side-by-side (albeit remotely in this instance) to generate effective work products that were better than either participant could have created alone. It was also informative and enjoyable for both of us.

I like these collaborative engagements the best. It's stimulating and fun to work with smart, creative, and energetic people. One thing I felt lacking in my career as soon as I became an independent consultant was the opportunity to kick ideas around with other people. There was no chance to scribble on a whiteboard together, get their feedback on work I've done, and put our heads together to come up with better solutions. I felt isolated. That's probably why I enjoy the collaborative engagements; they help to fill that gap in my professional interactions.

The collaborations provide good learning opportunities as well. They always leave me better prepared for the next project, with a broader base of knowledge and experience to rely on when I confront the next thorny challenge.

I recommend that you keep these different consulting modes in mind when future client opportunities arise. Understanding your own preferences will help you select those gigs that are likely to be most enjoyable and fulfilling. It's also a good idea to match the consulting mode with the needs of a specific project. Your client might ask to hire you to perform some work in a pair-of-hands mode, but your assessment of the project might indicate that a collaborative approach would be more effective. Shaping the engagement's parameters to yield the best client outcome is part of your responsibility as a consultant.

Next Steps

- Classify several of your most recent consulting experiences into one of these three engagement modes.
- Which of those engagements did you enjoy the most? The least? Did the consulting mode influence how much you enjoyed them? Why?
- Which of those engagements gave the client the best results? Did the consulting mode influence how effective they were? Why? Do you think a different consulting mode would have affected the outcome?
- If you conclude that you favor one mode over the others, seek to structure your future consulting engagements to emphasize that mode, where appropriate.

6

THE CONSULTING LIFESTYLE

By GARY K. EVANS

Anyone who's flirting with going independent must consider a number of issues. Consulting (or contracting) isn't just regular employment without a boss—it's *qualitatively* different from a traditional corporate position, and it's not for everyone. It affects both you and your family in a myriad of ways. It's not a move to undertake without carefully considering the implications.

WHY BECOME A CONSULTANT?

When I considered going out on my own, the fundamental question I had to face was: why do this? What inspires someone to walk away from the security of a salaried job?

The answer varies with the individual. Some want more income or more control over their professional lives. Others are running from a bad corporate position or seeking a challenging, and possibly exhausting, world of untapped potential. Still others are forced into the choice by a layoff. Regardless, you should examine your motives ruthlessly.

Survey the field in which you wish to market your services and ask yourself if it can supply your financial needs on a sustained basis. In 1999, the Y2K problem put COBOL and RPG programmers in high demand, and many with those skills jumped to contract or independent work. But by the end of 2001, it was the end of the road for many who had only those skills to bring to the market. You can't let your skills go stale.

Be brutal in your self-examination. Remember, you can't count on working whenever you like—you work when work is around, because it might not be available when you want it. If the thought of cold calling gives you chills, perhaps you're not ready to take the plunge. Are you ready to always be looking for work? Are you ready to accept each holiday and vacation period as unpaid days? Give the potential downside serious consideration.

If you do decide to give consulting a fling, please do not burn your former employee relationships. You might despise the company you're leaving, but don't ever say so publicly, and that includes on your social media accounts. Although you might think your former managers are all idiots, if you ever speak of them publicly, make sure you describe only what they did right. You can never know if you might someday need to rely on those very people to hire you or to act as a reference. In 1993, I was included in a layoff by NCR Corporation in the United States. Five weeks later, my first consulting client was NCR-Canada, with whom I had experienced zero prior contact. You just never know what the future may bring. Keep it professional, never personal.

What if you move to consulting and then realize this really is not for you? Always have a backup plan, as well as some money in the bank. As I discuss later on, consulting affects everyone in a family or a relationship. You might find that the stresses of job search, continual job uncertainty, weeks away from home, living in hotels, and eating meals alone is too high a price to pay. It all takes a toll. Eventually you might conclude that being an independent consultant is not a good fit for you, at least not now.

A simple recommendation if you want to test the consulting waters is to plan to spend six to twelve months building a consulting presence, while retaining your full-time job. If you find yourself unemployed and the job market is good, you might be able to fill your calendar with consulting work and perhaps even capture some full-time employment offers as well. In the latter scenario, one approach I embraced was to offer my services to a potential employer on a contract basis for, say, three months, so we could "test drive" each other. This way I was building my consulting credentials and history. They had already acknowledged that they thought I would make a valuable addition to their full-time staff, so their risk was low.

Two of the facets I love most about consulting are the flexibility it offers and the creativity it allows. You just have to think of how you can construct a win-win both for your own goals and for each company that engages you. If you decide that independent consulting is not to your taste or the work just doesn't materialize, consider joining a small consulting firm that needs your skills or even returning to a full-time employment position.

The flexibility that consulting provides lets you structure your work to best suit your life objectives and priorities. One consultant decided how much money she wanted to make each year. When she reached that magic number, she would then take the rest of the year off from consulting to spend time on other activities that were more important to her: family, hobbies, travel, self-education, whatever. Of course, this strategy works best when you're confident you'll be getting enough work to hit your income target before December 31.

The notion that consulting isn't a job, but rather is a way of doing a job, came home to me when I read Alan Weiss's excellent book *Million Dollar Consulting*. Essentially, we must have a field in which to conduct our consulting. You can choose to align yourself with a product, a vendor, a technology domain, a platform, or a project role. But beyond those choices, you must also find a focus, which should become your personal mission statement. Without this, you'll never know when to say no to a job offer. And if you don't say no to the wrong engagement, you won't be available to say yes when the right one comes along.

IT'S A FAMILY BUSINESS

Unless you're a hermit, don't fool yourself: consulting affects everyone in a family or a close relationship. For contractors as well as regular employees, time away from home takes its toll. In the expanding global marketplace, our industry requires more traveling than ever before. I recently checked my frequent-flier balance with Delta Airlines. It's over five hundred thousand miles, even after cashing in several tens of thousands of miles for family flight tickets. And this is only for Delta, which I have flown just four times in the past three years! I estimate I logged very close to one million miles across all airlines in my first seventeen years of consulting.

But even the grinding tedium of air travel does not compare to the stress that comes at the end of a contract when no other opportunity is present. Essentially, you're out of a job—again and again. The stress of finding clients, negotiating fees, terms, and schedules, and delivering what you promise can be a killer if you don't have confidence in your abilities and support from those closest to you.

All of this will take a physical toll also. I have been very active all my adult life—lifting weights and playing soccer. This physical activity is crucial to maintaining both my mental and physical well-being. Make time for yourself so you can stay as healthy as possible and be strong enough to support your family even when you're not there with them. Having work is great, but you need to take enough breaks to stay mentally and physically healthy.

When you disappear into a distant town, don't become just a vague memory for your loved ones. When I travel, I call home every single night to talk with my wife and my children so I can still have a presence at home. When my children were small, I helped them with homework over the phone. Math isn't easy to do by voice alone. All those years ago, my wife would fax or email the kids' assignment sheets to me, and I would go over the assignments with them, usually sending back examples of how to solve the problems.

It would have been infinitely better to be sitting at the kitchen table with them, but I could not, so this was a creative alternative. It required more effort from me, but it helped them and kept us in touch. And that's the whole point. Although today's technology makes maintaining a family presence much easier, you are still away from home.

If you work out of a home office and you have small children, you will face a special challenge. When I started consulting, my children were seven and one. My seven-year-old understood the signal of my office door: when Daddy's door is closed, he is working and you should not interrupt him; he will come out later to play. But my one-year-old knew no such restraint. When he heard me through the door typing or talking on the telephone, all he knew was: Daddy's home . . . play time! It broke my heart—and his—for me to have to gently move him out of my office so I could work.

For several years, I resorted to setting up shop with my laptop in a local public library several days a week. It was there in a (really) little room that I wrote my Object-Oriented Analysis and Design course of more than seven hundred pages. Getting out of the house insulated me from the many appealing distractions.

Another unanticipated possibility if you're working out of your home is that your spouse or partner really might not like having you hanging around all day. You think you're at work, but your partner sees you as interloping on what was private turf. "This is my kingdom during the day, when you should be at an office somewhere else!" is the unstated attitude. Your partner might not hesitate to ask you to fix the cord on the vacuum cleaner, invite you to drive to the hardware store to look at faucets, or generate any number of other innocent interruptions. Those interruptions add up and sap your productivity. You could find yourself staring at a screen at 10:00 p.m., realizing you accomplished nothing billable that day on the project your client is paying you to complete.

Expect that your days will not go as smoothly as you hope, and accept that both you and your family will have to make some lifestyle changes and accommodations. Assess yourself and your loved ones honestly. If you do decide to take the plunge, put the burden on yourself, so it looks easy from your family's point of view.

WORKING WITH FAMILY MEMBERS

Some people who set up a new self-employment business intend to work with some of their family members, either officially as paid employees or unofficially just to help out. In some cases this works out well. In others it can seriously threaten the domestic tranquility. One of my colleagues shared the following story:

> *When I started my consulting business, I had a second phone line installed in the house for my home office. Occasionally, I wouldn't be able to get to my phone in time when it rang, so I asked my wife if she could please answer it when that happens and take a message. She kind of glared at me. She had previously been a secretary for twenty-six years and had had enough of that gig. I explained that I was asking her to answer the phone not as my company's secretary, but rather as the other person who lived in the house with me. That mollified her somewhat, but she still wasn't thrilled about it. Clearly, the consulting business was my company alone.*

Before you decide to pull family members into your business, think carefully about the potential impacts on the family dynamics and economics. You might be passionate about your foray into the world of independent consulting, but your spouse, nephew, or second cousin once removed might not share your commitment to the cause. Sit down together to work out the specifics of expectations, communications, and compensation. A spouse who's already busy taking care of children and running the household while you gallivant around the countryside might not care to adopt any responsibilities for your business. She didn't have to help with your work when you went to a normal office; why should she now?

If a family member has the knowledge, time, and inclination to help out with certain aspects of your business, great. Bring him or her on board, and treat it like a business relationship, but with someone you already know well and enjoy being around. Otherwise, either plan to do all the work yourself or hire an assistant when necessary to help out with small or periodic tasks.

Next Steps

- Make a list of the significant lifestyle impacts you and your family might experience if you were to change from your current work mode into independent consulting. Rate each of those as a plus or a minus.
- For each important person in your daily life, list the positive and negative impacts that your becoming an independent consultant working out of a home office could have on them. Highlight any impacts that could be unduly disruptive. Can you think of ways to mitigate those negative impacts?
- Examine the previous two lists and judge whether the positives outweigh the negatives enough to make you—and your family—willing to give independent consulting a try.

Part II

On the Job

7

MAKE A LIST, CHECK IT TWICE

When I began giving presentations at software conferences in the early 1990s, most speakers used plastic transparencies on an overhead projector for their visuals. Only a few speakers had begun using laptop computers with Microsoft PowerPoint or other presentation software.

In those early days, I once presented a full-day tutorial at a local conference. I packed up my boxes of transparencies and headed to the conference site, clear across town from my home. Near the middle of my talk, I noticed that I was running out of plastic faster than I was running out of time. Suddenly I realized that I had brought only two of the four boxes of transparencies I needed for this full-day tutorial. Uh-oh. Seriously embarrassing and highly unprofessional (a descriptor I strive mightily to avoid).

Fortunately, the man who was running the conference saved my bacon. I had sent him an electronic file of my slides in advance, which he had loaded onto his laptop. After lunch I was able to complete my presentation using his laptop in lieu of my missing transparencies. That was my first live Power-Point experience and among my most awkward professional mistakes.

That was a close call. I learned my lesson, though. From then on I have *always* used a checklist to prepare for my speaking and consulting engagements. I already had created a travel checklist, but as this was a local event with no travel involved, I didn't bother to think carefully about what I needed to bring with me. I never made that mistake again.

TRAVEL CHECKLIST

My travel checklist has evolved over the years. I use it for both business and vacation travel. Different sections of the checklist remind me what to take along depending on which class I'm teaching. A separate section lists items to throw in the car when I'm driving somewhere instead of flying, like my favorite pillow and my stuffed teddy bear (just kidding about the teddy bear; not kidding about the pillow). I have a supplemental checklist for international travel that reminds me to pack my passport, foreign currency, power plug adapters, international SIM card for my phone, and so forth.

I am religious about using the checklist to plan each trip and pack my bags. It helps me to take along the right amount and right kinds of clothing, all of my toiletries and medications, the appropriate frequent-flier and car-rental cards, and the noise-canceling headphones that make long flights more bearable. It's also convenient to have a record of everything that's in my suitcase, should the airline's subterranean baggage-handling creatures devour it. Thanks to these checklists, I have never reached a destination and discovered that I was missing my laser pointer or a pair of socks.

You might scoff at my little checklists, but I tell you, they work. When I described my travel checklist to a fellow consultant, he chuckled, held up his index finger, and said, "My checklist has one thing on it: slides." But then he related the time he attended a conference to deliver a half-day tutorial, only to discover that he was scheduled to teach—but had not brought along materials for—a full day. My colleague needs a better checklist.

You can see the current version of my travel checklist at the Web Added Value™ (WAV) Download Resource Center at www.jrosspub.com. That page also offers several checklists graciously provided by consultant Mike Cohn. One is a comprehensive travel packing list, which is nicely organized into clothes, Dopp kit (what I call a toilet kit), gadgets, and other categories. A second list provides a comprehensive reminder of all the items he needs for the specific class he is presenting. When you're teaching a class that involves a variety of student activities, you don't want to come up short on any of the necessary workbooks, cards, sticky notes, or other materials you need. My classes are simpler than some of Mike's, so I put all that information right on my main travel checklist.

PLANNING AND TRACKING

A third list from Mike Cohn is a planning form for a specific client engagement that provides a place to organize all the necessary information. It's easy to overlook some of these bits, to your peril. For instance, I always get the cell phone number for my primary contact at the client site in case I encounter travel difficulties on the way there. Mike's engagement checklist has a place to record that sort of useful information. I've needed those numbers several times, like when an airline's pilots went on strike just hours before I was supposed to fly from one client site to another in a different country. I simply couldn't get there; we had to reschedule the event.

Mike also shared some checklists that identify the tasks he must perform to book a venue for a public class his company is presenting, as well as the items to take along when he's speaking to a regional group. I suspect Mike's events all run smoothly with the help of these planning aids.

Besides checklists, I've developed other forms that I use for various purposes in my consulting and training business. They are nothing fancy, but if you need similar forms for your own business, you are welcome to download those from the WAV page at www.jrosspub.com and tweak them to suit your purposes. One form lets me track the time I spend doing off-site consulting work in my home office for a client. I provide these kinds of services on an hourly basis, so I need to keep track of how much time I spend each month on project activities so I can send the client an appropriate invoice.

Perhaps this looks too lawyer-like to you. That's not the intent. I'm not trying to wring every dollar I can out of the client, but I do need an accurate record. I always round my time in the client's favor. If I ever have to do any rework because of a mistake I made, of course the client does not pay for that time. No client has ever asked to see these logs. They are useful for providing a client with cost updates and future estimates as we go along though.

I use the event tracking form to record information about speaking and consulting gigs I have scheduled. There are many bits of information to keep track of, and there have been times in my career when I had numerous events pending or awaiting payment. I don't want to overlook anything associated with such activities. I note when I sent out my speaking agreement and when it was returned with a signature, as well as the dates I made my airline, hotel, and rental car reservations. I can log the date I sent the course handout master to the client for duplication, and also when I ordered copies of my books to be shipped to the client for a class I'm teaching.

I don't want to arrive at a destination without my presentation files, so the form lets me note whether I have loaded all the necessary files onto my laptop (L) and also onto a backup flash drive (B). Finally, I record the dates when I completed the event, submitted the invoice to the client, and received payment (my favorite step in the process). Putting all of these items onto a single page shows me at a quick glance where each of my business events stands.

You might think my checklists are a waste of time, just another example of unnecessary process overhead. Perhaps you're right. Let's do an experiment. We'll both pack for the same trip. I'll use my travel checklist to help me. You just do whatever you normally do to pack. We'll see who runs out of underwear first.

Next Steps

- If you don't already have a travel checklist, download the ones from the Web Added Value™ (WAV) Download Resource Center at www.jrosspub.com and customize them to suit your specific needs.
- If you do already have a travel checklist, compare it to the ones on this book's WAV page for ideas of useful changes to make.
- Download the other forms from this book's WAV page and consider whether any of them, or forms like them, would help you plan and track your consulting events. Modify them as appropriate to suit your needs.

8

NO EASY ANSWERS

I've spent a lot of time helping organizations improve how they develop and manage the requirements for software projects. Most people realize this is a challenging task without many shortcuts. Yet some people have asked me questions in a way that suggests they hope I will provide a magic, easy solution to their difficult problem. If only I could.

IF IT WAS EASY, ANYONE COULD DO IT

Someone once asked me during a training course, "What should you do if your requirements are written in Japanese?" This American software development organization was collaborating with a Japanese company, which supplied their requirements initially written in their native language. I could think of only four possible ways to deal with this situation:

- Learn to read Japanese
- Have someone translate the requirements they receive from Japanese into English
- Persuade the Japanese originators to write them in English in the first place
- Have a Japanese speaker work closely with the Japanese company to do the translation as the requirements are being developed

This seems obvious to me. But I could tell from the inquirer's wistful expression and tone of voice that he was really hoping I knew of a painless solution to this problem. I'm pretty sure he already realized that there was none. (This was long before services like Google Translate existed.) Nevertheless, he asked. I hope he wasn't terribly disappointed with my response.

I would like nothing better than to offer amazingly effective and easy solutions to such challenges. Just think how much I could charge as a consultant if I knew those secrets! Alas, there are no such secrets. There are no magic wands, talking mirrors, genies in lamps, or all-knowing wizards. Sorry.

ABRACADABRA

In a second case, a business analyst told me that another BA she worked with sometimes proceeded with his part of their project without respecting the needs and limitations that her portion of the work imposed on his. She wanted ideas about how to deal with this problem.

My suggestion was to try to forge a more collaborative relationship with the second BA so they both could identify their interdependencies, partition the work appropriately, and work together effectively. However, she was reluctant to talk to the other BA. She didn't seem to think the strategy I proposed was feasible in her environment, so she dismissed it out of hand.

I wonder if she thought I had a secret code phrase that would make this other BA cooperate with her. Perhaps she was seeking some trick to make him more reasonable. Hypnotism, maybe? The best I could do was to propose that she sit down with the other players on this kind of project and have everyone tell their peers, "Here's what I need from you for us jointly to be successful. What do you need from me?" All project participants should be able to join in a conversation like this.

That's a more collaborative approach. It's not magic, it might be uncomfortable, and it might fail if the other participants refuse to play along. Sadly, not all project stakeholders are interested in being flexible and collaborative. I point out at the beginning of all of my training classes that none of the practices I'm going to describe are likely to work if you're dealing with unreasonable people. But people sometimes appear to be unreasonable when they are merely uninformed. I have seen apparently unreasonable people change their tune when presented with information they were lacking. If certain people you're trying to work with truly are being uncooperative, though, that's an interpersonal issue, not a technical problem.

FANTASY PLANNING

This desire for painless solutions also shows up when planning a project. Project managers and team members often are asked to estimate how much time, effort, or money it will take to accomplish a proposed—but often ill-defined—body of work. If you're asked for such an estimate, you might return an answer your manager or your customer doesn't like. Perhaps it requires more resources than are available, or it will take longer than the customers desire. These disappointed people can exert considerable pressure on you to change your estimate, even if there's no good reason to. Simply cutting the estimate doesn't make the project smaller or reduce how long it will take to do the work. It just moves everyone deeper into a fantasy world. It's comforting, perhaps, but it's not helpful.

I saw a striking example of this phenomenon once with a project manager (I'll call her Melanie). A senior manager asked Melanie in a heavily-attended department meeting how long it would take to complete a particular project. Melanie replied, "Two years." This manager said, "That's too long; I need it in six months."

So how did Melanie respond? She simply said, "Okay." In other words, she just pretended it was feasible to execute this project in six months. I'm not a huge fan of pretending at work.

But what *really* changed during those few seconds? Nothing! The required work did not shrink by a factor of four. Melanie's team did not instantly quadruple its productivity. No additional people were assigned to the project. Nor were Melanie's estimation method and assumptions questioned. Perhaps Melanie and the manager who asked the question had different perceptions of the project's scope, but that possibility wasn't discussed. Melanie's answer simply stated what she knew the senior manager wanted to hear.

Not surprisingly, the project took more than two years. Even thoughtful estimates often are optimistic and don't account for risks, unexpected events, and the inevitable scope growth.

It does no one any favors to pretend that the world is different from how it really is. It's fruitless to seek magic solutions for difficult problems when there aren't any. At times, I'm not that crazy about reality, but it's all I have, so I must deal with it. So do my clients, whether they like it or not. Sometimes, that means we encounter technical barriers or interpersonal challenges we cannot easily fix, no matter how badly we want to.

Instead of searching for secret solutions, we have to rely on skilled technical practitioners, adroit project managers, and legitimate leaders who can steer teams of people toward effective communication and collaboration. That's a special kind of magic in itself.

Next Steps

- Reflect on conversations you have had, or observed, in which someone appeared to be either applying or responding to performance pressure in an unreasonable way. Is there a more realistic way the parties could have approached the conflict to reach an acceptable agreement?
- Have you encountered situations in which a client or fellow team member seemed to expect a magic solution to a thorny problem? Can you think of effective ways to sell more realistic and practical solution ideas to them?

9

CONSULTANTS AS LEGITIMATE LEADERS: THE GOLDILOCKS APPROACH

By JEANETTE PIGEON

Today, many people are protesting a perceived lack of legitimate leadership in private industry and government. By *legitimate leadership*, I mean power that is exercised fairly and is based on a relationship of trust between a leader and followers. Followers grant this leadership of power and authority because they believe an individual exhibits the characteristics to lead and to create win-win outcomes. A *leader* is a guide whose ideas define the paths for a group to follow to a shared goal or outcome in a collaborative way.

As a consultant, you might have wondered how you can effectively lead a team of professionals during the short tenure of a contract assignment. Because you are an outsider to the organization and have a limited amount of time to complete a project, you need to establish yourself quickly as a capable leader who can win over the hearts and minds of others. They need to see you as a confident and highly competent guide who knows the path for them to follow, built upon a foundation of trust and reinforced through consistency of behavior and communication.

The big question is how to build this trust quickly. Do you try to satisfy everyone by being overly friendly and flexible? Or do you aggressively assert your dominance, so everyone knows who's in charge? I recommend you use a Goldilocks approach: not too weak, yet not too strong.

As in the Brothers Grimm's tale of *Goldilocks and the Three Bears*, legitimate leadership is earned using a just-right approach. Being either too weak or too strong will not develop team cohesion nor motivate others to pursue a common goal to reach successful outcomes. These approaches are one-sided; neither establishes a trusting relationship. To build trust, you must practice the 3 Cs of legitimate leadership: *confidence, competence,* and *consistency* of behavior and communication. Practicing the 3 Cs will help you establish and maintain a relationship of mutual trust to create win-win outcomes. Let's consider each of the three possible approaches and their efficacy in creating legitimate leadership.

TOO WEAK

You attempt to build trust by trying to satisfy everyone. You're unable to articulate a common path. You appear to have no sense of direction, to be a flip-flopper with no consistent vision. When you speak, you are inarticulate or inconsistent about the team's goals or how they can achieve those goals. You try to be nice to your team members and to give them as much time and leeway as they want, even though this might conflict with what your project requires to be successful. Your stakeholders don't see substantive progress, so their expectations are not met. As a result, you create a leadership vacuum.

In a leadership vacuum, one or more team members may rise and become implicit leaders of the team, undermining your leadership authority. When working in a matrix organization or with a newly formed team, members don't collaborate effectively. Some might constantly challenge your authority over the team.

In the process of trying to accommodate everyone individually, you satisfy no one. You do not appear to be a competent leader of a fully functioning team. Your confidence in the face of these obvious capability and trust gaps makes you appear out of touch and ineffective as a leader.

TOO STRONG

You dominate the team members and other stakeholders and create a dictatorship. Team members are dragged down a path that is fraught with difficulty, delays, and failed projects. Stakeholders and team members become intimidated. They won't open up to you and tell you the truth. Instead of establishing a trusting relationship with your people, you achieve the opposite. You ignore the organizational culture and hierarchy, and you reject or fail to solicit input from others. People resent you and what you are trying to achieve. The results can include a failure to follow your lead and perhaps even attempts to sabotage your efforts.

Leading others through fear and intimidation is never effective when collaboration is your goal. Although you might appear to the stakeholders to be a competent subject matter expert, you don't appear effective as a leader. Consequently, you don't earn the trust or legitimate leadership of your team or your stakeholders.

JUST RIGHT

You've taken the time to meet with key members of your team and other stakeholders. You've established a bond with each of them as a person and as a professional. You are sensitive to their needs and desires, and you have set appropriate expectations about working together and what will be achieved. You maintain an open-door policy, encourage questions and ideas, and work openly to address concerns and to mitigate risks.

As issues arise, you seek to resolve them fairly and face-to-face without creating added tension or causing others to become defensive. You walk the talk and roll up your sleeves, working alongside the team members when necessary. Your team is cohesive; the team members understand how to engage you and what you expect of them. They are not afraid to seek your counsel and will let you know if issues arise before you're aware of them. Morale is high; people put in extra effort without being asked. Stakeholders are satisfied, and they appreciate how efficiently and effectively your team performs.

Legitimate leadership is the reward of those who build a relationship of trust and exhibit the 3 Cs: confidence of leadership, competence as a subject matter expert, and consistency of behavior and communication. The just-right approach to legitimate leadership will allow you to more easily assert the leadership role among your team and stakeholders, enjoying the collaborative synergy that results. Your team and its stakeholders will enjoy working with you, satisfied in having achieved the stated goals. A series of such win-win outcomes will contribute to a long and professionally fulfilling consulting career.

Next Steps

- Think of two or three people you have encountered whom you consider to be legitimate leaders. What behaviors did they exhibit that gave you confidence in their leadership?
- Think of two or three people you have encountered who were not effective leaders. Why not? What could they have done differently to give you confidence in their ability to lead?
- Have you known leaders or managers whom you did not trust? Why didn't you trust them?
- Examine your own leadership style and see if the analysis from the preceding three steps offers any ideas about how you could transform yourself into a more effective, legitimate leader.

10

OMG, WHAT HAVE I DONE?! ANTICIPATING RISKS WHEN WORKING WITH OTHERS

By VICKI JAMES

I quit my public-service project management job a few years ago to enter the world of independent consulting. I thrive on change and the idea of bringing new and better ideas, processes, and tools to as many people and organizations as possible. Unfortunately, I made a mistake along the way. This mistake could occur with a variety of working relationships, including corporate employment, project collaborations, consulting for clients, and business partnerships.

The story begins about six weeks after I had left my civil service position, where I had been a business analyst and project manager for eleven years. I had started talking with one of the owners of a local technology company about subcontracting opportunities in both of those fields. Instead, they offered me a job as a salaried employee. Great! I could earn a salary doing what I wanted, consulting with different clients while helping the company to expand its business opportunities. The difference was that my work would be through an established company rather than my own startup.

What did I have to lose? I was prepared to postpone establishing my own consulting business for one year as a worst-case scenario. This company hired me without even an interview, which seemed at the time like a vote of confidence and a sure sign of success. In hindsight, I went to work for them with too little information, and I paid the price.

Interviews are a funny thing. Most of us fear them. What questions will they ask? Will they like me? Will I sound knowledgeable? Do I have spinach in my teeth? I often counsel others who are considering a change that the interview also is a chance for them to find out about the prospective employer and judge how well the company might align with the candidate's professional goals and expectations.

Too bad I did not listen to my own advice. I did not take the opportunity to explore how the company would help—or hinder—my own professional aspirations. Instead, I envisioned a world in which they would leverage my expertise to expand their own business, both in terms of the client projects I took on and by relying on my experience and tendency to act to bring better process to my own work environment.

The management structure of the company consisted of four officers: three investors and a hired operations manager. By one officer's own admission, there was not a single decision maker. Instead, the company philosophy was management by consensus. This approach did not allow for serious consideration of my ideas for process improvement within the company.

I felt as if my expertise and experience were not valued because of this. Initially, I chalked it up to being the new girl on the block. Eventually, though, the reality became clear that adding another perspective to their dynamic would confuse things more than they already were in their leaderless decision-making processes.

Things began to unravel almost a year into the position, when they assigned me to manage a troubled project. I had been working directly with various clients on contracts away from the central office and bosses until this time. It was while working with the bosses on managing a high-profile client that I began to recognize the extent of the differences in our business philosophies and professional ethics. Here are some examples of the struggles I encountered:

- Management often questioned and criticized my actions, decisions, and communications because we did not share the same client- and team-management principles. I am generally forthright and candid; I communicate everything to all. They preferred to hold information close to the vest. Rarely did a week go by that I was not "counseled" by one of the bosses. Often, this was after I had previously discussed some strategy with another boss. They did not have a shared philosophy among themselves, and I often paid the price for their lack of continuity.
- I am an analytical and process-oriented individual. In this fast-moving technology company, I always felt that projects were in chaos. The

managers believed that process slowed down development and, there-fore, billing. I don't agree.

- The management team as a whole did not buy into the value of project management. One or more bosses would often ignore or overturn my recommendations and actions in relation to project process, clients, and team development. On at least two occasions, the Chief Technology Officer made derogatory comments to me regarding "you project management types."

This was clearly a clash of working styles and values. I now realize that an interview and more exploration up front might have kept me from taking a job at a company where I would not be happy. I might have avoided the position altogether or been able to propose conditions of employment. Because I leapt at this appealing opportunity without performing due diligence, I missed an important opportunity to identify and manage some of the risks of working with other people. Instead, I spent fourteen months in a position that was not satisfying.

Different professional relationships come with different risks. I now see how important risk analysis is when I consider this from the perspective of an independent consultant and the opportunities that might come along. Let me give you some examples.

CLIENTS

Some clients will come with a cost greater than the benefit you hope to receive. It may be that there is too little—or no—money if the client does not pay as agreed and you end up in the hole. There may be other financial consequences to the company, such as the cost of employee turnover or the impact on the company's reputation if things go badly.

Get to know your clients and document all agreements, both financial and operational, before beginning work. You always have the option to turn the work down. This should be given serious consideration when the risk is high.

BUSINESS PARTNERS

Taking on a business partner is much like getting married in the sense of financial and legal obligations. The unfortunate ending in either case is called *dissolution*, and it can be very damaging. You should understand your future business partner well enough to be able to identify the risks and benefits of working together. See Chapter 18 (*When One Is Not Enough*) for some suggestions about how to lay a solid foundation for effective partnerships. Risk mitigation is far easier and less painful than crisis resolution.

COLLABORATORS

You will need to rely on your collaborators to uphold their end of the bargain and to treat you fairly when you join forces to complete a project. Get to know them. If you need to, check references either formally or informally. Discuss and document all agreements up front to avoid misunderstandings. I recently began collaborating with a colleague on a writing project. This time I was much more careful to consider what could go wrong and how likely it would be to happen. That's the essence of risk analysis.

Whether you're exploring a client-vendor relationship, an employee-employer relationship, or partnering with someone in a business or on a project, consider the following questions to begin recognizing the potential risks:

- Do you share a common vision for the business or project?
- Do you know, accept, and respect each other's work ethics, dedication, commitment, and constraints?
- Do your skills complement each other? For instance, do you have a skill your client lacks, or does one partner have a strategic, big-picture outlook for the company, while the other can focus on the details?
- Is there mutual respect for each other's expertise? That is, can you be confident that your ideas will be fairly considered, or does your client or partner believe she already has all the answers?

Once you've acquired more information, you can ponder further. What are the likely benefits of the collaboration? What can you imagine possibly going wrong? What impact could those outcomes have on you mentally, financially, or professionally? What is the likelihood of each of those risks materializing into an actual problem? Do the benefits outweigh the risks?

This is where I failed in my own situation. While I had considered that the worst-case outcome of employment was deferring my move into independent consulting for a year, I did not take the time to adequately explore the range and likelihood of other potential unpleasant outcomes from taking this position. I hope you will gain some valuable insight from this experience so we can all learn from my mistake.

Next Steps

- List several qualities you would want to see in a collaborator or partner with whom you might work.
- Identify several behaviors you could exhibit that you think would make you a more effective business partner or project collaborator and someone people would like to work with.

11

THE DREAM CLIENT

What makes an ideal client, a company or an individual that you hope will call you back over and over? The best clients are fun to work with, appreciate your value, benefit from your contributions, and treat you well. They don't waste your time or make you feel as though you are wasting theirs. They pay you on time and without hassle. They present interesting challenges and opportunities that give you a chance to apply all of your skills and knowledge and to grow from the experience

Can such terrific clients really exist? They do!

DREAM CLIENT #1

I've been fortunate to have had several ideal clients over the years. My very first consulting client, Sandy, was in that category, so I got a bit spoiled early in my career. Sandy was a mid-level manager leading software process improvement efforts in a company in Rochester, New York. I met her when I gave a presentation for a local professional group while I was still working at Kodak. She read my first book, *Creating a Software Engineering Culture*, and then she hired me to help with their improvement efforts in several capacities. I worked for Sandy and others in her company at various locations for several years, mostly in the collaborator consulting mode.

Sandy and I worked well together and became friends. We're still in touch today. I like it when I stay friends with some of my clients long after our collaboration has ended. Some consultants prefer to maintain a professional distance from the people who hire them. Not me. We can work together, exchange money for services rendered, and be friends without any of these various connections tangling each other up. It was great fun last spring when

I just happened to bump into a former client, with whom I've stayed in touch for more than ten years, when we were both visiting a winery in Washington State—totally random and a real treat. Plus, the wine there was excellent.

Sandy demonstrated another characteristic of a first-rate client. She was highly skilled at reading the politics of her corporate environment and navigating them successfully without getting caught up in the politics herself. She knew how to pitch proposed process changes in a way that would grab the right managers' attention and make the changes politically acceptable.

This talent made Sandy quite effective at incorporating the changes we advocated into her organization so they yielded the maximum benefits. It was educational to watch her chart the political and management minefields and cruise around the obstacles. If you can't read the politics and steer them to your advantage, then you might be victimized by them.

DREAM CLIENT #2

I've worked for another great client for more than fifteen years. Bill leads the software process activities in a large company with dozens of divisions worldwide that make complex software and hardware products. I've provided many types of services to Bill's company, including teaching classes, speaking at their internal technology conferences, writing process documents, reviewing requirements specifications, and consulting on a variety of special projects. Bill employs several consultants who specialize in various areas to augment his personal efforts. He can direct consulting opportunities to whoever is the best fit and is available when he needs them.

Bill is an ideal client for many reasons. He gives me as much work as I'm interested in doing, while respecting the times I decline an offer from him. He has never given me any hassle on contracting, always accepts my standard speaking and consulting agreements, never challenges my fees, and insulates me from his corporate legal department. Bill has referred me to managers of numerous divisions in his large company to provide consulting and training services. My dozens of invoices have always been paid on time. Sometimes he even gives away many copies of my books to his colleagues.

Bill also has been generous about sharing ownership of our work products. Occasionally he has asked me to develop some artifact, such as a document template or a process description, that I was interested in adding to my own collection for use with other clients. Bill has always agreed to do so, in exchange for a discounted rate on my consulting fee for that portion of the work.

On top of all that, Bill and I have become good friends. We've socialized outside our professional engagements, visited some wineries together, and even visited each other's homes, even though we live more than twenty-five hundred miles apart.

It has been a real pleasure to work with clients like Sandy, Bill, and a few others with equally desirable characteristics. I didn't do anything special to find these dream clients. We just connected at some point and found that we fit together well. Perhaps you'll be as fortunate. You might contemplate the characteristics you'd like to see in your own perfect clients so you can target your marketing efforts toward such folks and cultivate a long-term connection if you find one.

I've had a handful of clients who rose above the norm in a different way: they actually paid me bonuses! After teaching a one-day class at one company, the payment I received included an extra five hundred dollars. When I inquired about this (I know, don't look a gift horse in the mouth), my client contact said the feedback on my class was excellent and made him look good. Hence, he thought I deserved a bonus. The same sort of thing happened with one or two other clients also. It's always great to know that people enjoy both the work you do and their relationship with you.

Alas, not all clients fit in this ideal class. The next two chapters describe some far less appealing clients and what you might do when certain problems arise.

Next Steps

- Identify some of the clients you have particularly enjoyed working for. Which of their characteristics or behaviors did you find appealing and rewarding? Could you influence any of those factors through your behaviors as a consultant?

12

CLIENTS WHO GIVE YOU GRIEF

I have worked with about 130 clients in my years as a consultant and trainer, including companies in the United States and abroad; government agencies at the federal, state, and local levels; and individuals. I've sold my products to hundreds more customers worldwide. Nearly all of these have been easy and trouble-free to work with. But a few have given me headaches. This chapter relates some of the problems I've encountered, so you can be alert for those in your own consulting work.

GETTING STIFFED

Several consultants I know have been stiffed by one or two of their clients— they simply never paid for services rendered. This has happened to me just once (see Chapter 19, *It's a Matter of Policy*). I've come close a couple of other times. I once did a two-week European seminar tour sponsored by a software tool vendor, teaching six one-day courses in three countries. Afterward, I simply could not get the company to pay me. It wasn't a trivial amount of money, either.

After multiple requests, I finally received payment. The check required the signatures of two company officers, yet no one at all had signed it! I was fed up. In a pretty sour mood, I called the company's president. A check for the full amount—signed, no less—arrived the next day by overnight delivery. Amazing, eh? It just shouldn't be that difficult to get paid for the work you've done.

On two occasions, individual customers did not pay for products they had ordered from me. They ignored my invoices and follow-up emails. As it happens, both of these customers were outside the United States. Consequently, I changed my billing policy: now I will no longer ship a product to a purchaser outside the U.S. until their payment is sitting in my bank account. It's a shame that a very few people make life more difficult for everyone through their irresponsible actions.

I have occasionally had problems with delayed payments when a client required my little sole-proprietorship company to enter into a subcontracting arrangement with one of their established contractors. The contractor typically waits until the client pays them for my services before they will pass the funds along to me. This can add a month or more to the usual payment cycle.

Last year just such a contractor did not pay me on time and would not respond to my inquiries. No one at the state government agency for whom I had done the work seemed to have any influence over the contractor, whom they had already paid. It took several months of inquiring, cajoling, threatening, and escalating (I consulted with a contracts attorney), but I finally did get paid in a series of biweekly installments. Such income uncertainty—let alone the hassle factor—is just one of the issues you have to get used to as an independent consultant.

I suspect the contractor was having some cash flow problems that led to the delayed payment. Now, I'm not an unreasonable man. If they had simply told me about the situation, we could have worked out a payment schedule without this level of acrimony and frustration. I'll never work for that client again, and I'll never work as a subcontractor again.

On the plus side, for the first time in my twenty-four-year consulting experience, I had to invoke the interest-due-for-late-payments clause that I include in every client agreement. Amazingly, the contractor paid the extra money without argument. So the situation resulted in a good financial outcome for me, although it wasted a lot of time, energy, and goodwill, and for a while I feared I wouldn't be paid at all.

FIRING A CLIENT

One year, when I was still working at Kodak before going independent, I helped plan our internal software engineering conference. We were considering a speaker for the keynote presentation, a well-known figure in a particular software area. However, one of the planning committee members said that the consultant we had in mind had experienced a previous unpleasant incident with Kodak, and that he was no longer willing to work at the company. No one knew exactly what the details of the problem were.

At the time, my reaction was, "How arrogant!" When I became a consultant myself, however, I discovered that some clients simply aren't worth the trouble. There are a very few clients that I won't work with again for various reasons, including sluggish payments, too many problems encountered with contracting or invoicing (like invoices that disappeared simply because one particular individual changed jobs), and incredibly slow or erratic decision making. If the opportunity arises and you need the income, you'll probably just bite your tongue and tolerate difficult clients. But if you have the luxury of having enough work, it sometimes makes sense to say, "Thanks, but no thanks" when certain clients call you again.

One of my consultant friends tried for nearly eighteen months to receive a payment from a large technology company, to no avail. Ultimately, they offered to pay him a discounted amount within thirty days or the entire balance at some indeterminate future date. Totally fed up, my friend contacted the office of the president of this huge company. To his relief, he was paid right away. Wouldn't it have been easier for everyone if the company had just paid the bill as promised? My friend refused to do any further work with that client. Coincidentally, I had so many problems with that same company myself that years ago I decided not to deal with them again either. They just aren't worth it.

Problems with clients sometimes lead to changes in your business practices. When I encountered a couple of clients who took far longer to pay me than I thought was reasonable, I adopted a new policy. Rather than invoicing a new client after I deliver a training class for the speaking fee plus my travel and lodging expenses, I began quoting an all-inclusive fee, submitting an invoice in advance, and requesting that payment be delivered when I arrive to present the course.

Nearly all of my clients accepted this policy. I might relax the policy when I have a sustained and successful relationship with a client or in other special circumstances, like when I wish to defer income into the next calendar year for tax reasons. Otherwise, though, the class starts when I receive my check.

Some consultants request payment of a portion of their fee in advance, which they retain if the client cancels the event. I've never done that, although I do include a cancellation fee in my speaking agreement. See Chapter 17 (*Everything's Negotiable*) for more about cancellation fees.

QUESTIONABLE ETHICS

I use a simple written consulting agreement to itemize the specifics of each client engagement. A prospective client once asked me to state in the agreement that I would be performing a certain kind of work, because that's what they had funding for. In reality, though, I would be doing something different while I was on site. My client told me that if the agreement stated what I would really be doing, his management wouldn't approve it.

This struck me as unethical. What if a senior manager had discovered that I was doing something other than what had been approved and funded? Not only would I probably not get paid, I wouldn't be hired by that company again, and my professional reputation could be damaged. Maybe I could even get sued.

Perhaps there are some gray areas when it comes to integrity. But if someone explicitly asks you to lie about work that you do, that's black-and-white. I declined this invitation and never dealt with that company again.

A POOR FIT

The notion of being scrupulously ethical in professional dealings applies to consultants as well as to clients, of course. While I was at Kodak early in my software development career, my team needed to bring in a database consultant from a major vendor for some short-term help. I spoke to the prospective consultant and asked how much experience he had in the area with which we were struggling.

"I haven't done that before," he replied, "but I can learn along with you." I'm sorry, that answer is incorrect, but thanks for playing. It seemed unethical for him to request that we pay $1,200 a day for him to learn alongside us. We found a different consultant who knew what he was doing.

As a consultant, it's important to acknowledge your limitations as well as your capabilities. Once in a while, I receive an inquiry from a client who's seeking help in an area in which I lack expertise. I never offer a proposal in such a case because I know there are more appropriate people available. If someone can do a better job for the client than I can for a particular service, that's who the client should hire. I'm always happy to refer a potential client to another consultant who's a better fit for their needs. Similarly, I'm grateful when other consultants point clients toward me.

I neither pay nor accept finder's fees for these sorts of referrals, although I have known other consultants who did. I figure that if everybody is willing to help match up prospective clients with the right consultants, then everybody's back gets scratched. It all averages out in the end.

KNOCKING YOUR HEAD AGAINST THE WALL

A consultant friend of mine, Peter, pointed out that when you've lost hope of having any effectiveness with a client, it's time to move on. You should also bail if a company is abusing or taking advantage of you in any way.

Peter once consulted for a company that practiced what he termed *management by rage*. Peter made it clear to his contacts that there had better not be any rage directed at him. The relationship worked for a while, but then Peter became viewed as a threat by one of the managers. One day that manager raged at Peter behind closed doors for twenty minutes, complaining, "You're trying to take over my job!" In reality, Peter had no interest in the manager's job. The man was simply being unreasonable. Peter did get the manager to apologize to him at one point during the meeting for making such outrageous statements.

Afterward, Peter was understandably shaken by the experience. After he calmed down, he thought about whether he still wanted to pursue that consulting engagement. He decided that he didn't, so he quit. The company's management sent a more reasonable person to see how much money Peter wanted to come back, but Peter still said no and walked away.

Again, a very few clients simply are not worth the aggravation they cause. Try to identify them early and make your escape.

CLIENTS WHO GO DARK

I once had a client who brought me in twice, both to deliver some training classes and to do some consulting work. I thought the events all went fine, and the manager who hired me seemed happy with the results. At the end of my second visit he said he wanted to set up another engagement soon.

After I returned home, I sent this manager a speaking agreement for the dates he had requested. No reply. I emailed him several more times to follow up. No answer. I phoned and left several voice mails. No response.

This client literally never contacted me again. I don't know what the problem was, but I would have appreciated it had he simply told me they were no longer interested in my services. This would have saved me the time and trouble of repeatedly attempting to contact him, which I was doing at his request, after all. Weird.

Actually, I did hear from him a few years later, in a way. I received a flood of virus-infested messages that appeared to come from his email address. Somehow, that seemed fitting.

Next Steps

- Think of any specific problems you have had with clients. Perform some root cause analysis to understand why each problem occurred. Is there anything you could have done to detect the issue earlier and keep it from becoming an actual problem?
- List any clients you've had that you wouldn't want to work for again. Why not? Are you being reasonable in blocking them out? Are there warning signs you could look for in the future to see if another client might pose similar problems?
- State any conditions or actions that would make you reluctant to work with a client again.

13

DIFFICULT CLIENT?
TRY THESE QUICK TIPS

By MARGARET MELONI

Your hands are sweating; your stomach is in knots. Once again, you have a client who has become truly obnoxious. Somehow, he is driving you crazy. If you say *left*, he says *right*. The hiring honeymoon is over, and now you see that your client is—believe it or not—a difficult person.

Part of your challenge is that your attachment to your client is both financial- and relationship-based. Oh, and it is tied to money. Wait, did I already say that? Well, which of you are *not* in business to make money?

What about being respected for your knowledge and your expertise? And—dare I say it—what about your ego? How can this person, this client, hire you to do something and then turn around and disregard your advice? Or, even worse, ask for your input and then do the exact opposite? I mean, really, what's up with that?

You know that your reputation either attracts or repels potential clients. You also know that your ability to get along well with your clients is a strong component of your professional reputation. I would suggest that most of the burden of resolving a difficult situation resides with you. As a consultant, you are hired to be the best of the best. Frequently you serve as a role model to your client and their team. There are expectations that come with being hired for your skills and experience; you are expected to represent professional behavior at its very best.

It is not likely that your difficult client will change for you, but you can change the way the two of you interact. You can take more control of the situation and work toward a positive outcome. To accomplish that, I must ask you to do two things: let go of your attachment to finances and, if applicable, set your ego aside.

When you let money and ego drive the situation, it shows. I recently overheard a consultant speaking about one of his clients in this manner. "I do not have time for their problems; I have money to make," the consultant said. I'll bet his client thinks of *him* as the difficult person. Unless this consultant has some very rare expertise, this might not be a long-term assignment, and this client probably will not look to him for future engagements. However, this doesn't mean that if you *do* have rare expertise, it's okay to be difficult. No one enjoys dealing with difficult people.

If you can let your concern for building an effective working relationship take charge, you are well on your way to a positive outcome. Once you're ready to speak to your difficult client about the friction points, consider the following approach.

- Prepare for the conversation in advance. Identify what you hope to gain from the interaction, and begin with this end in mind.
- Be flexible. Do not be so focused on your end goal that you can't take a detour in the conversation. This detour may help you better understand your difficult client's point of view.
- Select a time that is convenient for both of you, a time when you both can listen and exchange ideas.
- Listen—really listen—to what your difficult client has to say. If he says something like, "I cannot do that" or "that won't work," ask why. Whatever issue he has might not be about you at all. Try to get the real problem out in the open.
- Consider letting the client speak first. If he seems comfortable taking the lead in the conversation, let him.
- Maintain emotional objectivity. Remember, whatever drives him to be difficult is about him, not about you. Again, try to turn off your ego and stop thinking about your checkbook.
- Stay calm. An individual who is upset may become defensive and verbally attack you. If this happens, take a deep breath and pause before responding.

If the discussion becomes too heated, you might suggest to your difficult client that you both take some time to cool off. Then agree upon a time when you will reconvene.

No matter how challenging, you both need to resolve the issue. Create an agreement between you and your client to stick with the situation until you have both been able to understand one another. You want to create a relationship where you and your difficult client can work together and respect each other as individuals and professionals, even if you'll never be best friends.

Next Steps

- Have you encountered any particularly difficult clients yourself? If so, how did you try to deal with them? Could you put the issues on the table and confront them calmly and objectively? If not, why not? How might you change your approach on a similar situation in the future?
- Have you ever worked with a client who thought *you* were being difficult? Did they have a legitimate point? If so, is there anything you could change to avoid having a future client think you're being difficult?

This book has free material available for download from the
Web Added Value™ resource center at *www.jrosspub.com*

Part III

Practicalities

14

WHAT ARE YOU WORTH?

One of your first challenges as a self-employed person is determining what to charge for your services and products. There isn't a guidebook for setting prices. It's very much a matter of what the market will bear. As with most service providers, the more experience you have and the better known you are in your field, the more you can ask. I've known some consultants who charged less than they could probably get away with. It's hard to know how much you can command until you push the limits and see what happens.

HAPPY EITHER WAY

The best advice I ever found on setting prices came from an insightful book by Gerald M. Weinberg called *The Secrets of Consulting: A Guide to Giving & Getting Advice Successfully*. Weinberg's Principle of Least Regret states: "Set the price so you won't regret it either way." In other words, choose a price so you're happy whether the client says yes or no to your proposal. I keep this principle in mind every time I prepare a price quote for a prospective engagement.

As an example, I have taught a particular training course, most often in two-day format, 187 times. Put another way, I have spent more than one full year of my life presenting this material! It's not very exciting for me anymore. If a client asks me to teach this course now, I often would rather not do it. Therefore, I might ask for more money to teach that course than for another one that's more interesting to do. If the client accepts my offer, fine—I'll be there. I'll do the best job I possibly can because that's what the students deserve, regardless of how I feel about it. I'll smile all the way to the bank.

Weinberg's principle also helped me regulate how many commitments I made during those years when I was fortunate enough to receive an abundance of inquiries. If you're hungrier, you might be tempted to charge less to boost your chances of landing the gig. During the rich times, though, you can quote higher fees to make sure you don't exhaust yourself by accepting every opportunity that comes along. It's all a matter of balancing your supply of time with customers' demand for your services.

WHAT THE MARKET WILL BEAR

When I launched my independent consulting career in the late 1990s, I set my fees based on what I saw other consultants were charging. Back then I charged $1,500 a day for consulting and $2,500 a day for training. I figured that training was a higher-leverage activity. Providing useful information to 25 students at a time is more valuable to the client than a one-on-one consultation. Therefore, I believed I was entitled to more compensation for teaching a class.

Over the years, those rates went up. But I still know some established consultants who are charging only around $1,500 a day to deliver training. In my view, they are underpricing their services. Obviously, you'll make less if you're working through a parent company that contracts out your services—such as an established training company in your field—or an agency that finds jobs for you. They're working on your behalf and are entitled to their slice.

There is a school of thought that says the higher your price, the greater the perception of value to the prospective client. Therefore, you will get more work if you charge more. Sometimes this strategy does work, at least up to a point. I have some colleagues who said they landed more gigs when they raised their training rate. Of course, there's an upper cap beyond which clients will seek lower-priced options.

Raising your rates with existing clients is a bit tricky. They'll probably want to know what the justification is for the increase, and they may or may not buy your argument. You might want to keep your current rate schedule in place with ongoing clients, applying any increases to future engagements with new clients.

One of my colleagues gradually increased his hourly rate for custom software development projects by telling prospective new clients what he was currently charging and then inviting them to beat that number, thereby procuring his services. At one point, he actually had representatives from two client departments standing in the same room and bidding for his services! Few consultants will be so fortunate as to get into an auction situation, but if you have a reputation for doing fast, high-quality work, you can set your fees to the maximum the market will tolerate. Again, it's all about the basic economics of supply and demand.

I suggest you base your fee for a specific engagement on the value you're providing to the client. Delivering a presentation that has an unlimited audience provides more value to the client than a class with restricted attendance. If I'm helping one person with some project questions, I will provide less value than if I'm developing a new requirements process to be deployed across a company's entire software development organization.

I've done some experiments with pricing the products I sell through my website, such as e-learning courseware, e-books, and template collections. I wanted to test the notion that increasing the price also increases the perceived value, thereby leading to more sales. I've tried raising prices, lowering prices, running half-price sales, offering discounted bundle packages, and offering buy-one-get-one-free and other discount promotions. Nothing seemed to make much difference in how many items I sold, except possibly cutting the price in half. I've concluded that if someone wants a particular product, they're likely to just buy it, if the price is not totally out of line. They're not going to buy something that they're not enthusiastic about, no matter the price.

Having more competitors enter your domain can exert downward price pressure. I observed this in the field of software requirements training. I got into the game early, with a well-received book and numerous articles and presentations in this area. I could command substantial fees for teaching classes. However, as more and more people wrote books about requirements and business analysis and developed their own training materials, requirements training became more of a commodity. I couldn't quote the same fees and still be competitive, although certain clients did want me personally to teach the class because I wrote the textbook. So, I adjusted my fees just enough to retain the level of work I was interested in doing.

YOU WANT FRIES WITH THAT?

I often present a client with the option to bundle multiple services and/or products at a discounted price. For instance, if they're bringing me in to teach a class, I might suggest they also engage me to provide some follow-up consulting to help them leverage their training investment for maximum benefit. A colleague refers to this sort of enhancement offer as *fries*.

As another example, I'll offer a hefty discount on the purchase of an e-learning course site license after I present a live class at the client's location, so they can extend the training to people who couldn't attend the initial class. My standard proposal for e-learning courses always offers bundle discounts, typically 10 percent off any two courses purchased at once and 20 percent off three or more courses purchased together. Basically, once I have a client who recognizes the value I can provide to his organization, I make sure he knows about all the resources I have available. There might be more money lurking in the client's budget that I can tap into.

FIXED PRICE OR HOURLY?

You can choose to set your fees in two ways: fixed price for a defined engagement, or time and materials (T&M) for something that is more open-ended. A T&M contract will pay the cost of your labor, at either hourly or daily rates, plus the cost of any materials you might need to purchase or supply, which should be small for most business analysis and project management consulting engagements. Other expenses, such as travel costs, additionally must be built into the agreement.

Clients often prefer a fixed-price contract because they know exactly what they will be paying and how that fits with their budget. They might be nervous about an unbounded T&M contract, perhaps fearing that you will work more slowly or create unnecessary or highly complex deliverables to pad your fees. If you have an ongoing relationship with the client such that they understand and respect your work efficiency, they'll be more comfortable with a T&M agreement, particularly on a project in which size and deliverables are not well defined early on. The consultant's risk with a fixed-price contract increases with the amount of uncertainty in the project definition and scope. Work with the client to get as clear a statement of work as possible, so you have a shared understanding of the scope of the effort.

When you calculate the fee that you wish to quote for a fixed-price contract, you need to estimate the number of hours the project will require, and then multiply that by the hourly rate you wish to earn. As usual, predicting the future through such estimates comes with considerable fuzziness. If you have performed similar work before, your estimates will be better—provided you kept records of the time you spent on the previous jobs (hint). If you perform similar kinds of work routinely, develop planning checklists to help you identify all the tasks you might have to do on a specific job so you don't underestimate the work involved.

If you're collaborating with client staff rather than handling the project entirely yourself, your estimate should include the hours you'll spend reviewing materials received from the client. Be sure to plan for some rework effort after the client reviews any work products you deliver. People often overlook rework when preparing estimates, but it's nearly always needed. If you're working off-site, anticipate the time needed to communicate with client staff. The more participants and the more geographically separated sites that are involved, the more time you can expect to spend on communication activities. Those phone calls and emails add up.

Projects almost always turn out to be larger than anticipated. It's critical to build substantial contingency buffers into every fixed-price fee you calculate to account for the parts of the iceberg you can't see yet. You also need a clear understanding with the client regarding how to handle scope changes during the project's course. The client might request additional work, in which case it's obvious that you're entitled to be paid for that work under the same terms as in the original agreement. (Write that language into the contract!) A trickier situation arises when the project is larger than you expected based on your understanding of the initial scope definition. The client might conclude that's your problem and be reluctant to pay more than originally agreed, especially if the scope statement seemed detailed and accurate at the time. Agreeing up front on the process for handling scope changes on a fixed-price contract can avoid hard feelings later on.

The vast majority of my consulting contracts have been based on T&M, which is really just my time. I've done a lot of work in that mode for one client in particular. My primary contact there knows that I work fast and do high-quality work. He doesn't worry about me dragging my feet or milking him for excessive fees.

For the handful of fixed-price contracts I've done, it seems that no matter how carefully I estimate the work and build in thoughtful contingency buffers, the effort still exceeds my plans. I'm not off by a huge percentage, but I can feel my hourly rate dropping as I slip into overtime. If this happens to you, resist the temptation to cut corners or let quality suffer in the rush to get the work done and keep your hourly rate up where you want it to be. That will come back to bite you if your client doesn't feel he's getting adequate value for the money. Record your time estimates and the actual time you spend on tasks to help improve future estimates. In fact, if you don't use this sort of historical data when you prepare estimates, you really aren't estimating—you're guessing.

During all of your fee negotiations with clients, keep in mind the objective of a win-win outcome. Most of the time, a client and a consultant can agree upon a fee structure that satisfies all of the participants and seems fair to everyone. If you can't, walk away.

Next Steps

- Review the prices you charge for your various services and products. Try to learn what similar products and services cost from other companies. Make sure you're competitively positioned with regard to the nature and quality of your offerings versus alternatives.
- Consider experimenting with adjusting your prices to see how that affects sales. Do you think you could raise your rates and still keep your existing business load, or maybe even get more? If you're already getting all the work you want, raising your rates is probably safe to try.
- The next time you need to prepare a price quote for a potential client, list the pluses and minuses of making a fixed-fee bid versus a time-and-materials hourly rate. Try to learn which is customary with that client and whether there is latitude to propose an alternative without losing the bid at the outset.

15

MONEY MATTERS FOR
THE NEW CONSULTANT

By GARY K. EVANS

You probably didn't become a consultant as a hobby. You're looking to make a living from it, which means you need to deal with money. This chapter addresses some of the economic practicalities of running your business, as either a self-employed independent consultant or a free-lance hourly contractor.

FIRST, HIRE AN ACCOUNTANT

If you're a professional, I assume that you're very good at what you do. Unless your areas of expertise include accounting and tax law, you should hire a fellow professional—an accountant—to take care of these matters. Shop around and find one with at least some self-employed clientele.

As with technologists and other professionals, accountants differ in their skills and specialties. My accountant makes more per hour than I do, and he's worth every penny. Each year, he has saved me money that otherwise would have slipped through my fingers.

Some self-employed consultants buy Intuit QuickBooks or an equivalent package to help them track their business income and expenses. I use Quick-Books myself, and so does Karl. Whether or not you enlist the services of a professional accountant, you must keep meticulous track of your finances. QuickBooks does this. It will let you generate invoices for your clients, flag receivables that are past their due date, track your travel expenses, and so forth. If you try to do this with Excel, you are more adventurous than I. Spring for the money to buy a proper accounting package. It's a deductible business expense, and you will be very glad you have it. So will your accountant, if you have to provide a categorized general ledger file so you can claim the proper deductions and depreciations at tax time.

A relationship with an accountant can also be helpful when you have to make estimated federal and state income tax payments. Unlike corporate employment, where taxes are withheld from each paycheck, self-employed people must pay their own estimated taxes to the Internal Revenue Service (IRS). To make your life more difficult, these payment periods are not of uniform length. Due dates are January 15, April 15, June 15, and September 15, pushed back as necessary for weekends and holidays. You can mail in the payments or pay online with the Electronic Federal Tax Payment System®.

If you are reasonably skilled at preparing your own tax returns, you can estimate these necessary payments yourself. Otherwise, enlist your accountant to help. There are penalties for substantial underpayments and late payments of estimated taxes. It can be difficult to guess correctly at the amount of tax due if your income is erratic throughout the year, as is typical for an independent consultant. It's just one more of the complications you face when you go it alone.

RATES: DON'T BE A CHEAP DATE

Setting rates is neither a science nor a crapshoot. You can peruse some of the many books on this topic to learn exactly how to do this, whether you do fixed fee, daily rates, or hourly rates. Karl offered some suggestions on setting rates in Chapter 14 (*What Are You Worth?*). Here, I'll comment only on some of the issues I've personally encountered.

You don't work every day. Regular employees get up in the morning, go to work, and come home in the evening—every weekday. An independent consultant or a contractor gets up every morning, but what happens after that is somewhat random. In a good economy, you should expect to be unemployed for about a quarter of each year. You do want to have some kind of life, don't you?

Another way to think of this is that you work for three weeks and then have no engagement the fourth week of each month. Factor this downtime into your price setting. In a bad economy, prepare for surviving up to six months without work. (Actually, this is good advice for anyone who has any form of employment.) In my worst year, I worked only four months out of twelve. It was tough, but my past discipline in setting aside savings got us through.

Should you match the going rate? Finding the going rate for, say, C#/.NET developers in New York City or anywhere else is easy. The internet is the most accessible source of such information. Recruiting companies often publish salary surveys organized by skill and geographical region. Starting out, be aware of what clients are paying both salaried employees and contractors. Independent contractors must cover business expenses that employees don't have, so they're expected to request hourly-equivalent rates from 40 to 100 percent higher than do regular employees—but you do have to be good enough to justify these higher rates.

I've found considering your value to be a tremendous factor in determining your consulting rates. Value is often equated with price, and I'm not the first person to note that when I increased my rates, I got more and better work because my perceived value increased. If you have extensive experience and real expertise, you can command higher rates.

Lowering your rate to get work. This is a disaster, both now and for the future. Small clients all want to get top-quality workers for $25 to $35 per hour. If you're willing to go that low just to work, I urge you to get a corporate job that pays the same rate and comes with some benefits.

Paying your own expenses from your daily or hourly pay. I did this once—for four weeks. Never again. Now I bill the client for my services and invoice separately for my expenses, perhaps up to an agreed-upon maximum amount. I don't even negotiate on any other arrangement. Unless you're bidding on a fixed-fee project, reputable companies who work with independents expect to pay services and expenses separately.

However, this is just my policy. Karl has approached this issue rather differently than I. He quotes fixed rates for short on-site training engagements that include a portion to cover reasonable travel, hotel, and meal expenses and the cost of books he supplies. His clients like this because it simplifies processing the invoices, as no receipts are required. They know right up front what the total cost will be. And it gives Karl the flexibility to stay in a luxury hotel or sleep in a tent, depending on his choice. That approach also simplifies matters if the trip involves events for multiple clients, where expenses would otherwise have to be allocated among the clients.

Non-billable time. I was stunned when I discovered how much time I spent doing invoices and expense reports, cold calling and warm calling, organizing files and contact lists, learning new technology, and developing new material—and I couldn't bill anyone for the time! Estimates vary, but an independent consultant or contractor should plan to spend 20 to 30 percent of his working week on non-billable activities. Those books, articles, and conference presentations don't write themselves while you sleep.

The 2X/3X rule. Independent consulting is costly because you have to cover all your own expenses and benefits. That means you must consider yourself as an employer, and price yourself with the mindset of an employer selling your services to clients at a rate that ensures a respectable profit margin. To this end, I offer the 2X/3X rule, another piece of wisdom I received from a successful consultant.

First, identify the amount you'd be paid as a salaried employee at a corporation doing what you do as a consultant. Doubling this number will provide you a break-even target as a consultant. But if you triple your salary figure, you'll be able to reinvest in your business and grow it. When I first started out and determined the doubled figure, I almost choked. After just a couple of years, though, I learned how right my more experienced colleague was.

There are roughly two thousand working hours in a year, so a before-tax employee salary of $100,000 equates to $50 per hour. A consultant doing the same work as an employee earning $100,000 should be asking for $100 to $150 per hour. Why? The consultant will probably work for a few weeks or months, and short-term engagements carry a higher hourly rate. The independent consultant has no employment security and must pay his or her own overhead: life and disability insurance, business liability, health care insurance, retirement funding, computer equipment, maintenance and repairs, office supplies, telephones, and more. That is why the 2X guideline only brings you to the breakeven point.

DON'T BURN CASH ON AN OFFICE

I was amused by a colleague who decided he should go into independent consulting and immediately spent $5,000 on a new PC, laptop, fax machine (it was a while ago), answering machine (a long while ago), preprinted business forms with his color logo, and a bucket of really marginal items. Yet he didn't have a single client or even the prospect of one at the time.

I suggest you build an office as you need one. When I started consulting more than 25 years ago, I bought an answering machine first so I'd be able to return calls. When my first client called to say he had selected me and was faxing me a contract, I asked him to delay sending it until after lunch. Then I ran out and bought my first fax machine and hooked it up. I received the contract, signed it, and faxed back the signature page. That machine lasted seven years, but it had to pay its own way first.

SOLE PROPRIETORSHIP VERSUS INCORPORATION

This is an important issue. Incorporating gives you some legal and financial protection, but it incurs costs, such as extra accounting and filing fees, among others. Some people incorporate right away (presumably as an S corporation designation, not a C corporation like Fortune 500 companies). Others wait to incorporate until they have an established business and want to shelter their income. Part of the issue is image: corporations have a cachet of stability. Another part is cultural: some companies work only with corporations and won't hire a sole proprietor, except perhaps as a subcontractor to one of their established corporate contractors.

As a sole proprietor, you can set up bank accounts and credit cards in the name of the business. You'll file Schedule C with your personal federal and state income tax returns each year to report your self-employment business income and expenses. You shouldn't need to file any other special business tax forms, other than perhaps Form 4562 to claim a deduction for, or to depreciate, business property you buy, such as computer equipment. You can also ask the IRS to issue your company an employer identification number (EIN). When a client requests a Form W-9 from you for income reporting purposes, you can give them your EIN instead of your personal Social Security number. Every bit of protection against identity theft helps.

Another option is to set up a limited liability company or LLC. This is a business structure that is simpler and less expensive than an S corporation, still allows money to flow directly to the LLC owners (that is, you), and presents a more business-like image than being a sole proprietor. An LLC also offers some legal protection to its owners, reducing their liability for acts and debts of the LLC.

I was a sole proprietor under the DBA (doing business as) designation for more than six years before I incorporated as an S corporation. I now have a second business for software product development, set up as an LLC. The company structure you choose is a business and legal decision. You should listen to your accountant and legal advisers for guidance on the structure that is most appropriate for you, your goals and growth plans, and the financial risk exposure associated with the kinds of work you do.

It's important to recognize that the IRS expects your small business to turn a profit from time to time. Otherwise, it's a hobby, not a business. The general rule is that your consulting business should turn a profit in at least two years out of five to keep the IRS happy. As a business, you can take tax deductions for your legitimate expenses, including travel and (half of) meals, office supplies, advertising, books, business insurance, possibly your home office, and the like. However, you may not take such deductions for a hobby.

To assess whether you really are running a business, even if you aren't turning a profit (yet), the IRS will want to make sure you are acting as though you're intending and attempting to make a profit. If you're struggling to get your consulting business off the ground such that you are operating at a loss, check with your accountant to make sure the IRS will continue to regard your company as a legitimate business activity and not reclassify it as a hobby.

PLANNING FOR RETIREMENT

As a self-employed person, you're also responsible for planning for your family's financial security after you retire. Perhaps you're already skilled at navigating the befuddling world of investments. If not, look for a fee-only financial planner to help you set up and fund appropriate retirement accounts.

Beyond traditional and Roth individual retirement arrangements (IRAs), sole proprietors, LLCs, and those who have incorporated can set aside additional money in accounts such as a SEP-IRA (Simplified Employee Pension Individual Retirement Arrangement) or various types of pension plans. If you participated in a previous corporate employer's 401(k) plan, you should be able to roll over the contents of your account into a traditional IRA that you then manage yourself. There are all sorts of income tax implications (including tax deferral), maximum contribution limits, and other issues with retirement planning that cry out for professional guidance. It's complicated, and there can be very significant long-term implications if you choose poorly.

A fellow consultant once got some advice from an older coworker when he began his career in corporate America years ago. His coworker told him that the people he knew who were most financially comfortable during retirement had saved every penny they legally could in their retirement plans.

My colleague took that advice to heart. He and his wife did the same, even after he left corporate America and became an independent consultant at age 44. I guess his plan worked, as he retired just 10 years later with a sizable nest egg.

Regardless of your age, don't put off planning for retirement. It's too important.

Next Steps

- If you already have an attorney and/or accountant, ask them about helping you with financial and legal matters for any company you might establish as an independent consultant. Are such matters within their field of expertise? Do they have recommendations for how you might structure your company and why?
- If you know some other independent consultants, ask them how their businesses are structured, the pluses and minuses of that approach, and what they would recommend in your situation.
- Look for publications or reports that contain average salary data for people employed in your line of work in your geographic area. Use the guidance presented in this chapter to determine what you would feel comfortable charging for the services you can provide.
- Even if you're young, revisit your retirement plans. Do you have an individual IRA or a 401(k) plan or traditional pension with your current employer? Does your spouse have an individual IRA? If not, set up retirement accounts and begin funding them regularly.
- Use an online calculator to estimate how much money you should try to sock away in your retirement accounts each year. Determine how much money you could realistically save for retirement based on three possible scenarios for how your consulting career might turn out: not very successful such that you need to go back to regular employment; moderately successful; or exceptionally successful.

16

GET IT IN WRITING

True confession: I'm a process kind of guy. Recognizing that memories are imperfect and details can easily become lost, I like to write down important information so everyone involved in some activity knows what's happening and agrees to the plan. For this reason, I record the particulars of significant agreements I make with clients to avoid confusion, mistakes, and hard feelings. In this chapter I'll describe some of those agreements. You can download templates for the various sorts of simple agreement documents I've created from the Web Added Value™ (WAV) Download Resource Center at www.jrosspub.com.

SPEAKING AGREEMENT

I've spent much of the past two decades traveling to companies and government agencies around the world to deliver training courses. I always use a simple speaking agreement for these events. This agreement contains information such as:

- The particulars of the event, including location, the maximum number of attendees, dates and times, and contact person
- Instructions for setting up the room and my needs for the facility, such as a projector for my laptop, flip charts with easels and markers, and a lavalier microphone (essential for me)
- Information about the student handouts and textbooks we will use
- Financial details, including my money-back guarantee
- Contingencies for unexpected occurrences that could disrupt the event, including cancellation and rescheduling fees

This information all fits on one page. It works just fine for most engagements. However, sometimes the client's legal department wants to get involved. They always create a vastly longer and more complex contract that we have to negotiate. It took a full month to work through issues on the last such client agreement I had to deal with, although that was unusually long. I like my simple template much better.

This agreement has worked well for me for years. I rarely undertake an engagement without one. I won't make travel arrangements or order books until I've received a signed speaking agreement back from the client. Otherwise, I'm not confident they have fully committed to the event and the date. Several prospective clients never returned the agreement for an event they had requested. It's frustrating for me to have to hold those dates open and keep checking back to see whether the client wishes to proceed or not. If you've changed your mind, dear client, please just tell me.

I have a consultant friend who loathes paperwork. He never uses a written agreement with his clients if he can get away without one. Luckily, he hasn't encountered any problems with this approach—yet. But I've had some experiences for which having a written agreement was quite valuable; other consultants have shared similar stories with me.

One winter I traveled to the New Jersey countryside to teach a three-day class at a large company. The next morning, I went to the building where the class was to be held. No one was there to meet me. I finally reached my contact person on the phone. She thought the class was going to begin the *next* day and run for three days. Ah, that explained why the receptionist didn't know what I was talking about.

I pulled out the speaking agreement—I always take it with me. Sure enough, I was there on the correct date. By not reading the agreement carefully, my contact had miscommunicated to all the students in the class. We now had only two days to cover everything we originally planned to cover in three. If I had shown up a day late for a class I was supposed to teach, I'm sure there would have been financial consequences, not to mention the inconvenience to all the students. In this case, we were able to work it out, but it was a mistake that didn't have to happen. At least I had a day to myself during a snowstorm in rural New Jersey. Fun.

CONSULTING AGREEMENTS

I use two different templates for consulting (as opposed to training) engagements, one for work performed at the client site and the other for work I do at home. I call this second sort of activity off-site consulting; others might call it virtual or remote consulting. You can find the templates I use for both kinds of engagements at the WAV page for this book at www.jrosspub.com.

My template collection includes an alternative on-site consulting agreement template (#2) that was contributed by a colleague. This one is a little more formal and richer in legal details than mine, which might be a good idea. If you decide to create such templates for your own consulting business, I suggest you study these and any other examples you can locate from experienced colleagues, then pull together the best ideas from all of them to suit your situation.

When I have an established long-term relationship with a client, I might skip writing an agreement for a specific engagement. I have one such client at a company with whom I've worked for many years. We work together very well, and I never have to worry about him not paying me or encountering some other misunderstanding. In a case like this, I dispense with the formal written agreements as an unnecessary overhead step.

COURSEWARE LICENSING AGREEMENT

In keeping with my general business philosophy of trying to earn a living while I'm asleep (see Chapter 21, *A Kind of Business Plan*), many years ago I began licensing my courseware to other companies. Some of these are training companies or independent consultants who can deliver my classes to their own clients and pay me a royalty when they do. Other licensees are companies or government agencies that wish to use my materials for internal training, employing their own staff as instructors.

I have crafted licensing agreements for these two different situations. Again, you may access the templates for my licensing agreements at the WAV page for this book. These agreements specify the materials I'm providing, the licensing fees and payment terms, and how the licensee may and may not use the materials.

The terms in my various agreement templates are not cast in concrete. Periodically, a prospective client or licensee raises particular concerns or has a situation that's a little out of the ordinary. They might ask me to adjust some of the terms. Making that adjustment could be the difference between closing a deal or not. So I certainly have some negotiating flexibility in portions of these agreements.

But there are limits. For instance, I will never remove the cancellation or rescheduling fee clause from my speaking agreement, although I might agree to adjust my initial terms if the client pushes back in a reasonable way. Also, I never license courseware to a company without some payment up front. That essentially would be giving away my content for free, something I just don't do.

THE USUAL DISCLAIMER

Although I have used these agreements for many years without any problems, they may or may not be suitable for you. I recommend you have an attorney look over whatever agreements you create to make sure they cover all the important bases and provide you with adequate protection, while still being fair to your clients. Most of the time, a well-crafted and simple agreement suffices to establish the parameters of your client engagements so both parties know what to expect. I do feel better having it in writing.

Next Steps

- If you don't already have written agreements that you use for your consulting and training engagements, download the ones described in this chapter and see if they would be useful for you. Adapt them as appropriate to your specific needs.
- If you do already have written agreement templates, compare them to the ones described here and see if there are any useful improvements you can make.

17

EVERYTHING'S NEGOTIABLE

The previous chapter described the simple agreements I use to record the details for each of my speaking and consulting engagements. These usually work fine, but occasionally I will get some pushback from the client on specific terms in the agreement. Sometimes, the client's legal department rejects my simple agreement and sends me a massive document to sign.

But I don't just sign that contract. A contract is naturally written to the benefit of the entity that created it, so you need to watch out for any terms that are unacceptable to you. I read the contract carefully, looking for anything that makes me uncomfortable. It turns out that many of the terms in a boilerplate contract can be adjusted if you aren't happy with them. This chapter describes some typical categories where you might need to negotiate with a client to reach a mutually acceptable agreement.

I'm in the midst of such a negotiation this very day. So far, this client is proving quite flexible on my requested changes. For instance, the client's standard services contract demands that the consultant take a drug test, something I've encountered only once before. I explained that I don't take drugs—and I don't take drug tests. The client dropped the requirement. Sometimes you just have to ask.

But in a previous situation, a client decided not to hire me to teach a class because I declined to take their drug test. Some years later, I discovered that they had instead hired a trainer to whom I had licensed the course to come into my home city and teach my class. That instructor, who happened to be Canadian, told me that the client never even asked him about taking a drug test! Some things just make no sense at all.

I'd like to believe that reasonable adults can find a way to reach an agreement that they can all live with. Sadly, that's not always true. A highly experienced consultant friend of mine has shared horror stories about her futile attempts to negotiate egregious clauses out of consulting contracts with several companies. As one illustration, consider this:

> *I was supposed to start that Monday, but in the security badge pa-perwork they sneaked in one more document that I refused to sign because I'd be signing over to them all intellectual property rights to anything I was currently working on and (get this, it's literally in their contract) anything I'd ever work on in the future. I refused. I explained why it's unreasonable; they stonewalled and simply refused to change it.*

No consultant in her right mind would ever sign a contract like that. Some people undoubtedly have, perhaps not fully appreciating what they were giving away or expecting that the clause would not be enforced. Maybe the client contact you're dealing with recognizes that such terms are unreasonable and unacceptable, but the purchasing or legal people won't budge. You can reluctantly sign on the dotted line—and if you're hungry enough, perhaps you will—or you can walk away.

START AT THE TOP

Whether you're in the early stages of exploring a possible engagement or finalizing the contract details, it's best if you can work directly with the client's key decision maker. Otherwise, all conclusions are tentative, and you can waste a lot of time on discussions that do not lead to fruition. Numerous seasoned consultants gave me this same advice when I was starting out. Unfortunately, I soon learned that the decision maker rarely makes the initial contact with me.

My first client communications typically are with a low- or mid-level manager who is passionate about improving some aspect of the organization's software work and wants to bring me in to help. That manager still needs higher-level approvals before anything can happen; the process frequently stalls out at that stage. It can be difficult—or impossible—for a consultant to reach that ideal decision maker to expedite the negotiation process.

There are several reasons to negotiate as high up the food chain as possible. A senior client has more leverage in keeping a project from becoming a technical success yet a political failure. It also helps you understand what would constitute a win for upper-level management, so you can keep your focus on that objective. If a high-level manager wants to bring you in, it's more likely that he will go to battle with any resisters in purchasing or the legal department and make it happen.

Recently, a new client contacted me about providing training in software peer reviews across his organization, something I've done for 25 years. He had seen the benefits of peer reviews in his previous company and wanted to bring them into his new organization. His management seemed enthusiastic about it. We had multiple email and telephone exchanges over a span of weeks, and I wrote a formal proposal with several options for them to consider. My revenue from this engagement could have ranged from about $6,000 to $50,000 depending on which package of live courses, e-learning, and courseware licensing the client selected. The last I had heard, my contact was just waiting for his CIO to approve the engagement.

After I didn't hear anything more for several weeks, I followed up and learned that his company now had a new CIO—the whole thing was off. Quite a few of my potential engagements have been thwarted because of management turnover like this. Had I been able to interact directly with the first CIO early on, we might have been able to reach an agreement quickly. At least that way I might have received a cancellation fee if the new CIO abandoned the effort. Instead, my revenue turned out to be zero. It's frustrating, but this is a common outcome for a consultant.

At this very moment, I'm waiting to hear back from another prospective client who was eager to discuss some requirements training. I told him I was free to talk any time. That was three months and two follow-up email pings ago. My phone sits, silently waiting.

FEES

The most obvious negotiable item is the fee you're requesting for your services. In my experience, clients don't challenge this as often as you might expect. I have standard rates for certain services, but there's some flexibility in them. I'll offer a nice discount if a client opts to acquire a site license for some of my e-learning training courses in addition to having me present a live class. I'll also drop the price if the client wants a combination of consulting and training services or requests multiple presentations during the same trip.

Once, a prospective client asked for a discount of several thousand dollars off a two-day training course simply because my quote exceeded her budget. She said she hoped I would knock the price down just because I'm such a nice guy. Sorry, I'm not *that* nice. I lowered the price some, but I wasn't willing to do the job for the price she suggested. We never did come to an agreement. That's the way some negotiations turn out.

Bringing an expert consultant into a company is not cheap. The price I quote a prospective client for delivering a training course could be high enough to scare them away. Rather than lowering my price to land the gig, I try to sell my services on the basis of value, not cost.

The majority of the work I've done as an independent consultant has involved delivering training on software requirements and business analysis topics. If I sense that my quoted fee is making the client hesitate, I suggest they think about the price their organization is paying for the way their teams are operating today. That is, what's the cost of *not* bringing me in to help their BAs and other team members learn how to work more effectively?

I encourage my clients to think in terms of the potential return on investment (ROI) they might achieve from my services, rather than focusing on the size of the check they'd have to write to me. A software team doesn't have to go very far wrong to waste a lot of money on rework because of requirements shortcomings. If I can teach their BAs how to do a better job of defining and communicating requirements, they can recoup the cost of the training quickly.

Unfortunately, it seems that not all software organizations consider the price they're paying for their current ways of working. This is sometimes called the *cost of quality*. It's not common for people to measure how much of their project costs can be traced to problems with requirements or other process shortcomings. Organizations often accept defects and rework as a normal part of doing business. Some of it certainly is, but rare is the organization that cannot improve its business analysis processes in ways that will pay off big time.

Consider the following angle to make the case for your services. Suppose the fully burdened cost—salary, taxes, benefits, overhead—of each BA in the client company is $125,000. If the company has eight such employees, and if you can provide them with knowledge that could make each of them just five percent more efficient for the next five years, that works out to a cost savings of some $250,000 (not accounting for inflation). Wouldn't it be worth it to the company to spend, say, $20,000 to bring you in to provide those capability-enhancing services? Companies should be thrilled at a potential ROI like that.

I often caution my training clients that if, after attending the class, their team members go right back to working how they always have in the past, their investment of time and money will be wasted. I don't want that to happen. Therefore, my classes emphasize practicality and ways to begin applying new techniques quickly on their current projects. Getting clients to consider the *value* that training or consulting engagements can provide—not just their cost—can help turn a proposal into a contract.

CANCELLATION

My speaking agreements always include a fee for canceling or rescheduling the event. Some clients balk at this. My premise is that when I sign the agreement, I am committing a certain block of days for the client event, plus preparation and travel time. Should the client decide to change the agreed-upon date or to cancel the event entirely, it's unlikely that I can re-book that time slot with another client on short notice. If I purchase a nonrefundable airline ticket or have some books shipped to the client, changing the date or canceling the gig will cost me money and inconvenience.

Therefore, I ask the client to make a similar commitment to me in the form of agreeing to pay me 20 or 25 percent of the price as a cancellation or rescheduling fee. Sometimes we negotiate a lower such fee. Or, we might put some time bounds around it. Maybe no payment is due if I can reschedule at no cost to me or if they cancel at least X weeks prior to the event. If the client does need to reschedule and it doesn't inconvenience me or cost me out of pocket, I will generally waive the rescheduling fee. But I always insist on including some language about rescheduling and cancellation fees in the agreement. If the client won't accept that, we don't make a deal.

One client tried waiting until immediately prior to the scheduled event to sign the speaking agreement. She wanted to minimize the likelihood of having to cancel or reschedule, thereby incurring a fee. However, my policy is to not commit specific dates to a client until I receive the signed speaking agreement. I felt no qualms about giving that client's requested dates to another who was willing to make the commitment. I didn't appreciate the game of schedule chicken this client was playing with me. That gig ultimately fell through.

I've only had to invoke the cancellation or rescheduling fee four times during my career. To my surprise, those invoices were all paid faster than my regular invoices. Go figure.

USAGE RIGHTS

I've seen some consulting-service contracts that claim unreasonably broad rights for the presentation materials used in a training class. They might stipulate that the client has a perpetual free license to use the class materials in any way they wish, simply because someone taught it once at their company. In principle, this right could extend to unlimited distribution of the material throughout the company, teaching the class themselves within or outside their company, posting the materials publicly on the internet, or even licensing the courseware to other companies without the copyright owner's knowledge or permission.

This is the first clause I ask to remove from every such service contract. My clients do not have the right to use my training materials for any purpose other than the courses I am presenting myself, unless we execute a separate licensing agreement. I've never had any problem getting this clause removed.

VIDEO RECORDING

Once in a while, a client wishes to record my live presentation and show it to other people throughout their company. This represents a lost revenue opportunity, because they might use the video rather than hiring me to come in and teach another class.

I'm not totally averse to video recording. If my session is open to anyone in the company who wants to come, it's fine with me if they record it for employees who couldn't attend the live session or work in other locations. Usually, though, my training courses are capped at a certain number of attendees for the agreed-upon fee. If they want to make a recording available to other people, I will generally permit this but charge them extra for the privilege.

INSURANCE

Contracts coming out of the legal department stipulate the various types of insurance the consultant is expected to carry. If your company has multiple employees, you might be required to provide workers' compensation insurance coverage. To my understanding, though (and remember, this book contains no legal advice), sole proprietors with no employees are exempt from carrying workers' comp. Make sure to check your state laws on this.

I do carry business liability insurance, which offers some protection if, say, I injure a student with my laser pointer or damage client property with my rental car. If the coverage amounts stipulated in the contract are higher than I carry, I request to lower those coverage expectations to match my policy limits. The clients' legal departments have always approved such requests. Some clients request to be listed as a named insured on my business liability insurance policy. This is easily accomplished with a phone call or email to my insurance agent.

I do not carry professional liability or malpractice (errors and omissions— aka E&O) insurance, although some companies request that. Clients have always been willing to remove that requirement when I point out that I don't carry it and that E&O coverage isn't necessary for the sorts of engagements I perform. Refer to Chapter 20 (*For Your Protection*) for more information about insurance concerns for the self-employed consultant.

OTHER EXPENSES

Not long ago, for the first time in my career, a client required that I undergo a criminal background investigation. I have no objection to that (so long as they don't find out about all my secret offshore bank accounts or the yachts), but they wanted to charge me $49.79 for the privilege of being investigated. I persuaded the client to cover this unexpected cost.

That's the way most negotiations go. I agree to something the client is requesting, but then I issue a request of my own of comparable magnitude. We both feel as though the other party is being reasonable and flexible, which makes us amenable to reciprocating.

That same client also asked about pulling a credit report on me. Also fine, if peculiar, as they would be paying *me* money, not the reverse. However, I have security freezes on my credit accounts with the three major consumer reporting agencies (Experian, TransUnion, and Equifax) as a protection against identity theft. Until late 2018, if someone needed my credit report, I would have had to pay ten dollars per agency to temporarily unfreeze my account. I asked the client to pay for that also, but they decided they didn't need to do a credit check after all. What a surprise. Fortunately, freezing and unfreezing your credit file is now free of charge throughout the United States.

NON-COMPETE CLAUSE

A very few contracts I've received contained a non-compete clause. The client demanded that I not perform similar services for any other company in their same area of business for some years following our engagement.

I will not sign a contract that contains a non-compete clause. I don't permit any client to tell me who I may and may not work for in the future. I am always happy to sign a nondisclosure agreement (NDA) with a client to mutually protect our own intellectual property, trade secrets, product information, and the like. Even if we don't execute an NDA, I always respect every client's privacy and any secrets I might learn during the engagement.

If I see a non-compete clause in the contract, particularly if I'm simply delivering a training course, I explain that I can't allow any one client to block me from providing similar generic training on some topic to other companies. So far, clients have always been willing to remove that clause after I explained that there really isn't any risk to them.

THINKING WIN-WIN

Each party involved in a negotiation strives to adjust the outcome in its own favor, but they should also respect their counterpart's legitimate needs. We all have limits to our flexibility. If the people with whom we're negotiating insist on finalizing the terms beyond our tolerance limits, we won't reach a mutually acceptable outcome. You won't win every negotiation, but you might be able to do better than you expect just by asking. I will sometimes concede a minor point to resolve something I feel more strongly about in my favor.

For more on effective negotiation, I highly recommend *Getting to Yes: Negotiating Agreement Without Giving In* by Roger Fisher, William Ury, and Bruce Patton. This classic book provides excellent advice on how to successfully negotiate from an understanding of each party's interests, rather than by passionately defending immovable positions.

As an aside, Chapter 24 of my memoir of life lessons, *Pearls from Sand*, describes many ways I've been able to negotiate better deals in daily life. Just by asking in the right way, I've saved money on shoes, delivering a newly purchased treadmill to my house, magazine subscription renewals, cable TV bills, satellite radio for my car, medical services, clothing, land-scaping services, and much more. Until you ask, the answer is always no, so go ahead and ask. The tips in that chapter alone will more than make up for the book's cost.

Next Steps

- If a client wants you to sign an elaborate contract that seems like overkill, ask if the two of you can use your own (presumably simpler) agreement template instead.
- The next time a client presents you with a contract, read it carefully and consider whether there are any terms there that make you nervous. Mark up the initial contract with any questions you have and terms you would like to negotiate. If some issue makes you a little uncomfortable but you can live with it, don't make a big issue out of that one. Instead, focus on terms that are particularly inconvenient for you, heavily skewed in the client's favor, or shift risk onto you.
- If you have a previously executed contract available to study, read through it and identify categories in which you anticipate having to negotiate on future contracts. Use the categories discussed in this chapter as a starting point.
- For each category in which you anticipate possible future negotiations being necessary, make a note of any relevant policies or boundaries, such as insurance coverage limits, that will help you efficiently detect and respond to problematic terms in future contracts.

18

WHEN ONE IS NOT ENOUGH

One disadvantage of being an independent consultant is that you might miss out on interesting projects that are not quite an exact fit for you. A client might present an appealing opportunity that's bigger than you feel comfortable handling on your own. Another client could have a project that's a fairly good match for your skills, but you know someone else who could handle a portion of the work better. A client job might require specialized certifications, licenses, or insurance that you don't carry, but perhaps you know another consultant who does. Or maybe a client calls with an interesting opportunity but some aspect of it doesn't appeal to you, such as an extended on-site period, an excessive time commitment, or more travel than you want to do.

Responding to such opportunities in order to both give you some work and satisfy the client's needs might require you to partner with other consultants. I've been involved in several successful such partnerships, which were a pleasant change from doing all the work solo. I'll describe two of them here, along with some tips for making these collaborations work.

COMBINING RESOURCES

Many years ago, a consultant named Linda suggested that her current client hire me to present some training on software requirements. Linda previously had taken a requirements class from me, and she thought that same class would help her client's organization. They brought me in; the class went fine. Linda and I became friends and stayed in touch.

Several years later, Linda landed an engagement with a county government agency in the area where we both lived at that time. The gig involved developing some requirements processes, as well as creating and delivering a customized class aligned with the new processes. Linda thought of me as a possible collaborator for this fairly large project. She knew I had considerable experience with developing requirements processes and training materials. It seemed like an interesting job that I could handle easily, I got along well with Linda, and it was in my backyard. What's not to like?

Linda had extensive experience in contracting with government agencies, so we structured the partnership with her being the prime contractor to the client agency and my company subcontracting to hers. We drew up a formal agreement that described the scope of work, stated that my company was an independent contractor to hers, and stipulated the compensation amount and payment terms. The agreement also defined the duration of the partnership, termination conditions, and protection of confidential information. Because Linda's company was the prime contractor, the client would pay Linda, and then she would pay me.

Note that if you partner through a subcontracting engagement like this and are paid more than $600 in a single calendar year, the prime contractor must issue you a 1099-MISC tax form before January 31 of the next year. The prime contractor can deduct amounts paid to a subcontractor as a business expense, and of course the amount paid is income to the subcontractor. The 1099-MISC informs the IRS about all that. This is the same arrangement as when you contract directly to a client company on a typical solo gig; they'll send you a 1099-MISC the next January.

My partnership with Linda worked out just as well as we had hoped. We both brought a lot to the project. Putting our heads together resulted in better deliverables than either of us could have produced on our own. It was great to have an experienced collaborator review the deliverables each of us created before we handed anything over to the client. When I develop proprietary materials for a client on my own, I can't show them to another consultant for confidentiality reasons. The client was happy, and the customized course I taught—based largely on my pre-existing courseware—was well received. Best of all, Linda and I stayed friends after the project was completed.

PROVIDING A BACKSTOP

Early in my independent consulting career I provided extensive training and consulting services to a large federal government agency (is there any other kind?). My principal contact there, Patty, later approached me with a project intended to help their BAs and developers do a better job of specifying and implementing various quality attribute requirements. Such requirements encompass availability, installability, scalability, security, testability, and similar properties of a software system. Many of these attributes were of vital importance to that agency's applications, but they hadn't been doing a good job on them. (To be fair, few organizations are great at handling quality attribute requirements.) Patty wanted me to develop some comprehensive guidance documents regarding these kinds of requirements.

As Patty explained the project, I realized that it would require an extended on-site period to interact with various stakeholders in person. I couldn't make that level of commitment at that time. As an alternative, I suggested that Patty consider working with Andre, another consultant I knew well who had a lot of expertise with both requirements specification and software development. I had a good relationship with Andre on both professional and personal levels.

Andre was very familiar with my approach to requirements, which gave Patty a comfort level with this new consultant. The three of us lived in different states, so I offered to provide backup assistance to Andre from my home office. This dropped my travel commitment to zero and kept me engaged on an interesting project that I couldn't do myself. The three of us all felt that the project had a higher chance of success with both Andre and me participating. Andre would handle the on-site interviewing of stakeholders and draft the initial guidance documents, coming to me with questions along the way. I would then review his deliverables carefully before he handed them over to Patty.

I was already established as a consultant with this federal agency, so they could simply pay Andre and me separately for the time we spent working on the project. Therefore, there was no need for an official business connection between Andre's company and mine for this engagement. This contrasts with the formal subcontracting arrangement Linda and I established on the project I described previously. Both kinds of arrangements can work fine, provided it's okay with the client and that the partnering consultants have a clear understanding of the scope of work and who will do what.

I'd like to say this project was a complete success, but that would be a stretch. The collaboration among the three of us went fine. However, major cultural and management issues within the client's software community posed profound barriers to implementing all the useful materials Andre had written. As a consultant, you're limited in the extent to which you can effect cultural and practice changes in your client's organization. The organization must be receptive to change. Its leadership must make the case for change with the staff, set expectations, provide resources, and demand accountability. It's discouraging to put in a lot of work to create high-quality products, only to see the implementation founder on the rocks.

On the plus side, Patty resurrected the project some time later. The last we heard, several of the quality attributes Andre had tackled in his guidance documents were well on their way to implementation success. Patty seemed happy, so therefore Andre and I were happy.

MAKING IT WORK

If you want to engage in these sorts of partnerships, you'll need to develop a network of contacts among fellow consultants whom you could approach with opportunities. I've met many such peers through IT conferences. You might get to know others by reputation through their writing or presentations. There is more risk in working with someone you don't already know well, so lay the groundwork for an effective partnership at the outset. I recommend writing a formal agreement that you both sign, even if it's just a statement of work so that you both know—and agree to—your responsibilities to each other and to the client.

Collaboration Process

The two (or more) of you should plan from the outset on just *how* you will work together, particularly if you are geographically separated. Consider how you will exchange and manage versions of documents on which you are both working concurrently. Agree on how to communicate, track status, and resolve issues. Make clear who is responsible for assembling the final package of deliverables and presenting it to the client. You might also discuss how you will make decisions if the partners disagree on some issue. It's worth considering how you would handle a situation where one of you has to drop out of the partnership for some reason. Could the other one pick up the slack, or would the client face a delay or an uncompleted project?

The time you spend laying this foundation can prevent friction points and hurt feelings later on. For another story about the benefits of laying out in advance how you plan to work together, see Chapter 35 (*On Co-Authoring a Book*). There I describe how Joy Beatty and I joined forces to write the third edition of my *Software Requirements* book, a long-distance collaboration of nearly one year that worked out great and was a lot of fun.

Even if you already know each other fairly well, watch out for ego clashes and power struggles. Just because you're an expert in a certain area doesn't mean you know everything about it, so be open to suggestions and fresh ideas from your partner. The two of you must present a unified front, being careful to avoid providing conflicting input that will only confuse and annoy the client. You might select one of you to serve as the principal point of contact with your client. Keep your interactions with all stakeholders—including each other—professional and cordial.

Intellectual Property

Another topic worth exploring at the outset is the ownership of any intellectual property (IP) you develop during the course of the collaboration. Some examples of such IP are document templates, presentation slides, white papers or guidance documents on specific topics, and spreadsheet tools.

As I explain in Chapter 26 (*On Intellectual Property*), the client owns any IP that is considered to be a *work for hire* that they paid you to create. However, during the course of the engagement, one of you might develop some material you'd like to be able to use with other clients. It's not fair to charge either the client or the partner (if you're working in a subcontractor mode with your collaborator) full price for any item you create in which you retain an ownership interest. Your partner and you should discuss how you will handle such situations if it looks like the project could spin off these kinds of useful items. Agree on who would hold the copyright to such items—it could be joint—and who would pay for the time to create them. Negotiating these kinds of issues in advance can help you avoid infringement complaints, hard feelings, and lawsuits in the future.

Properly structured, well planned, and thoughtfully executed, a consulting partnership can let you work on projects of a size or nature you wouldn't take on yourself. This broadens your experience base for future work. You'll experience a productive synergy and be able to learn from your partner, something that I sorely missed when I did so much work on my own as an independent consultant. Plus, it's fun to work with smart people.

Next Steps

- Contemplate whether you have ever taken on a job that was larger than you could realistically handle alone or that wasn't a great fit for your skill set. What were the consequences of that decision? Would it have made more sense to look for a partner to share some of the work?
- Make a list of fellow consultants you know with whom you might enjoy partnering on a project sometime. Look for people with skills similar to yours and for those with complementary skills. Consider how well your personalities might fit together. Let those people know you would be interested in partnering should the opportunity arise, and ask if that's something that would be appealing to them.
- If you have a possible consulting collaboration opportunity ahead of you, work with the potential partner to outline carefully how you would structure the partnership in terms of contracting, client interactions, work sharing, communications, and other factors that you anticipate could affect a successful outcome.

19

IT'S A MATTER OF POLICY

Every organization operates according to a set of policies, or business rules, whether explicitly documented or merely integrated into the culture's oral tradition. You should adopt policies for your consulting practice too. This chapter presents many operating policies that I've accumulated for my one-person consulting and training company, Process Impact, as well as some I've heard from other consultants. I encourage you to formulate your own analogous policies.

ON TRAVELING

A central aspect of being a consultant or trainer is that you usually have to go where the work is. This isn't always true today, thanks to virtual consulting, webinar tools, and online collaboration technologies (see Chapter 24, *The Challenges of Remote Consulting*). Usually, though, you can expect to have to travel to client sites.

Early in my consulting career I had no idea how much work I was going to get, so I gratefully accepted every opportunity that came along. I was fortunate to get traction with the business quickly. As a consequence, I was doing a *lot* of traveling. My busiest travel year involved 137 flight segments and 131 nights in hotels. It didn't take me long to decide that I:

Don't travel during more than three weeks of each month.

This doesn't mean that I was gone three-quarters of the time, just that I might travel one or more days during three out of every four weeks. It's important to set time aside at home to get caught up, maintain relationships with family and friends, develop new training material and other content, write articles and books, and even relax and enjoy yourself (or so I've heard).

This policy also has helped keep me healthy. Two consultant friends became ill and couldn't fully recover for several months because their back-to-back travel commitments were so exhausting. The only thing worse than traveling a lot is traveling while you're sick. Leave time in your schedule to treat yourself well.

Along that same line, I find it very tiring to teach more than two days in a row. It's hard to be witty and charming—both on your feet and on your toes—all day long, day after day. Therefore, if a client asks me to teach two sessions of a two-day class, I will:

Take Wednesday off between a pair of two-day training sessions.

I might do some sightseeing, visit friends in the area, or take in a movie. My vocal cords, feet, and disposition all benefit from the break. Of course, I don't charge the client for my expenses or time on the day off.

Anyone who travels a lot has had the experience of being trapped overnight—or longer—in an airport or at a hotel. It happens, whether due to bad weather, mechanical problems, missed connections, or terrorist acts. I was stranded at a client site far from home for several days after 9/11. Another consultant friend was stuck in a distant city for more than two days after a canceled flight. With today's crowded planes, there simply was no space available on numerous later flights to accommodate all the affected passengers. I don't worry much about such delays on my way home, but it can be disastrous on your journey to a gig. Therefore, I decided long ago that I would:

Never take the last flight of the day to a client site.

I'd rather arrive several hours early than miss the engagement because I'm stuck in an airport hotel a thousand miles away.

It's unnerving to have to search for your destination early in the morning on the first day of a gig in an unfamiliar city. Traffic can be heavier or more confusing than you expected, and you might encounter construction delays. The meeting location could be cleverly hidden somewhere in a vast corporate campus, or parking might be problematic. Maybe even all of the above. To avoid beginning the workday with excessive stress, I like to:

Practice the drive from the hotel to the event location the prior evening.

I've only arrived late for an event once in my consulting career, heading into Jersey City from a hotel near Newark one morning. Who knew the highway to the Holland Tunnel into Manhattan would be so popular during rush hour? Everyone except me, apparently. I never again groped my way to an unfamiliar location without a dry run beforehand.

I've done some work outside North America, going to Europe a couple of times and taking several trips to Australia and New Zealand. This led me to my next traveling policy. Now I treat myself. I will:

Only fly across an ocean in business class or better.

Yes, it's expensive, and no, you don't get there any faster. But it certainly is a lot more pleasant. I arrive at my distant destination better rested and ready to work. I build the fees for business class airfare into the price quotes I provide to my overseas clients. If they are unwilling to pay the cost, that's no problem—I just thank them for their inquiry and stay home. Unless, that is, I really want to go anyway, in which case I'll pay the additional airfare myself or upgrade with frequent-flier miles.

I have a consultant friend who thrives on international travel. He and his wife are adventurous people who love to explore exotic locations. They really suck the marrow out of life. (I tried to suck the marrow out of life once, but I chipped a tooth on the bone.) I haven't adopted this policy myself, but Ken has decided to:

Spend one extra day sightseeing for each time zone change.

So if Ken goes to some faraway place like China or India, he takes his wife along and they spend several extra days touring, hiking, or camping. Every Christmas I receive their where-we-went-this-year photo montage. This isn't a bad way to see the world if you can afford the time and cost.

You know all those little bars of soap that hotels give you? I don't let the extras go to waste. Instead, I:

Collect unused hotel soaps and shampoo bottles, and donate them to a homeless shelter.

Some people think it's unethical to "steal" soap you didn't use. I view the soap as part of what I'm paying for in the hotel room, so it bothers me not one whit to take the leftovers home. Over the past thirty years I've given hundreds of little bars of soap and shampoo bottles to people who needed them more than I—or the hotel—did.

Some years ago I figured out an interesting traveling trick. I learned how to:

Leverage airline frequent-flier programs against each other.

At the time I concocted this scheme, I held second-tier premium frequent-flier status on United Airlines. I wrote to American Airlines, which flew on some of the same routes, and invited them to match my premium status on United. They didn't bump me up two frequent-flier levels, but they did bump me up one. "Hmm," I said to myself, "that was easy." The next year I tried it again, and it worked again. Then I mailed a copy of my United card and my new American Airlines premium-level card to Delta and made them the same offer. Again, they said yes.

I pulled off this scheme for several years, parlaying premium status on one airline into others and enjoying the ensuing benefits. It cost me only a few postage stamps. There was nothing underhanded about this—I was simply presenting each airline with a business offer. One year, I held premium status on four airlines without having earned any of them! The scheme didn't always work, and at the moment I don't have premium status on any airline because I don't fly that much anymore. It was enjoyable while it lasted though.

Another trick I learned is to exploit the fact that prices for hotels, flights, and rental cars change frequently. Now I will:

Check the prices for hotel rooms and rental cars I've already reserved before I leave home.

If I find a lower price online, I simply call the hotel or rental car company and they readily change my reservation to the lower rate. I can find better rates this way roughly half the time.

Recently I performed this check for five hotels and a rental car I had reserved for a vacation coming up soon. With fifteen minutes of mousing around online, I saved more than sixty dollars off three of my original reservations. I checked again the day before I left and saved another thirty dollars. It's worth the few minutes it takes to look (unless your client is reimbursing all of your expenses).

I'm a planning kind of guy. Having encountered my share of unpleasant surprises when traveling, and having read about others that I've dodged so far, I now:

Adopt small contingency plans to help make each trip run smoothly.

For instance, I wear clip-on sunglasses over my regular glasses. Those are quite fragile and hard to find in stores, so now I carry two pairs of sunglasses along in case one breaks (as has happened to me). I place a printed copy of my boarding pass inside any checked baggage in case the suitcase handle with my ID tag breaks off and I need to prove the bag is mine (as has happened to me). I also carry a printed boarding pass in case my phone dies. For overseas trips, I upload scanned images of my passport and other key travel documents to a secure cloud location as backups.

I've read numerous horror stories about drivers who were billed for damage to a rental car that already was present when they picked it up. Consequently, I now take photos all the way around a rental car before I drive it away from the lot and again when I drop it off. So far I haven't needed that evidence to prove the car was already scratched or dinged when I got it, but it comforts me to have the photos available—just in case. I also carry printouts of some key maps for navigation when I'm driving in the event my electronic navigation device dies (as has happened to me).

I view these little precautions as risk management. Bad things like these don't occur very often and might never happen to you at all. I just feel more confident being prepared. But even the most thorough risk management and contingency planning won't anticipate an oddity like the toilet in your hotel room overflowing when you flush it first thing in the morning, barely awake—as also has happened to me. (Is it just me?) Sometimes you just have to roll with reality when it slaps you in the face.

ON FINANCES

In Chapter 14 (*What Are You Worth?*), I said that one of the most helpful tips I picked up about consulting was to:

Set my price so I'm happy whether the client says yes or no.

I have a standard daily training fee, which I adjust based on numerous factors for a given situation. I might knock the price down a bit if the destination is someplace I want to go anyway or if the gig sounds interesting. I'll quote a higher fee if I'm not that interested in the job or if the travel required is excessive. Most of the time, that high price scares the client away. If not, then I'll sigh, get on the airplane, and cash the big check at the end.

One famous consultant I know was invited to travel from the east coast of the United States to Asia to deliver a half-day presentation. Not wanting to spend that much time traveling for such a short gig, he requested an outrageous fee and first-class airfare. The client agreed; off he went.

Partway through my career I also decided to:

Quote an all-up fee that includes my expenses.

This way I don't have to provide receipts that are potentially subject to client pushback for travel and lodging expenses, textbooks, printing student handouts, and the like. This policy has greatly simplified my invoicing. Knowing the final price for an event up front also permits me to submit an invoice to the client in advance and to:

Request payment at the time of the event.

I adopted this practice after having a ridiculous number of invoices get lost in clients' accounting systems. Getting paid right away reduces my aggravation level and saves me the time of chasing down late payments. I also do not let clients get away with their occasional attempts to give themselves a discount for payment within ten, or maybe even thirty, days. My standard terms are net thirty days, with no discount for early payment and an interest charge of one percent per month for late payment, which I waive if it's just a bit late. Some clients request 45 days for payment. I'm okay with that, but I'll push back if they ask for 60 or more days. Remember, everything's negotiable.

One of my colleagues insists that:

New clients outside the United States must pay half the fee in advance.

This is a good idea if you have any concerns about whether you're going to get paid, in what currency, in what form, and when. A Canadian friend suffered a significant loss because of changing currency exchange rates, thanks to a client company in the United States that dragged its feet on payment. Of course, that could have gone the other way too, with exchange rates evolving in his favor. Mainly, he just wanted his money promptly. That seems fair to me.

A recent experience caused me to contemplate a new business policy. A small company that sold a certain software development tool invited me to deliver a webinar as part of their marketing outreach. I gave the talk, but my invoice wasn't paid on time. When I followed up, I learned that the company had just gone out of business—I am never going to get paid. Should

I establish a new policy to ask small companies with potentially dodgy finances to pay me in advance? Maybe.

Early in my consulting career I was invited to speak at a meeting of a local professional society chapter. The contact person asked what my fee would be. Not having done this sort of event before, I wasn't sure how to answer. However, after thinking about it, I concluded that I:

> *Do not charge a fee to speak at a local meeting of a professional organization.*

It's reasonable to have any travel expenses reimbursed, but I don't charge anything for the presentation itself. Delivering such presentations is a way for me to contribute to my profession, as well as providing a marketing and networking opportunity. The organization often presents me with a gift card for $25 or so as a token honorarium, a thoughtful touch.

Conversely, I:

> *Do not provide services to a company for free.*

A big corporation invited me to travel from my home in Portland, Oregon, to their site in Atlanta, Georgia, to present a 90-minute lunch-and-learn session to their business analysts. They couldn't pay me, although they offered to reimburse my airfare. I'm astonished that people think any established consultant would be willing to spend nearly two days on cross-country travel without compensation. I declined, but I always appreciate that people are interested in my work.

Companies sometimes invite consultants and authors to speak for free, arguing that it is a good advertising opportunity and maybe they'll hire you later on. I don't play that game. If I'm delivering value to a company's employees through a presentation or other interaction, I'm entitled to be compensated for that value. I've sometimes given a short presentation as a kind of audition, which has indeed led to a more substantive engagement. But I still insist on being paid for the short talk.

ON CLIENT RELATIONS

A client who engages a new consultant is taking a risk. What if she doesn't have as much experience or knowledge as she claims and doesn't offer good advice? What if a trainer is a poor presenter and the students don't find the class interesting or useful?

One time I brought a well-known consultant and author into Kodak to teach a one-day class. He was highly entertaining but provided little useful content, stimulated no class discussion, incorporated not a single exercise into the presentation, and provided no pointers to reference materials for more information. The course evaluations were mediocre, and I felt a little foolish. We never brought him back.

I don't want to be a consultant like that or to have my clients telling stories about me like this one. To help my clients reach a comfort level with hiring me, I always:

Provide a money-back guarantee.

My goal is for every client to feel that they would happily work with me again. Fortunately, no client has ever asked for a refund, but I'm fully prepared to reduce the fee if they don't feel they got their money's worth.

Periodically I receive emails or phone calls from people who have read one of my books or heard a presentation and want some advice about their situation. I'm happy to:

Answer the first question for free.

Sometimes this reply leads to an ongoing dialogue, but of course it's not feasible for anyone to provide unlimited free consulting to everyone who writes to them. Therefore, if the person who contacted me has more questions, I will offer him an off-site consulting agreement so we can continue the discussion at my usual hourly consulting rate. That offer generally terminates the discussion. Occasionally, though, it leads to an interesting, short-term consulting engagement.

I do always try to provide a substantive response to the initial question if my personal circumstances permit, so I'm frankly surprised at how seldom the questioners even acknowledge receipt of my reply or thank me. That seems kind of rude.

So there you have some of the policies I've adopted during my quarter-century as a consultant, speaker, and trainer. It's worth thinking about your own business policies, writing them down if necessary, adjusting them in the face of reality and experience, and applying them consistently. Except when it makes more sense to do something different, of course.

Next Steps

- Write down five to ten business policies that you have adopted for your consultancy, even if they've always been tacit before. How are these working for you? Are there times when you violate them, or are they rigid rules?
- Read through the business policies stated in this chapter and judge whether any of them apply to you. Modify them as appropriate, and add them to the previous list of policies you have adopted.

20

FOR YOUR PROTECTION

With GARY K. EVANS

As an independent consultant, you must provide for yourself and your family the health care, life, and disability income insurance that regular employees get from their employers. You must also obtain coverage to protect your business practice. Insurance is a significant expense, but it's mandatory—you're conducting a business, not playing a game of chance. Coverage and exclusions vary widely, so shop around and carefully compare the coverages each type of policy provides.

You're tempting fate and gambling with your home, livelihood, and future if you don't consider at least the seven types of insurance described here. Remember, nothing in this book constitutes legal advice. Check with your lawyer and insurance agent to understand your coverage needs.

BUSINESS LIABILITY

This coverage affords protection against liability if you cause harm or damage while engaged in business activities. You should never even consider walking onto a client's location without liability coverage. If you hit a client's employee with your car in the parking lot, or if you trip over a power cord and send a workstation crashing to the floor, you'll want some financial protection. Your personal automotive or umbrella liability insurance might not cover you in such a case. Even if it does, the limits might not be adequate to protect your business. Consider coverage of at least $1 million per incident, with $2 million general aggregate coverage. Double that might be better.

BUSINESS PROPERTY

As you'd expect from the name, this type of policy covers losses you might suffer to your business property, such as electrical damage, a dropped laptop, theft, and so on. If you operate your business from a home office, your homeowner's insurance policy may or may not provide coverage if equipment or other materials that you use in your consulting practice are stolen or destroyed, as in a fire.

You can probably obtain business liability and business property coverage from the same company where you have automobile, homeowner's, and other personal insurance policies. Depending on the coverage limits and deductibles you choose, the combined business liability and property premiums should be around four hundred dollars per year.

I did have to file a claim under my business property policy once. My laptop experienced a static discharge that killed the mouse buttons. It couldn't be repaired. My insurance agent told me to buy a new computer and then send him the bill. The insurance company immediately reimbursed me for the cost of the replacement laptop, less my deductible of one hundred dollars. That one claim made up for several years of premiums.

PROFESSIONAL LIABILITY

Also called professional indemnity, errors and omissions, and E&O insurance, this is malpractice insurance against liability caused by negligence or a mistake on your part that results in financial loss or bodily harm to a client or a client's customer. This is for civil liability, not criminal. Certain types of consulting services are more likely to need E&O coverage than others. You might consider an E&O policy if your business includes designing, developing, testing, or certifying products for your clients. Ask a lawyer about this one.

I (Karl) have never carried E&O insurance. I do not create software or software-containing products that my clients use themselves or sell to their clients. I primarily provide advisory and training services, although for certain clients I have also created process-related documents such as templates for project deliverables, process descriptions, and the like. To be sure, malpractice could extend to providing bad advice or failing to provide appropriate advice. I think my risk exposure is low here though.

Along with my money-back guarantee (see Chapter 19, *It's a Matter of Policy*), my consulting and training agreements include a limitation of liability clause, which states that I am not responsible if the client experiences any loss or lack of benefit from the services or products I deliver. My intent here is to avoid being sued if the client complains that a class was no good just because, say, the students never applied any of the practices I taught them. So far, no client has ever asked for a refund, and I haven't been sued. I'm keeping my fingers crossed.

You might feel more comfortable carrying actual insurance coverage instead of just crossing your fingers. Evaluate your risks, and have a discussion with your attorney before deciding.

LIFE

If you're single, make sure you have enough life insurance—or money in the bank—to bury yourself. If you have a family, carry enough to protect them for the years you would have provided for them had you survived. Carrying too little life insurance means your spouse might have to go to work or get a second job to provide replacement income for your children's education or the million other necessities of daily life.

To determine how much coverage you really need, explore available life insurance calculators on the internet. Term life insurance policies are cheapest for younger workers, but a whole-life policy might be a better choice if you have trouble saving money on your own, as it builds up cash value over time. You can take out a loan against the cash value that a whole-life policy accrues, but not against a term life policy. Talk with a trusted insurance agent to understand the options and trade-offs.

HEALTH CARE

Although it's a necessity, concerns about health care insurance frighten many people who are contemplating the move to independence. But it need not be such a scary proposition. As a short-term solution, if you leave your employer—voluntarily or not—you are generally entitled to continue receiving the same health care insurance coverage through a program called COBRA, the Consolidated Omnibus Budget Reconciliation Act of 1985.

You pay the full cost of the premiums that likely were subsidized by your employer for up to 18 months of continued coverage. The benefits office at your company should be able to help you with COBRA coverage. After those 18 months, you are on your own to find health care insurance.

If you're used to getting your health care insurance from a traditional corporate employer, be prepared for sticker shock, particularly if you are—how do we say this?—older (like us). Coverages, deductibles, out-of-pocket maximums, provider networks, and premiums vary widely. If you're self-employed, your health care insurance premiums may be tax-deductible; your accountant can advise you.

Prior to passage of the Affordable Care Act, health care insurance could be prohibitively expensive or even unavailable if you or your family members had a history of medical problems (pre-existing conditions). As of this writing, the health care insurance market is undergoing significant turbulence. Carefully consider your insurance needs, and explore the offerings from every insurance provider in your area to obtain the best value for your family. Seek out advisers who hold the PAHM® (Professional, Academy for Healthcare Management) certification, indicating that they are thoroughly knowledgeable in health insurance.

You skip this kind of coverage at your peril. Nasty things can happen even if you're young and healthy, and being a road warrior increases the chance of an incident. While on a consulting job in December of 2000, I (Karl) slipped and fell on some ice-covered steps in Dallas, Texas. I tore two of the four rotator cuff tendons in my right shoulder. I'm very dominantly right-handed—my left arm exists mainly for visual symmetry—so this was not a fun injury. My insurance covered the visit to the emergency room that night. I didn't have surgery, but I needed quite a bit of physical therapy after I returned home. Had I not had health care coverage, this could have been an even more unpleasant experience.

Consider setting up a health savings account (HSA) if you have a qualifying high-deductible health insurance policy. The HSA allows you to set aside several thousand tax-deductible dollars per year in a special bank account. You can use this account to pay out-of-pocket medical expenses, such as deductibles, prescriptions, and even over-the-counter medications. Not all policies might qualify, and periodically the rules regarding HSAs do change, so check before you set one up.

If your consulting business involves international travel, check whether your health care policy provides coverage outside your home country. Many consultants work well into their seventies, at which point they are likely on Medicare. With only minor exceptions, Medicare does not provide coverage for medical services outside the United States. Supplemental Medicare insurance plans may or may not provide such coverage. If they don't, and you want the protection, you'll need to get international medical coverage through another source, such as by purchasing travel insurance for an overseas trip.

Navigating the plethora of plans available for health care can be overwhelming. It's almost impossible to compare them apples-to-apples, as there are so many variables. An independent insurance broker can help you choose the most appropriate plan for your family situation from among the many possibilities.

DISABILITY INCOME

Everyone knows that carrying life insurance to protect your family when you die is worth considering. However, you are far more likely to become disabled than to die in any given year. Statistically speaking, a twenty-year-old in the United States has a greater than 25 percent chance of becoming disabled and unable to work for at least a year during his working career (www.disabilitycanhappen.org/chances_disability/disability_stats.asp). That's a long time to go without income.

As the name implies, disability income insurance provides you with some income if you become disabled through illness or injury and can't work. Shop around with multiple agents and providers, because many insurers no longer offer this type of insurance. The coverage that is available comes in various flavors, specifically short-term and long-term disability. Policies vary in their monthly benefits, the waiting (or elimination) period before benefits kick in, how long benefits are paid, and so on. Disability policies obtained through professional organizations or your university alumni association might be cheaper than buying an individual policy directly from an insurance company, but they might not offer as many options. These things always have trade-offs.

Becoming disabled without having disability insurance means that you'll have no life insurance payoff because you're still alive, yet you'll be a cost liability: you might need to be fed, bathed, cared for, rehabilitated, and so on. Coverage is based on your current income, so review your coverage yearly as your income changes. Depending on your policy, your disability insurance payments might stop when you reach the age of eligibility for full Social Security retirement benefits—but your disability could remain far longer.

As with all insurance, you hope you never have to cash in, because that means something bad happened. But bad things do happen. Karl has a close friend who was a highly-regarded software consultant. At age 47, Norm suffered a traumatic brain injury in a car accident while driving home from a consulting gig, thanks to an idiot talking on a cell phone. (Please don't talk or text on your cell phone while driving.)

Norm has not worked since that accident in 1999. He will never work again. Norm said that having private disability income insurance made the difference between him being able to continue living in his house and living under a bridge. But when he turned 65, his private disability insurance payments stopped. After that, all he had to live on were his remaining savings and Social Security retirement payments.

By the way, if you are finding this book useful, please consider making a donation to the Norm Kerth Benefit Fund at www.processimpact .com/norm_kerth.html. Every dollar helps. Thanks!

LONG-TERM CARE

Losing your income for awhile as a result of becoming disabled is bad enough, but what if you were to suffer an injury or illness that necessitated ongoing care for an extended period of time, perhaps for the rest of your life? Caregivers might have to come into your home to assist you. At some point, you might need to move into an assisted-living residence, a nursing home, or a memory-care facility.

These kinds of care are very costly, easily adding up to several thousand dollars per month. You can burn through even a sizable pile of savings quickly, leaving your family to struggle financially. Normal health care insurance policies typically do not provide any coverage for such extra daily expenses over an extended period of time. Government programs like Medicare or Medicaid provide limited assistance under only very strict conditions. The likelihood of requiring such care is low during one's working years, but it isn't zero.

Depending on how concerned you are about such a possibility, you might look into purchasing a long-term care insurance policy. Some insurance companies have stopped writing such policies in recent years, but your insurance agent or an independent insurance broker should be able to find candidate policies for you to consider. The younger you are, the less these policies cost. I (Karl) bought a long-term care policy at age 50 that provides decent coverage at an annual premium of about $1,500. I hope I never need it. If I don't, then I wasted a bunch of money on premiums. But if I do, it will make a big difference in my family's financial stability.

A USEFUL TIP

A client might present you with a contract that lists multiple, unusual types of insurance and the coverages the hiring company expects you to carry. I (Gary) have had several clients ask me to carry insurance such as: automobile liability insurance ($1 million per incident); commercial crime insurance ($5 million per incident); and networks security and privacy (cyber) insurance ($5 million minimum limit). The first time I saw this parade of policies, I was stunned. The automobile liability request bothered me more than the others: I am a consultant, not a chauffeur.

The resolution to this dilemma was a simple matter of negotiating with the client's legal department. These insurance demands were part of their service contract boilerplate, and when I explained the nature of the work I would perform, I invariably heard, "No problem. Just strike what you think does not apply, and send us the red-lined contract." Problem solved.

A fellow consultant once gave me some great advice on insurance in general. Whenever a client insisted that he carry some obscure type of insurance, he would request that the client pay for it for the duration of the project. That would be factored into the overall cost structure. It never hurts to ask.

Next Steps

- Go through the sections in this chapter and judge whether you currently have adequate insurance coverage for you and your family in each of these categories.
- If you are thinking of going independent, list the types of insurance and the coverage levels you would have to buy on your own that you might be currently getting from your employer. Contact your insurance agent or an insurance broker for provider recommendations and price quotes. Build the cost of new premiums you would have to pay into your budget planning for becoming self-employed.

Part IV

Building the Business

21

A KIND OF BUSINESS PLAN

I didn't have an explicit business plan when I launched my consulting career. I hadn't set any particular goals, let alone devised strategies for achieving those goals. I just thought I'd see what happened and how my new career shaped up. I don't necessarily recommend this approach, although it worked out for me.

Once my business became established, I did think carefully about how I wanted my consulting career to evolve. Eventually I came up with a sort of rudimentary business objective: earn a nice living while I'm asleep. While that's not the same as a business *plan*, that objective did force the question of "How are you going to do that?"

As an independent consultant with no employees, every penny of revenue I generated came directly through my own efforts. The trick was to figure out how to generate as much income as possible with as little effort as possible. That is, to look for sources of passive income. I came up with several techniques for creating ongoing revenue streams after some initial investment of effort.

There are some excellent ideas about generating passive income in a fine book by Alan Weiss called *Money Talks: How to Make a Million as a Speaker*. I've never made a million dollars in a year, but my investment in that book certainly paid off. Weiss wrote another useful book titled *Million Dollar Consulting: The Professional's Guide to Growing a Practice*. These two books are valuable for both aspiring and experienced consultants.

INCOME WHILE YOU SLEEP #1: BOOK ROYALTIES

Book royalties are a gift that keeps on giving, with some caveats. First, you need to write the book. This is not trivial. I will talk more about that process in Chapter 32 (*You Say You Want to Write a Book?*). Second, it has to be a good book. Ideally, it will accrue many positive reviews, and readers will recognize the contribution it makes to the practitioners in your field.

Third, the book should fill an important niche in the literature of your domain. For several of my books, I identified gaps in the software literature and attempted to plug them, with generally good success. It's best if the topic you're writing about doesn't have a lot of competitive titles, or if you have something innovative and unique to share.

Fourth, people need to know the book even exists, which generally means going with an established, traditional publisher rather than self-publishing. You won't get as much money per copy that way, but you certainly will sell more copies. Chapter 33 (*Getting Your Book into Print*) has a lot of information about finding and working with a publisher. And fifth, it works best if you write a book that has a long shelf life, not one that deals with the latest fad in your field or with a technology that will be obsolete in just a year or two.

Most technical and professional books don't sell zillions of copies, so don't expect to live on your royalties. I only know a handful of people who make more—sometimes a lot more—than $100,000 a year from software book royalties. I've never approached that lofty pinnacle myself. Nonetheless, the royalties do add up.

Once the book is conceived, planned, outlined, proposed to a publisher, contracted, written, reviewed, revised, edited, proofread, published, and promoted, all you need to do is cash the royalty checks. What could be easier?

INCOME WHILE YOU SLEEP #2: LICENSING

Most of my work through my company, Process Impact, has involved training. The revenue stream from delivering training by yourself is linear: if you teach two classes, you make twice as much money as if you teach one class. To increase the income-to-effort ratio you must disrupt this linear relationship.

One option is to hire other people to teach classes for you and split the revenue. This lets you stay home while someone else wrestles with airplanes, hotels, rental cars, weather, and students. However, having employees or subcontractors complicates your accounting and taxes, at the very least. It forces you to rely on other people. They might not do quite as fine a job as you would yourself, at least not at first, yet you are ultimately responsible for the quality of the client's experience with your company. Of course, if you aspire to grow your consultancy into a larger company, hiring an employee or two is a necessary first step. Before you take on an employee, think carefully about whether you want the onus of being responsible for someone else's livelihood, negotiating salary, providing insurance and other benefits, and everything else that goes with it. I did not.

I tried a different approach. For many years I have licensed my courseware to other companies. Some of my licensees teach the courses internally to their own staff. Others deliver classes to their own clients or through public seminars. Licensing has worked out well for me.

Obviously, first you must have content available that others find valuable. The content must be structured and packaged such that other people can easily learn to present it effectively. Whenever I developed a new course for my own use, I created detailed instructor notes and supporting information as I went along, with the intent of licensing the material to others.

Some people who license their courseware tell the licensee to let them know when they will be teaching a class. The licensor will then send the requisite number of copies of the student handout to the client site. To me, this suggests that the creator of the materials believes this is the One True Course on that topic, and that it always must be presented in precisely the same way.

I don't take that approach. My licensing agreements give licensees the right to modify, extend, and subset the licensed material to best meet the needs of each audience. I do this with my own clients; it's only reasonable to permit my licensees to do the same. I described the licensing agreements I use in Chapter 16 (*Get It in Writing*).

After we execute the licensing agreement, I'm not involved with how a licensee uses the courseware. I often point prospective clients to two or three of my licensees so the client can consider alternatives to having me teach the class personally. I don't know how much my licensees charge, and I don't care. At the end of every calendar quarter, I send an email to each licensee to ask if they delivered any courses. If they did, I get the particulars about location, duration, and number of students, and then I send the licensee an invoice for the appropriate royalty amount.

Could a licensee lie to me and tell me they only taught three courses when in fact they taught 87 that quarter? Sure. I'd never know. There's a certain amount of trust involved with a licensing arrangement like this. I'm thoughtful about who I'll license the courseware to, as I consider it to be valuable intellectual property. Some of my licensees have never presented a class; others have taught dozens. On average, all of us have benefited from the arrangement, as have thousands of students I could not have reached personally with my message.

I've also licensed various other items I created to people who wished to incorporate them into their own products, courseware, and publications. These materials include white papers, articles, project document templates, figures or tables from books, slides to accompany one of my books when it's used as a university textbook, and the like. I typically charge nominal fees for such licensing.

Just this week, I made $100 by licensing three pages of content to a training company. The total effort involved on my part consisted of a brief email exchange and a faxed licensing agreement. Okay, I wasn't asleep when we worked that out, but the effort was minimal.

INCOME WHILE YOU SLEEP #3: E-LEARNING COURSEWARE

After the attacks of 9/11, it occurred to me that people might be hesitant to travel for training. Therefore, I began exploring ways to package some of my presentations in a CD- or web-based format so people could take my classes from the convenience of their own chairs. After experimenting with different approaches, I settled on an e-learning format that closely mimics my live presentations. There are various ways you can approach e-learning, but this felt right for me because people seem to enjoy my live classes and conference presentations. You can see descriptions and previews of my current suite of e-learning courses at www.processimpact.com/elearning. I also created on-demand webinar versions of several short presentations in this same e-learning format.

Over the years, I've sold hundreds of both single-user and corporate-wide, unlimited-use site license versions of my e-learning courses. Creating the courses is a lot of work. I had to learn how to do all that. Preparing slides, writing scripts, recording and cleaning up the audio tracks, synchronizing slide animations with the audio, publishing the whole as a deliverable course, and testing it takes considerable time. I grew very tired of hearing my own voice drone on hour after hour during testing. But after making that initial investment, the delivery cost and effort is minimal, and the profit margin is high.

The e-learning courses also make great train-the-trainer aids for people who license my corresponding instructor-led courseware. Prospective instructors can hear exactly how I present each topic from the course, as many times as they wish. I generally offer my licensees a 50 percent discount on the corresponding e-learning course.

As a related venture, I have presented dozens of webinars on various topics through multiple channels, including websites devoted to business analysis or project management, companies that develop requirements management tools, and training companies. One of these companies that has a very active webinar program records their webinars and makes the recordings available to its members on demand. The company shares the revenue it receives from these viewings with the speakers who presented the sessions initially. It has never amounted to a lot of income for me, but it keeps trickling in. As a side benefit, some organizations that put on webinars will share the attendee contact information with the speakers, which you can use as leads to go looking for work if you wish.

INCOME WHILE YOU SLEEP #4: E-BOOKS

Some years ago, I wrote several e-books of approximately seventy pages in length on various topics. I have sold them as PDF downloads through my company's website, www.processimpact.com, both as single-user copies and as site licenses that allow a company to distribute them throughout their organization. These e-books are inexpensive, but they collectively constitute another small revenue stream that requires negligible effort on my part following the initial investment.

There are numerous web services that handle purchases of these sorts of downloadable products by customers, so the purchasing process is entirely automated from my point of view. Those services manage the shopping cart, the download process, discount codes, and so forth. I use e-Junkie, which has worked fine for me.

It is now quite easy to publish e-books like these through online retailers like Kindle Direct Publishing, Smashwords, IngramSpark, and many others. You can create versions for use with various e-book readers, including Kindle, iBooks, NOOK, and Kobo. Chapter 34 (*Being Your Own Publisher*) describes some experiences with self-publishing.

INCOME WHILE YOU SLEEP #5: OTHER PRODUCTS

I've developed and sold a variety of other products over the years through my website. None of them generated massive revenue, but it didn't take a great deal of work to create them, and the dollars continue to trickle in. Some products I've tried never caught on; others have yielded reasonable income over the years.

The most popular product by far has been the Process Impact Goodies Collection. This is a set of more than 60 document templates, spreadsheet tools, sample project deliverables, e-books, webinars, checklists, and other useful items for requirements engineering, project management, and peer reviews. Customers can buy small groups of these items in individual sets for a few dollars, or they can purchase the entire collection in a single big zip file for more dollars. Actually, it was a customer who suggested in 2006 that I package all of my downloads into a convenient and low-priced collection like this. Thanks for the excellent idea, mystery customer!

Best of all, the profits from these downloads go to a consultant who has been disabled with a traumatic brain injury caused by a motor vehicle accident in 1999.

INCOME WHILE YOU SLEEP #6: AFFILIATE PROGRAMS

Another way to get free money is to sign up for affiliate or reseller programs. When visitors to your website click through certain links to a vendor's site and buy products there, you get some percentage of what they spend as a commission. I've been a member of the Amazon Associates program for many years. If you want to see how it works, follow this link, amzn.to/2flYVAZ, to the Amazon.com page for my forensic mystery novel, *The Reconstruction*.

Even if you don't buy the book (what?!), once you've clicked in through a link like that, you may then browse around Amazon to your heart's content and buy lots of other stuff. I will receive a small percentage of whatever you spend, and it costs you nothing. Go ahead, try it. Buy many things. Feel free. Do it again later on. Tell your friends. I'll let you know how well it works.

Affiliate programs can work the other way, also. I have enlisted several companies to resell my e-learning courses, for instance. When one of their customers buys a course, we split the revenue. Their marketing reach extends to customers who might never find me on their own. Everybody wins. Of course, not all affiliate programs yield actual profits, but once set up, they provide one more way to make money while you sleep.

Is this a great business plan, or what?

Next Steps

- Survey the portfolio of useful materials you've developed and consider what you could turn into products to sell through your website. Can you identify any other channels through which you might sell such products or partners who could resell them for you?
- Consider whether any courseware you have developed is suitable for transforming into an e-learning format. What's the competition like, and how could you produce a superior learning experience with your material? Could you host that courseware on your website, or would it be better to partner with an established training company to sell access through them?
- Become familiar with the vendors of tools, methodology assets, and the like in your business domain to find affiliate programs you might be able to take advantage of.

This book has free material available for download from the
Web Added Value™ resource center at *www.jrosspub.com*

22

BE PREPARED FOR
THE UNEXPECTED

By CLAUDIA DENCKER

My career has taken many twists and turns and has been filled with amazing opportunities and successes, as well as its share of disappointments. While I am now an employee of Stanford University, I spent the bulk of my career as an independent consultant. And there truly is no better career.

Many authors have written about the business of consulting, such as how to set yourself up legally, financially, and with the tax authorities. But that's the easy part, because you are in control. You take action, you get results. Where many consultants, business people, and even candidates seeking employment fail is in securing the gig, closing the sale, landing the job. Without a stream of consulting assignments, you won't be able to establish or maintain your status as an independent consultant.

This chapter takes you through what I believe are the most important aspects of consulting: establishing a relationship with a client and maintaining that relationship, thereby securing repeat business. Many of these lessons can also be applied to interviewing for a job for regular employment.

I have a nontechnical background. But, I was fortunate enough to be in the right place at the right time when the economy was expanding. I left Hewlett-Packard in 1983 as a software quality engineer with little prospect for advancement unless I got an MBA. The job offer I received from a small start-up in Santa Clara, California, was a compelling step toward realizing the long-held dream of running my own business. This company, a contract software testing house, taught me the necessary skills to take my first step into consulting. I learned the great importance of salesmanship from two masters, one a long-standing salesman and the other a recent graduate from San Jose State University who came to sales naturally.

THE MEETING SURPRISE

Before I tell you just what I learned, let me relate a story. Years later, well into my independent consulting career, I was trying to secure some business with a medical device company in San Jose, California. I had already made contact with the decision maker. As part of his qualification process, he wanted me to meet some of the key team members before he made a commitment. I agreed, and we set a date.

On the day of the appointment, thinking that I would only be meeting with two or three people, I drove to the site. It was a stunning day with bright sunshine, blue sky, and a cool breeze blowing through the South Bay, a good omen for the day. As usual, I dressed in business attire and took along some company brochures and business cards in my briefcase, confident that I had a solid chance of landing the job after meeting with a few people.

Imagine my surprise when I entered the conference room and saw twenty people sitting around a large table all waiting to meet me. I took a deep breath, smiled at everyone, and relaxed. This would not be a typical session.

The people around the table introduced themselves. Then came the first question: "Tell us about your services." For those of you interviewing for a job, this is the same question as "Tell us a little about yourself."

I had practiced my pitch many times before in similar settings, in written materials, and through presentations, so I launched into a description of my services. This took about five minutes, as I had pared it to the essentials. I didn't want to talk too much about myself. I wanted to learn from the potential customers what they were looking for, what their pain points were, and how I could help. Only two or three attendees asked questions; everyone else sat and listened. I kept my answers short and to the point, being sure to answer only the question that was asked and nothing more. I even let the occasional silence set in.

Toward the end of the meeting, someone asked another common question: "How much is it going to cost?"

I responded with my usual answer: "Let me review your specifications, and I'll put together a cost for you quickly." I had learned years earlier to avoid giving off-the-cuff estimates. The goal of my meeting with the twenty participants was to get to the next step in the sales cycle. Off-the-cuff cost estimates can slam doors or paint you into corners. You might be providing a broad estimate—maybe even a guess—based on limited information, but to the client it sounds a lot like a commitment.

The meeting ended when I had gathered all the information I needed to finalize and price the proposal and to be confident of its success. I had spent much of the meeting listening to the customer, not rushing my answers, and, when I did speak, keeping my answers on point. I tried to keep the customer talking as much as possible.

As I left, I informed everyone that I was very interested. "I want your business," I said. "It would be pleasure to work with you and your team."

I'm happy to say that I landed the job. To this day, I still don't know why there were twenty people in the room, as I worked with only one of them.

LESSONS LEARNED

So what had I learned from the two sales masters that helped me land this contract? Here are the primary lessons:

- Listen, listen, listen. Have the customers tell you what their pain points are; don't assume that you already know. As you gain consulting experience, you'll often recognize the real problem and have some solutions in mind well before the customer has finished telling her story, because you've seen it before. But listen all the way through to catch as much nuance as you can.
- Keep the customers talking and elaborating on their situation. This will help you to form an airtight response to their needs.
- Only answer the question that was asked. Do not elaborate or expand unnecessarily.
- Be prepared for the unexpected (like a much larger interviewing group than you expected).
- Avoid ballparking the cost of your services off the top of your head. Even cost ranges can be booby traps unless they are ridiculously wide, and then everyone will recognize that. This will work against you.

- Be sure to tell the customer that you want their business. In an unexpected way, it is flattering to the customer and, of course, important to you. Your career as an independent consultant starts with that first sale.

Just as important, I also learned to relax in those face-to-face meetings. They can be fun.

Next Steps

- Write up a short paragraph to concisely summarize the kinds of work you do and the benefits you can provide to clients. This will help you to focus on precisely what your business positioning is, and it will help prospective customers determine whether you're the right person to address their problems.
- Make a list of the key points you wish to convey, and the essential bits of information you wish to acquire, when you're talking with a prospective customer and trying to land the job.
- For certain types of engagements you might perform, make a list of the standard questions you want to ask prospective customers to help you assess whether you are a fit for the job and to help you formulate a proposal. For instance, when talking with a possible customer about teaching a class, you might want to know how many people they wish to train, where the class(es)would be held, their preferred time frame, the students' backgrounds and prerequisite knowledge, what problems they hope the training will solve, and what they would consider to be a successful outcome of the training.

23

HOW TO GET REPEAT BUSINESS FROM YOUR CLIENTS

By ADRIANA BEAL

Any consultant, whether working independently or as part of a consultancy firm, knows that getting repeat business from existing clients is at least as important as finding new clients. When I started providing consulting services to a variety of clients in different industries, I realized that I could classify my clients into two groups:

- Organizations that needed my help for a specific reason that is unlikely to repeat for a long time (for example, a pension fund that no longer needed my services after implementing my recommendations from a fraud risk assessment)
- Organizations that could benefit from my services from time to time, if they liked my work (the majority of my clients)

Obviously, I provided the same level of dedication to clients that were unlikely to need my services again as I did to firms that I knew could offer me repeat business. However, based on this classification, I was able to adopt metrics to monitor my performance as a consultant. I estimated that two years was enough time for another complex software project—the type of work I specialize in—to surface in a typical organization. Therefore, one indicator of my performance was the percentage of companies from the second group that offered me repeat business within a two-year period.

After a decade in consulting, I realized that out of the fifteen consulting clients I have had since moving to the United States in 2004, only one had not yet asked me for repeat business. Even this exception didn't reflect dissatisfaction with my services, as a couple of executives kept in touch with me after the work ended. One of them even hired me to consult for his new employer when he changed jobs. Therefore, I thought I'd be a good candidate to answer a question Karl Wiegers posed: if you get repeat business over the years from the same clients, why do they keep calling you?

Combining my own observations with testimonials from former clients, the following are the top three reasons why I believe the same companies kept calling me back during the past decade. I suspect these practices would also help you retain your clients.

APPLYING SYSTEMS THINKING SKILLS

Systems thinking is a way of understanding reality that emphasizes the relationships among a system's parts, rather than the parts themselves. This is one of the most valuable skills for a consultant. Systems thinking doesn't apply just to information systems, but rather to any system—people, organizations, and so on—whose components are interconnected in such a way that they produce their own patterns of behavior over time.

It's difficult to provide an example of how systems thinking can improve project results without talking extensively about the characteristics of a particular system. I'll use a simple case to illustrate my point. One of my e-commerce projects received a change request to add a screening process during checkout to prevent certain products from being sold in regions where their sale was restricted by law. The business stakeholders approved the requirements, and the team was ready to start coding the solution.

However, I realized that what seemed to be a simple change affecting only one step during the checkout process also affected other business areas, including the call center operation. Without other changes, such as a new feature in the call center application to allow agents to filter out restricted items when recommending products to a customer, the sales process would suffer. Call center representatives would run the risk of wasting time convincing a customer to buy a product, only to learn at checkout time that the product could not be ordered from the customer's location. This would increase the risk of customer frustration, lead to a higher abandon rate, and increase the handle time of inbound calls. As is so common with software change requests, the real problem and its solution were considerably larger than anyone thought at the outset.

Systems thinkers aim to enhance total system properties, rather than try-ing to optimize certain parts of the system. A good resource is *Thinking in Systems: A Primer* by the late scientist Donella H. Meadows. Meadows ex-plains such phenomena as why everyone in a system can act dutifully and rationally and yet still have those well-meaning actions add up to a terrible result, and why a system might suddenly and without warning jump into some completely unexpected behavior.

By using systems thinking, you can forge more creative and satisfactory solutions for your clients, ensuring that separate groups keep the whole in mind while working on their individual parts. When a new challenge arises, the client will remember the benefit of bringing in an external consultant who understands such causal relationships.

BEING TRUTHFUL AND STRAIGHTFORWARD

I've always been very candid with my clients, telling them when I thought an idea didn't sound feasible or a solution didn't seem effective. Often, a team member would disagree with my approach. But throughout the years I kept my belief that speaking up early and honestly about problems improves your results and increases client satisfaction.

Here's an example, based on a common business problem. In one of my client companies, the IT group had not met a software release date in years; budgets were out of control. As part of the process improvement initiative I was leading, the head of development wanted his project teams to stop lying and hiding problems that threatened the completion date, something they did mostly to look good in meetings. This manager's proposed approach was to confront his subordinates and demand a change in behavior.

The problem, however, was that "lying to look good" was a practice that permeated even the top management layer. The only way to solve the prob-lem was to acknowledge the role executives and managers played in it. It wasn't easy to discuss this sensitive issue with my client, but being honest about the need for change to come from the top allowed us to modify the signals that senior management sent to the development teams.

Before we addressed this problem, team members would hide issues they were experiencing, opting instead to wait until another person reported a delay. Their hope was to get the extra time they needed without having to be identified as the source of the project slippage. With the change in behavior starting from the top, the teams became more comfortable speaking up and dealing with any problem that threatened project success as soon as possible. This change caused significant decreases in delivery delays, defects, and runaway costs.

During project retrospectives, clients who later went on to hire me again frequently provided positive feedback regarding my ability to speak up early and honestly about project issues. These clients saw this *culture of candor* as an essential early-warning system to eliminate or minimize project risks in a timely manner. It's better to deal with a concern before it becomes a crisis.

PUTTING YOUR CLIENT'S INTERESTS BEFORE YOURS

As a consultant, sometimes I saw that I was not the right person to take on an assignment or that the project I was being hired to assist did not have a solid business case. Even though taking the assignment would be financially desirable for me in the short term, my clients always appreciated my addressing such concerns directly with them. In several cases, the client and I were able to rethink the project's mission and purpose, if necessary canceling either the initiative or my involvement in it. Whenever this type of situation arose over the last decade, it led to repeat business with that client or to referrals to other companies that could use my services.

By being candid with your clients, even when the truth is not in your best short-term interest, you help paint a picture of the real problems. You also reassure the clients that you will stay with your mission and purpose and not compromise your principles. Most clients will appreciate your transparency. It opens an opportunity for you to build solid relationships with those with whom you're working.

Getting repeat business from your clients, as well as referrals from them, is one of the most effective ways of growing a consulting business. Ironically, a really effective consultant enables her clients to do a better job on their future projects so they don't need additional help with those previously problematic issues. Fortunately, clients who recognize the value you can bring to diverse project situations will remember you when they encounter new thorny problems. My approach is not the only successful strategy to achieve the goal of landing repeat business, but the practices described here have helped me develop lasting and profitable relationships with my consulting clients. As with everything else in life, there is no one-size-fits-all solution. Each consultant needs to find a system that works well for him or her.

Next Steps

- Think of any clients that have brought you back for repeat business. Do you know why they wanted to hire you again? Were there specific aspects of your services or your connections with individuals at the client site that resonated with them? If so, are those factors you can consciously replicate to try to land repeat business from future clients?
- Identify any one-time clients from whom you would like to get repeat business but have not yet. Do you know why they haven't called you again? Were there any problems with the engagement or with your interactions with individuals that might have turned them off? If so, are there insights there that could increase your chances of getting repeat business with other clients in the future?
- If there weren't any obvious problems with those previous one-time clients, think of ways to reconnect with them and see if there are other services you could provide.
- Do you have any previous clients you could contact about referring you to other prospective clients, either within or outside their company?

24

THE CHALLENGES OF REMOTE CONSULTING

Partway through my career, I began offering a service of off-site consulting at an hourly rate that works out to less than my usual daily on-site consulting fee. This way I can provide useful services to clients who have only a few questions or a small project, want me to review some documents for them, or seek a little coaching on specific topics. I've conducted even large-scale and long-term engagements for remote clients, which has worked out well for everyone. I don't have to travel, I can work in my pajamas if I like, and I can work however many hours per day I wish, so long as I meet the client's deadlines. This hourly rate reduces a new client's risk too. They don't need to buy an entire day of consulting time and hope they'll get their money's worth.

Such off-site (also called remote or virtual) consulting is increasingly common in today's distributed, yet connected, work environment. It offers business analysis, project management, and other IT consultants—and their clients—considerable flexibility. However, not working in physical proximity poses challenges as well. It's not much of a problem for short-term interactions, but longer or more complex remote engagements must be thoughtfully planned and carried out. This chapter explores some issues to keep in mind if you want to try consulting at a distance.

BUILDING THE RELATIONSHIP

Even if you will be working at arm's length on an extended project, try to meet face-to-face at the beginning of the project and periodically throughout. It's valuable to get to know your client counterparts so you have not just faces, but also personalities and attitudes, to go with the names. Virtual collaboration doesn't permit casual hallway conversations, meeting up socially after work, or taking coffee breaks together (unless you arrange "virtual coffee" times both to talk work and to catch up on family doings, as one remote BA consultant does). This makes it harder to get to know each other and to form personal bonds. One of my consultant colleagues expressed it this way:

I come from a delivery and sales perspective. I find it invaluable to spend time early on building rapport in person so that our interactions go smoother when I'm remote. As I get to know the clients, I can detect subtle issues in our texts and emails. That in-person time should include both business and social components: coffee, lunch, dinner, happy hours.

That get-acquainted process is also important for your clients. They don't know you yet. You're an outsider, coming in to tell them how to work in different ways, or perhaps to lead some BA or PM activities on a project team. How can they grow to trust you—except perhaps by reputation—if they hear from you only occasionally through email and over the phone? If you can't introduce yourself in person, at least arrange a video chat with each of your coworkers just to get to know them better.

Once you've met, think of ways to sustain the human connection outside work, like becoming friends on social media. Communicating with your clients and coworkers in a context outside the (virtual) office helps to humanize the relationship and strengthen the bonds. Perhaps you can learn what TV shows you both like and make it a point to chat about them. You know, like friends do.

In some situations you might encounter budget constraints or other factors that make it impossible to meet with your fellow team members face-to-face. This isn't necessarily a fatal impediment. As one seasoned long-distance consultant shared:

I worked with one team for two years and never once met any of our developers face-to-face. We still had a reputation for being one of the best teams around. We could solve tough problems other teams couldn't, and I still consider each of the other team members a good friend today. In the end, the fact that we didn't meet in person had little bearing on our ability to succeed as a team. Where there's a will— and a culture that supports it—there's a way.

Speaking of culture, the context of the client organization and its openness to—and capability for—working remotely plays a huge part in determining success in a remote consulting engagement. If the client is a global company where employees and consultants have ready access to collaboration technologies, it should be easy and natural for them to work with people in multiple locations. In contrast, one BA consultant I know worked for a client with a long history of having exclusively on-site staff. They had limited capabilities for remote interactions, and people who didn't come to meetings in person were seriously judged for their absence. My colleague had to make the conscious decision to work locally with her team, because working remotely simply wasn't viable. It's nice to believe that remote consulting could always work. However, if the culture won't allow it, you'll likely never build the rapport you need to influence real change from afar.

As a remote leader, you'll need to take thoughtful culture-building actions to fuse your distributed group into a cohesive team of people who enjoy working together. When I managed a small co-located software group, I began a tradition of giving team members little bags of M&M's candies with notes attached to thank them for a particular action they took or to congratulate them for a success milestone. Everyone appreciates receiving recognition from both managers and their peers. It's hard to send candy through the wire, so look for some small fun things to do with each other virtually. One BA who worked with a widely distributed team began sending cupcake emojis to her team members over a chat system when someone did a good job and to help celebrate wins. Sending each other virtual cupcakes became the team members' way of patting each other on the back. Little in-joke actions like that can be powerful culture enhancers.

STAYING IN TOUCH

More than most other aspects of a software project, business analysis activities demand extensive verbal and written communications. Once you've connected personally, finding the right tactics to stay in touch will sustain a healthy working relationship.

As a remote worker, you have limited visibility into what's going on in real time. Make sure you don't fall off the grid—out of sight and out of touch. Just because you pushed some information out to your team members doesn't mean they read it and understood it. Without frequent communication and course adjustments, it's easy to have people move in the wrong direction for several days because of a misunderstanding or an overlooked revision in the project requirements.

Those of you working together must agree on how you will share information without deluging each other's inboxes. Seek to understand and accommodate your collaborators' individual communication style preferences. Think about how to balance a mix of synchronous (meetings, phone calls) and asynchronous (emails, posted updates) communications to keep the participants engaged without wasting anyone's time. Will you have scheduled conference calls, or will people just pick up the phone whenever they have a question or an update to share? How will the people in a one-on-one call share important information with the other project participants? Will you use threaded email discussions or a more powerful group communication tool, such as Slack, as a shared team memory? Consider whether to use a pull or a push model to notify your stakeholders, posting updates to an online workspace versus emailing status updates.

When people are not all interacting face-to-face, it's essential they all stay informed about project and task status, progress, and issues. Some remote consultants facilitate quick daily standups of just fifteen minutes with everyone connected by phone to sync up. You can couple those with weekly status reports about what got done, what didn't but should have, and what's on tap for the next week.

These standups are also good times to remind people about any dependencies between tasks to avoid bottlenecks and wait states. Quick periodic meetings offer opportunities to surface new risks that might require your attention; the weekly status reports can summarize risk mitigation status. Without being present physically to see what's going on, you need some structure like this to avoid getting blindsided by an overlooked task, a broken dependency, or a risk that turns into a problem.

Anticipate how you might handle a situation in which a team member at the client site goes dark on you: unresponsive to your calls and emails, not updating their work status. Without scheduled frequent communications, you and your client counterpart can waste time, each silently waiting for the other to call because of confusion about whose turn it is to get back to whom. Lack of contact could simply be due to a mix-up, or it could be a symptom of a deeper problem.

When dealing with global communications, be aware of differences in time zones, cultures, and technology access. It's important to respect everyone's schedule. One company that had people working on the same project sprinkled all over the planet scheduled their live meetings for various times of the day so that the inconvenience was shared among all involved. The same people shouldn't have to stay up until midnight for every meeting.

Taking turns dialing in to early and late calls sounds nice in theory, but in reality, the brunt often falls on the offshore team members to call during less-than-ideal hours. To more efficiently coordinate communications across large time-zone separations, consider designating one offshore team member as the primary liaison. Ask that individual to work a shift that shares hours with both onshore and offshore teams. That can help bridge the gaps of time and distance to avoid wasteful delays.

Don't underestimate the impact of time-zone differences on the challenge of working remotely. Round-the-clock coding with a distributed team is one thing, but because BA work is so intensively focused on communicating with stakeholders, physical separation poses substantially higher complexity and risks. I learned early in my software career that it takes remarkably little physical separation—sometimes even within the same building—to impede communication and slow things down.

Rather than using lengthy email exchanges for complicated back-and-forth discussions on a tricky issue, simply pick up the phone and call those involved. A phone call also helps you pick up on someone's tone of voice, which is especially vital when dealing with sensitive topics and controversial issues. With a big time difference, though, you cannot always just make a call to resolve an issue quickly. The turnaround could be as long as three days if you come up with a question on a Friday.

With the inherent time lag of asynchronous communications, be sure to allow more time for getting answers to questions and status updates than if everyone was working on site. You'll need to request feedback earlier than if you could just swing by a team member's desk and talk. I saw one long-distance project fall behind schedule almost from the outset because the plans didn't anticipate the friction of communicating only electronically and across three time zones. It's easier to remember that you owe someone a deliverable or some review comments when you see them several times a week. "Out of sight, out of mind" is more than just a proverb—it's real.

For a good illustration of how to plan a long-distance effort, read Chapter 35 (*On Co-Authoring a Book*). That chapter describes how Joy Beatty and I carefully laid out just how we were going to work together on a large book-writing project across a 2,000-mile gap. A two-person collaboration certainly is simpler than leading the BA activities on a large project remotely. Nonetheless, the principles of establishing mechanisms for communicating, sharing information, and monitoring status are much the same.

COORDINATING THE WORK

There's a certain expectation in business analysis that requirements workshops and other group activities will be facilitated from the front of a roomful of people. But if you're a lead BA or consultant working from a distance, the rest of the group might only see your face on a screen or hear your voice over a speakerphone. If you're present in the room only virtually, consider how you can ensure there is a rich, continuous group collaboration on the work that matters the most to success. This is especially critical when different national cultures, and perhaps native languages, are involved. You might provide the other participants with written materials prior to a meeting, so people who aren't totally fluent in your native language can prepare at their own pace. Not having to translate everything on the fly provides your collaborators with some comfort and confidence.

If you do opt to use live meetings as the hub of collaborative activities, lay the foundation beforehand. Define the agenda and assemble the inputs to each meeting before the synchronous (live) part begins. Don't waste expensive and hard-to-coordinate time together on sharing information that can be done in advance. With most of the groundwork completed ahead of time, the virtual meeting can focus on the key issues that are best resolved through real-time group discussion.

Asynchronous methods—Wikis, discussion threads, surveys, and the like—work well for collecting feedback and comments. An instant-messaging collaboration tool like Slack allows you to communicate directly with one or more people or to create channels that allow teams to form and communicate. Slack lets you call another person and share screens, as well. A conversation that begins as instant messages can be switched quickly into a voice call, and sharing screens helps with troubleshooting errors or reviewing documents.

As you work virtually with the team on more structured tasks, consider your role to be a facilitator of distributed dialogue. It doesn't matter if there are two people or 50 in the conversation. Listening is an integral part of being a consultant, whether face-to-face or virtual. However, as a virtual team leader you must promote *active* listening: prompting, rephrasing, and using open-ended questions to confirm understanding.

An important consultant attribute is being able to sense the client's reactions and read between the lines. Without the benefit of body language and other visual cues, it can be difficult to ensure clarity on all sides, to pick up what is *not* being said, and to confront sensitive issues. You can't see furrowed brows and puzzled looks over the phone, and a thumbs-up text emoji doesn't mean much. All of these remote collaboration problems balloon when groups of people are involved in multiple locations. Think about how you can make sure everyone has the opportunity to contribute to the discussion.

Videoconferencing software will help you see whether people are nodding in agreement or frowning silently. Using video during meetings helps you observe the dynamics of the group in a room. It also helps to cut down on the multitasking that tends to take place during a teleconference, because all the participants can see each other, including you.

I once moderated a technical peer review of a requirements document remotely. The other five participants sat in a room together at their company, while I was in my home office far away. Moderating a review meeting is a facilitation activity. I had to ensure that all attendees were engaged in the process and contributing constructively. The moderator must control any inappropriate or ineffective interactions, such as distracting side conversations. Effective moderation often requires reading body language, such as noticing when someone might be starting to say something but hasn't quite got there yet.

I found it challenging to keep this meeting moving along productively when I couldn't see the other participants, whom I had never met in person. I couldn't tell when someone was tuned out or if they were making funny faces at me during the discussion. Fortunately, we got through it and had a constructive outcome. It was quite a different experience from being able to look the others in the eye around the table though.

A good practice in a conference call is for participants to begin everything they say by identifying themselves and then proceeding with their comment or question. That way there's no burden on participants to recognize voices, which is especially helpful if someone has a cold. When surveying the group on some issue, ask each person to provide feedback in turn, just like going around a table. When you're directing words to specific individuals, say their name first, just in case they aren't listening or it's not obvious to whom you are speaking: "Karl, I have a question for you . . ."

Numerous internet applications facilitate long-distance collaboration activities. Cloud-based tools such as Google Docs, Google Sheet, and Box allow multiple team members to work with the same document at the same time, which can help during multi-location brainstorming sessions. Some tools also streamline communication, notifying team members when new documents are available or even when someone has downloaded a document. One remote BA illustrated how these tools can stimulate interaction:

On my current project, a subject matter expert of mine has been up-dating a document. When he saw that I was looking at it, he was able to quickly Slack me to say he was still working on it, and it wasn't quite ready for my eyes just yet. That saved me some premature review effort.

Business analysis work often involves developing and managing the requirements for a system. Look for a requirements management tool that stores requirements in a shareable database and facilitates real-time updates, collaborative interactions, and communications. Such tools can be expensive, but that's part of the cost of efficiently working remotely. Agile project management tools that stay constantly updated with the flow of the team's work are also valuable. Team members can refer to the tool's task list in their daily standups to ensure that expectations of who is doing what are clear, and to ensure all team members are aligned with the project's commitments and goals.

RESOLVING THE ISSUES

Every project encounters decisions that must be made, problems that arise, and issues to be resolved. Any group that must make decisions, whether co-located or geographically separated, should select one or more *decision rules* early on. That is, the stakeholders should determine in advance who will be making key decisions and how they will decide.

There's no single correct decision rule. You might require a unanimous vote, decide that majority rules (perhaps with an escalation path to a single decider in case of a tie), or insist that the group reach a consensus—these are all different. Perhaps the team will delegate certain decisions to specific individuals, but maybe one person has the authority to override a team decision.

It doesn't matter which decision rule you select, so long as everyone understands, accepts, and follows it. This one step can save you a lot of wasted time later on, when people continually want to revisit previous decisions or haggle over how to resolve some issue. Communicate important decisions promptly to all those who are affected by them. No one likes to feel they've been left in the dark because the key players, hundreds of miles away, forgot about them.

Numerous commercial decision support systems are available to help a distributed team of people address questions or problems and make decisions. Such tools provide asynchronous communications channels for threaded discussions, so the participants can get caught up and contribute at their convenience. This is a better option than using convoluted, extended e-mail discussions. The tools can also retain a single, collected history of the dialogue and the votes that led to making a decision.

Issues and problems will arise from time to time, of course. If you are working off-site, I suggest you pick up the phone at the first sign of an issue. When one of my colleagues had something bad happen on her remote project, she first learned about it through email. She immediately called the individual involved to discuss it. As my colleague said, "That way I could better hear his tone and sound sincere in mine." Video chat calls make it easier to make eye contact and to read body language. This helps to soothe ruffled feathers and to let project participants know how seriously you take their concerns, especially when you need to have a difficult conversation.

TREATING YOURSELF RIGHT

While working remotely offers numerous perks, it also requires consultants to put some personal limits in place to ensure they attain a sensible work/life balance. You have to be able to establish and stick to these limits; this is often difficult for hard-working entrepreneurs. It's easy to fall into the trap of failing to turn it off some evenings, because your home is your office and your office is your home. You might find yourself responding to emails while making dinner or at crazy hours, because that's when people in other locations are working. Put the phone down, and carve out time for yourself.

On one long-distance collaborative project, my high-energy partner made it clear right up front that she took weekends off for family time. As it happens, I don't work that way—all days look the same to me. Nonetheless, I respected her priorities and never expected to hear from her on a weekend. Of course, that doesn't mean that I didn't stuff her inbox for Monday morning.

All that said, if you are going to be in a leadership role and working virtually yourself or managing a virtual team, you have to recognize that 9 to 5 doesn't cut it. Sacrifices sometimes are required to succeed with a virtually structured team. Adopt an attitude that you will be extremely flexible with your schedule to respond to emails and participate in calls when needed. As a leader to whom others look in order to resolve issues or make decisions, providing timely attention to the team's needs is essential to keep things moving. Just don't burn yourself out in the process.

You might have a difficult time adjusting to working virtually at first, perhaps feeling insecure about the arrangement and being concerned about possible distrust between you and your client. You could end up overcompensating for this awkwardness by working excessive hours, lest you be judged if progress appears to be slow. Those concerns should abate when your counterparts in other locations come to appreciate your work ethic and the value you steadily provide.

Virtual collaboration can bring success to widely dispersed groups who need to share ideas, knowledge, or project work. The communication techniques you choose and the leadership you show can help the distributed team reach agreement on actionable responses to project situations. Your clients might come to accept that all the team members don't really have to be in the same room to work together effectively. And your family might be thrilled to have you sleeping in your own home instead of being away on yet another extended consulting engagement.

Next Steps

- If you have ever had to work remotely with a group of clients, consider which of the tips given here for remote engagement would have been helpful to you. List any other strategies or tips of your own for future reference when planning similar projects.
- If you anticipate an engagement involving remote participation, either only on your part or with client participants in multiple locations, spend time working with your primary client contact to plan the best techniques for bridging the distance gaps effectively. Identify any collaboration-support tools within the client's environment that you can leverage for the virtual work that lies ahead.
- Reach out to others in your network who have more experience working remotely and ask them to share their best-practice ideas about effective tools and approaches for maintaining engagement with remote meeting participants.

Part V

Media Matters

25

OUT OF ONE, MANY

When I began speaking at software conferences, I wondered if I needed to develop a new presentation each time I spoke. Some other speakers told me this was necessary. I quickly learned it was not. In fact, I have delivered certain short presentations more than two dozen times in various forums: conferences, professional society meetings, webinars, and for clients. Generalizing this insight, you should try to leverage the intellectual property (IP) you create as an independent consultant as many ways as you can. Let me give you a great example.

In 1999 a magazine editor invited me to write a short article, just 1,500 words, with "20 or 30 quick project management tips" to plug a hole in their editorial calendar. In about 90 minutes I banged out a piece titled "Secrets of Successful Project Management." Over the years, this small starting point grew in a surprising number of ways.

- By adding some more content, I created a one-hour presentation called "21 Project Management Success Tips," which I have delivered 12 times. The written version of the material—an enhanced version of the original short article—appeared in the proceedings of numerous conferences.
- I created an on-demand webinar version of the "21 Project Management Success Tips" presentation.
- The enhanced "21 Project Management Success Tips" paper was incorporated in a compilation of project management articles published by the IEEE Computer Society.
- By adding another dozen topics, drilling down into more detail on them and building in many practice activities, I expanded the one-hour talk into a full-day course called "Project Management Best

Practices." I've taught this course some 20 times at companies, government agencies, and conferences.

- I created an e-learning version of the "Project Management Best Practices" course, which I sell through my website, www.processimpact .com, and through another training company.
- I selected about three dozen slides from that e-learning course and packaged them as the "5-Minute Manager" e-learning series, with quick-hitting micro-tutorials on focused topics for busy people who don't need to take a whole course, also sold through my website.
- I wrote a series of articles amplifying on certain of the project management tips, which appeared in various print and online magazines.
- Next, I collected several of these papers into my *Project Initiation Handbook* e-book, again sold at processimpact.com.
- The *Project Initiation Handbook*, several other articles on project management, and some new material evolved into a book titled *Practical Project Initiation: A Handbook with Tools*, which was published by Microsoft Press in 2007.
- Going the other direction, I serialized selected chapters from *Practical Project Initiation* and republished them as articles on a project management-oriented website.

The moral of the story is this: as you create your own IP, look for opportunities to leverage it into other forms, both to increase your impact and visibility and to generate revenue. For instance, an article can turn into a podcast or a video, and vice versa. People learn in different ways, so packaging high-quality content for delivery in various media and through diverse channels increases its potential value to your audiences. It also helps your company's bottom line.

DO THE *RIGHTS* THING

If you publish an original article in a magazine or on a website, make sure the publishing agreement gives you the rights to reuse the material in a future book and to license it to other channels for reprinting. That is, you want to sell the periodical "first serial rights" (or, sometimes, "first North American serial rights") to the piece. A key word in the contract is "non-exclusive," meaning that you're not restricted from using the material elsewhere. You typically need to acknowledge the original publisher when you reprint materials and indicate that it is being reprinted with permission from that publisher.

Some publishers want only original material. Therefore, if you submit previously published material to another outlet, make sure to state that it has appeared previously so they can decide if it's right for them. I ask a lower fee for previously published material than I do for a new article.

If you publish a book with a traditional publisher, verify that the contract gives you the right to repurpose content adapted from the book into other forms, such as magazine articles, presentations, and blog posts. Publishers generally are happy to have you participate in promoting your book in this way. I have licensed many such derived articles to multiple websites, each of which generates a small amount of revenue. Starting the other way, if you write a series of blog posts, you might be able to combine them into e-books and perhaps ultimately into a full book. This book, for instance, grew out of my now-retired Consulting Tips and Tricks blog.

WHO OWNS IT?

You have to be careful how you use materials that you create exclusively for a single client at their request. You do not own the rights to such a work for hire—the client does. Therefore, you may not reuse or resell that material without their permission.

On a few occasions, I have negotiated with a client to retain the right to reuse items I created for them, usually by cutting my fee in half, such that we have joint ownership. These sorts of negotiations are perfectly fine, if the client doesn't mind. I recommend you get a statement of any such agreement in writing to protect yourself in the future. The person with whom you made the original agreement might move on after a few years, and you don't want to get into conflict with his successor, who might suspect you are violating the company's copyright to the material.

The same holds true if you create presentations or write articles while you're a regular corporate employee. Make sure you clarify who owns the material. I had to do this when I was writing for publication while I worked at Kodak before I went independent. I made sure that I wrote only on my own time and my own computer. All the materials I created for presentation or publication had to pass through Kodak's internal corporate clearance process for approval; I had the thickest corporate clearance folder at the company. When I left Kodak, I asked my manager to write a letter explicitly acknowledging my ownership of specified materials that I had created during my tenure there, as I expected to use them in my future consulting career. It's best to avoid any possible confusion and legal entanglements.

By the way, delivering your intellectual property to diverse customers in a variety of forms is a tip I picked up from Alan Weiss's highly useful books *Money Talks: How to Make a Million as a Speaker* and *Million Dollar Consulting: The Professional's Guide to Growing a Practice*. Those books were worth every penny I paid for them.

Next Steps

- Survey the collection of articles, blog posts, white papers, and any other short pieces you have written about your field to see if any of them can be leveraged into other publications or formats. Did you post a thoughtful response to a LinkedIn article that you can expand into a full article? Can you amplify a blog post into a more substantive piece? Can you use several articles as a starting point for an e-book? Can you develop a short presentation from an article or, conversely, write an article based on a presentation you gave?
- Consider whether you could adapt any of your writings to be pertinent to a related technical or business area. Perhaps you have an article about business analysis that could be modified slightly and be just as useful to project managers. If so, maybe you can place a modified article at a relevant website, blog, or trade journal and gain exposure in a new domain.

26

ON INTELLECTUAL PROPERTY

As a consultant, speaker, and writer, you will be creating valuable intellectual property (IP). You must protect your IP, because it's how you earn your living. The flip side is to make sure that you properly respect other people's IP. Most people I know are sensible, honest, and fair when it comes to these matters. Sadly, a few are not. This chapter addresses certain aspects of copyrights, IP rights, and courtesies. Let me reiterate that nothing I say here constitutes legal advice. Also, IP laws may vary from country to country.

COPYRIGHT NOTICES

People sometimes are confused about what can and cannot be copyrighted. You cannot copyright a fact, idea, system, or process. You *can* copyright the expression of an idea in an "original work of authorship" (language from www.copyright.gov). You cannot copyright a title, which is why you sometimes see multiple books or movies sharing the same title.

Also contrary to popular belief, you do not need to officially register your copyright on something you created with the United States Copyright Office to protect it. The act of creating the item automatically grants copyright ownership to the creator. However, placing a copyright notice on the item provides you with certain legal benefits.

According to the U.S. Copyright Office, a properly composed copyright notice consists of the following three elements:

1. The copyright symbol, ©; the word "copyright"; or the abbreviation "copr.," but not "(c)"
2. The year of first publication of the work, or the year of creation if the work is unpublished
3. The name of the copyright owner

It's not necessary to list all the years during which the material was copyrighted, only the year of its first publication or creation.

You might also wish to include a statement of the rights you are reserving. My copyright notices generally look like this:

> *Copyright © 2019 Karl Wiegers. All rights reserved.*

I have developed numerous document templates and other items that I intend for people to use as starting points for their own project deliverables. A copyright notice like the following appears on such templates:

> *Copyright © 2019 Karl Wiegers. Permission is granted to use and modify this document.*

I want to make it clear that people may use the document and modify it to best suit their needs, but that I own the copyright on the template itself. They may not claim it as their own, sell it to their own clients, post it on public websites (which, alas, happens all the time), or anything like that. Of course, I make no ownership claims on any documents a project team creates from my templates.

Although I do not register copyrights with the U.S. Copyright Office for most of the items I create, I certainly do for my books. A traditional publisher takes care of that as part of the publication process. It's the author's responsibility to register the copyright for self-published books. That process consists of filling out the appropriate form from the U.S. Copyright Office, paying a modest fee, sending them two copies of the book, and waiting many months to receive your certificate of registration. For more information, see the publication *Copyright Basics* at www.copyright.gov/circs/circ01 .pdf. A rich source of information about copyright is Stephen Fishman's book *The Copyright Handbook: What Every Writer Needs to Know*.

CITING THE WORK OF OTHERS

When I was a graduate student in organic chemistry, I read many journal articles and eventually wrote a few myself. I learned the importance of crediting other sources on which I relied in the books and articles I write. Citing other publications and their authors accomplishes two objectives. First, it gives credit to those who have done previous work in the area. With but rare exceptions, we all build on the work of others. If I incorporate what I learned from them into my own thinking and creations, I should acknowledge their contributions. And second, citing other sources points the interested reader toward resources for more information or supporting evidence for my positions.

I look askance at technical or professional publications that contain no references. It's unusual for an individual to invent a whole new domain of study entirely on his own. Omitting references suggests that the author is claiming credit for all of the knowledge presented in his publication.

If you have some sources that you want to cite in an article, learn how the periodical to which you are submitting it handles citations. Format your references in the same way you see done in other articles in the periodical. Books typically list references at the end, sequenced alphabetically by author, although sometimes each chapter will list the sources cited therein at the end. A bibliography of sources for further reading on certain topics isn't the same thing as a list of the references you cited at specific points in your text. Both have their place.

Check your citations scrupulously for completeness and accuracy. I've seen many erroneous references to my own publications: incorrect first name or middle initial, last name misspelled, incomplete or inaccurate title, incorrect publication date, and the like. No matter how carefully you check them, it's easy to have a mistake slip into a reference citation.

FAIR USE

Occasionally, you might wish to incorporate material from another source into your own work. Of course, the first thing you must do is to cite the original source, even if it's something you wrote earlier. If you don't own the copyright to a work, then you might also need to get permission from the copyright owner to reuse their material. The exception is if the amount and type of material you wish to use lies within the domain of fair use. The U.S. Copyright Office offers some comments on fair use at www.copy right.gov/fair-use/more-info.html.

Remember, a copyright notice does not have to appear on the material for it to be considered copyrighted. If you created some IP—a book, article, poem, play, or song—you own the copyright to it unless you've granted that copyright to some other party. For instance, with a work made for hire, the employer is considered the legal owner of the copyright to the work. Your contract with that employer should stipulate ownership of any materials created under the contract. If you don't own the copyright to some IP, please respect the owner's rights.

Unfortunately, precisely what constitutes fair use is not well defined. As I understand it, in general it is permissible to include short quotations or excerpts ("short" being undefined) in your own work without explicit permission, provided that you cite the original source. However, if either a significant fraction of your work is derived from someone else's work, or if you are incorporating a significant portion of someone else's work into yours ("significant" being undefined), then you need permission from the copyright owner. If you wish to include a complete table, figure, poem, or the like from someone else's work in yours, you must request permission first.

As stated in document FL102 by the U.S. Copyright Office, "The distinction between fair use and infringement may be unclear and not easily defined. There is no specific number of words, lines, or [musical] notes that may safely be taken without permission. *Acknowledging the source of the copyrighted material does not substitute for obtaining permission* [emphasis mine]."

I recently read an online article—adapted from a forthcoming book—that centered on a large table of information. That table was clearly based on a similar table from one of my own books. The author had added some value, but more than half of the material he presented was in fact my material, nearly verbatim. The author did not even include a citation to my original publication. I felt this went well beyond fair use, as he had essentially incorporated my entire table into his work, with neither acknowledgment nor permission.

I contacted the author, who replied that he planned to list my book in his book's general bibliography of resources. That did not seem adequate. I explained that a specific citation to my original source when he presented his table was necessary; requesting permission in advance was even better. The author balked but did check with his publisher, who wisely agreed with me. Citing another author's work costs you nothing; just do it.

LICENSING FEES

Citing another source costs you nothing, but it's within the rights of the copyright owner to request a licensing fee if you wish to reuse his or her material. For instance, I paid a licensing fee to include a Dilbert comic in one of my books. The comic was a perfect fit, well worth the modest cost.

I receive occasional requests from people to include content from my books, articles, or websites in something they are developing. Sometimes, what they're requesting lies within my understanding of fair use and it's no problem. If they wish to use my material for academic purposes or to share small items within their company, I'm generally happy to grant permission. I do try to be reasonable and fair, and I always appreciate people who go to the trouble to ask first.

Other times, though, someone wants to incorporate a figure, a complete document template, or some other resource I've created in a book or training course they'll be using for commercial gain. I generally ask a small licensing fee in these cases. They're going to make money in part from material I created, so I'm entitled to a little nibble of the pie. If that's okay with the person who made the request, we make a deal; other times they decide not to use my material after all. Either way is fine with me.

PROTECTING YOUR INTELLECTUAL PROPERTY

I've had both amusing and dismaying experiences in which people have misappropriated my IP. Let me share some of those so you can be alert for similar problems with your own creations.

The Paraphrasing

I once read an article about a software quality technique called inspection, a type of formal peer review, in a respected software journal. The author was a man of unimpeachable integrity, a titan of the software industry whom I admire greatly. Someone else, whom I didn't know, had written an accompanying two-page sidebar that presented an overview of software peer reviews. As I read the sidebar, I found myself nodding along, agreeing with what it said. Eventually, I realized why: I had written it!

This sidebar was nothing but a condensation and paraphrasing of an article I had published in a different magazine several years earlier. I'm the only person who ever would have noticed that connection—and I did. However, the author of the sidebar didn't cite my article, nor did she have permission from either me or that earlier magazine for this adaptation.

I easily convinced the journal's editor of the similarities between my article and the sidebar. He issued a clarification and apology in the next issue. I also wrote to the author of the sidebar, but she never replied. Had the author contacted me in advance and asked about presenting this summary—with due credit given to the original source—I would have said fine and thanked her for her interest in my work. Instead, she simply took my material, rephrased it somewhat, and presented it as her own. That's not fine.

The Mystery Slide

I was sitting with a friend at a conference. The speaker was presenting on some aspect of software requirements, a field in which my friend and I had both done quite a lot of work. The speaker showed a slide and said, "I'm not sure where I found this." My friend grinned at me and whispered, "I think I know."

The slide was pulled right out of one of my training courses. This was flattering, naturally, but it was also curious. I had never taught that course at the speaker's company, so I'm not sure how he got it. After the talk, I told him where that slide had originated. He apologized, and I told him he could continue to use it if he added a reference to the source.

The New Author

I recently discovered one of my articles posted on three unrelated websites. On one, no author was identified, implying that the website's owner wrote the piece. I called the owner, who agreed to show my name as the author, as he should have done in the first place. On the other two sites, different people showed their own names as the author, even though the article was lifted nearly verbatim from my site. It's highly irritating to have other people claim my work as their own. I work hard on the things I write; so do you.

The Incomplete Theft

I have long offered various templates and other project aids for downloading from my websites. Once I discovered another website that offered a use-case document template for downloading. Their template was identical to the one on my site, except that someone had replaced my copyright notice with her own. That is not legal.

When I pointed this out, the woman I contacted initially claimed she had created her template prior to mine, so therefore *I* was the copyright violator. I then called her attention to the Microsoft Word document properties for her file, where my name was still listed as the document's author! She reluctantly acknowledged that mine was the original and agreed to take hers down.

The Condensation

I keep an eye on how my intellectual property is misused, but not because of ego or to make sure that I always get full "credit" for anything I've ever said or written. Instead, it's a matter of making sure that the material from which I earn a living remains my property.

Some years ago, I received an email from someone I didn't know, asking if my *Software Requirements* book was now in the public domain. It was not. She had spotted an article that clearly was cribbed from that book, but the book wasn't referenced. I contacted the author and learned that this was the first in a series of three articles, indeed drawn from my book, without citation or permission.

The author was not an American, although he lived in the United States. He told me that summarizing another author's work like this was considered a compliment in his home country. I explained that it was considered plagiarism in the United States. Plagiarism involves claiming someone else's words as your own. Copyright infringement involves the unauthorized use of material that is protected by copyright. This instance appeared to be both.

It was too late to withdraw part two of the series from the publication cycle, but we got my name listed as a co-author for part three, along with the reference to my book. I'm not trying to be mean here, but I do have to protect the material I have created—with considerable effort—so that the ownership and any revenues ensuing from it remain mine. That seems fair.

The Reposting

Here's another interesting example of misappropriation. I discovered a website based in another country that had reposted numerous articles that were originally published in *Software Development* magazine, including several of mine. One problem was that the people who created this website had obtained permission from neither the publisher of *Software Development* nor the original authors to post these articles. Another problem was that they had moved the original author's name to the fine print at the end of each article, putting someone else's name at the top so it looked like that other person wrote it. I worked with the original magazine's publisher to get that website to halt this unethical practice. It's a never-ending battle to keep an eye on your IP—if you choose to do so.

A RISK OF PUBLISHING

My sister also is an IT professional. She once took a class on software require-ments at her company. During his presentation, the young instructor referred to something I had written, calling it "the Wiegers method." My sister didn't quite understand the point; she asked if he could expand on it. "Sorry," he said, "that's all I know."

"I'll ask him," my sister replied. We have different last names, so our con-nection was not apparent.

That night she gave me a call and told me what the instructor had quoted from my writing. I had no recollection of ever having said what he had attributed to me. I searched through both of my requirements books and didn't find anything like what he had said. She reported that back to the instructor, and I emailed him as well to follow up. I found the whole episode pretty amusing.

A risk of sharing your thoughts in public is that others may misunder-stand, misinterpret, or miscommunicate them. It happens in both positive and negative directions. Sometimes people have accused me of believing something that in fact I do not believe, because that's how they had inter-preted something I wrote after processing it through their own filters and biases. In other cases, I've received credit for some pithy quotation I had duly cited in my writing, but which I had not originated. If you're going to put yourself out there through writing or speaking, get used to this possibility. There's a fine line between recognition and notoriety.

PURE THEFT

Within a few weeks of publication of my most recent software book, *Software Requirements, 3rd Edition*, in 2013, I found dozens of websites that offered free downloads of the e-book version. I've also seen websites and discussion boards where people were offering free copies of my e-books to anybody who requested one. Of course, the author does not receive any royalties for such pirated book downloads.

This is unethical and illegal. It is called theft, and it is rampant. It's often hard to discover how to contact the managers of those sites and persuade them to remove the items that are being stolen. Some of them hide behind the façade that they are merely providing links to other sites that are actually doing the stealing, so they aren't responsible for any wrongdoing.

Consequently, I will not be writing any new technical books. It seems silly to spend hundreds of hours creating a product only to have unscrupulous people steal it. To be sure, not everyone who downloads a free book would have bought it anyway, but many industry experts agree that pirated downloads do hurt sales. If you're only concerned about getting your ideas—and your name—out there, don't worry about pirating. But if you want to make some money from your hard labor, or if you have an ethic of fairness and honesty, piracy is extremely annoying.

If you want a book, buy it. Authors work very hard on their creations, and they are entitled to compensation for their efforts, even in a world in which so many people seem to think anything available on the internet should be free. Oh, and if you obtain value from using a shareware application, throw the developer a few bucks. It's only fair.

THE FUNNIEST CASE

I have long made numerous document templates, checklists, and other resources available for downloading from the Process Impact Goodies web page at www.processimpact.com/goodies.html. Some years ago, I stumbled onto another consultant's site that offered a similar set of downloadable items; too similar, in fact. The boilerplate text on his page was lifted verbatim from my Goodies page, and about half of the items he had posted also were taken from there. (Copyscape.com is a website that lets you search for text copied from a website.) He did identify those items as being mine, but he hadn't requested permission to post them.

When I first contacted the consultant to inquire about this, he ignored me. I tried again. This time he replied but pushed back against my request that he remove my materials from his site. The guy said, "You don't have to be a <rude term> about it." Oh, great, I thought: name-calling escalation. He takes my material without permission and I'm the <rude term>? Ultimately, he apologized for that comment and complied with my request.

The funny part? The name of this dude's company, now long gone, included the word "maverick." A dictionary definition of maverick appeared at the top of each of his web pages: "someone who exhibits great independence in thought and action." Uh-huh.

Next Steps

- Check whether you have copyright notices on the materials you make publicly available through your website or in presentation handouts. Be sure they follow the guidance from the U. S. Copyright Office for a properly composed copyright notice.
- Reflect on articles and posts you have written, presentations you've developed, and the contents of your website. If you incorporated ideas, quotes, slides, figures, tables, images, or other content from others, make sure you've given them proper credit for it. If you think the scope of what you have included might go beyond fair use, contact the copyright owner and request permission to continue using the material.

27

SEVENTEEN TIPS FOR BECOMING
A CONFIDENT PRESENTER

I'm not quite sure how it happened, but somewhere along the way I became a public speaker. I never took a speech class or participated in debate in school. I never attended Toastmasters International or any other group that helps you become comfortable standing before an audience. Nonetheless, I've delivered well over 600 presentations in the past 28 years and enjoyed just about all of them. Somehow, I have become comfortable speaking for anywhere from 30 minutes to four days, to audiences ranging from just a few people up to several thousand.

Most consultants, business analysts, and project managers will be called upon to give a presentation or teach a class from time to time. Speaking in public is a terrifying experience for many people. That fear even has a name: glossophobia. The anxiety is understandable. Everyone is staring right at you, awaiting your words of wisdom. You feel exposed and vulnerable. It's one thing to say something foolish in a private conversation; it's quite a different matter to say it to dozens, hundreds, or thousands. The potential for embarrassment is enormous. However, so is the potential for sharing important information that can influence many people in a positive way, not to mention the potential for making a lot of money.

Just in case you—like so many other people—are nervous about giving presentations, here I share Karl's Tips for Confident Public Speaking. Keeping these ideas in mind will help chase the butterflies from your stomach. Maybe you'll even have fun the next time you're on stage.

DURING PREPARATION

Laying the foundation for a confident presentation begins long before you step into the spotlight. The following suggestions will help you construct a presentation that holds the audience's attention, achieves your objectives, and keeps you calm.

Presentation Tip #1: Determine your purpose

Think carefully about the goal for each talk you design and deliver. Is it to educate the audience or maybe to persuade them to adopt a particular point of view? Perhaps you're reporting the status of some project or strategic initiative, or you're trying to establish a shared vision toward a common objective. Occasionally, you might want to provoke controversy deliberately, stimulating the listeners' minds so they can break out of the box of traditional thinking and generate new ideas.

A motivational presentation can serve as a rousing call to action, so contemplate what you would like the members of your audience to think or do differently after they hear you speak. Considering these goals in advance will help you select the right content and delivery style to achieve your objectives. If people walk out of a talk without thinking differently or deciding to work in some new way, what was the point?

Presentation Tip #2: Know your audience

This is often stated as Rule #1 for giving a presentation or writing an article. I happen to believe that knowing your subject is really Rule #1, but knowing your audience is a close second.

Knowing your audience includes understanding the forms of communication that will resonate most strongly with them. Do they respond to textual bullet points on slides, or do they prefer tables, charts, and complex graphics? Will animations, cartoons, and videos hold their attention, or will they distract from your serious message? Do you need slides or other visual aids at all? Perhaps most important, what topics will grab their interest?

I once attended a lecture series on various science and engineering topics. One night an engineering professor spoke on the history of the toothpick. It was every bit as fascinating as it sounds. People began sneaking out of the auditorium within minutes after the lecture commenced. No visual aids could have livened up a topic that dull.

In addition, think about why the audience is there. What are their interests, concerns, assumptions, biases, and fears? This will help you set the tone of your presentation. If you're declaring a new strategic direction for the company, people are going to be nervous about the implications for their own jobs. Do you want to soothe their concerns? Or do you want to boldly set the new agenda and invite everyone to get on board?

Some 25 years ago I heard a top executive at a huge corporation describe his vision for the company to nearly 3,000 employees. He explicitly stated, "If you're not comfortable with this strategy, we can part friends." It was clear that he wasn't going anywhere. We all got the message: you can either stay on the train as it changes direction, or you can get off at the next stop.

Presentation Tip #3: Anticipate possible resistance

This is not much of a concern for educational talks, but certain types of presentations might not be well received by the audience, for a variety of reasons. If you're giving such a talk, take the time to anticipate what kinds of resistance your audience members might have to your message and how you might preemptively overcome it. Political speeches can certainly fit in this category, depending on to whom you're delivering them. Corporate presentations that deliver surprising news or announce new strategic initiatives can trigger resistance, dissatisfaction, and fear. Combine these first three tips to make sure your presentation goes over well and that it lays the foundation for moving forward, whether the news you're delivering is good or bad.

Presentation Tip #4: Go to the right place

I used to be a regular speaker at a series of software development conferences held in the San Francisco Bay Area. Some years they were at a convention center in San Francisco itself, other times in San Jose or Mountain View. Another regular speaker I knew once went to the San Francisco convention center, but the conference was held in San Jose that year! He had to frantically race the 50 miles to San Jose, barely making it in time for his presentation. It pays to know where you're heading before you make your travel arrangements.

I've been burned by location ambiguity a few times. At one client site, I was delivering a two-day course for business analysts, followed by a one-day management presentation. Not having been told otherwise, I assumed both would be held in the same location. So on the morning of day three, I went back to the same room where I'd taught the previous two days, only to find a different event underway. With some effort, I learned that my second class was scheduled for a building a quarter of a mile down the road. I had to hustle to get there.

Early in my consulting career, I arrived at a client's central location outside Washington, D.C., to teach a class, but the office was deserted. I didn't have a phone number for my contact person, a mistake I never made again (why do we learn so many important lessons from our mistakes?). It turned out the course was being held at a conference facility about eight miles away. Unfortunately, no one had thought to inform me. I had only the address for the company's main office, so that's where I went. One employee just happened to stop by the main office and gave me a ride to the training location. Had she not appeared, I'd probably still be waiting there today.

I had a similar experience just last year. This time I had phone numbers, but none of the three contacts I tried to reach the morning of the class answered their phone. A helpful receptionist did her best to figure out where the class might be held, to no avail. The location had been changed, and again I wasn't notified. A student in the class wandered by the reception area and recognized me, so I made it to the right room eventually. This is mighty frustrating. And the three contact people for whom I left voice mails never got back to me at all. Weird.

Presentation Tip #5: Take backups

I have my PowerPoint presentation on my laptop, a copy of the file on a flash drive that I carry separately from the laptop bag, and another copy stashed in a secured private folder on my website. Any cloud storage, like Dropbox or iCloud, will work if you don't have your own website.

The flash drive is in case my laptop dies, gets lost, or is stolen, or if it doesn't get along with the presentation room's projector and I need to use a different computer. I always save the PowerPoint file with fonts embedded, as another random computer might lack some fonts I need. The cloud backup is in case all else fails. You can't have too many backups.

It's also a good idea to carry electronic backups of any handouts that are supposed to be distributed with your presentation. I have occasionally had problems with staff members at the conferences where I'm speaking misplacing my materials. I always turn in my materials for duplication well before their deadline, but the staff at one conference where I was a regular speaker lost track of those files from time to time. Then they would follow up very late to remind me to send them my materials, which I had already done. That made me nervous.

One year I double-checked with the conference staff to ensure they had received the file I had sent them, a sizable handout for my full-day tutorial. No problem, the person I spoke to replied; we have everything right here, and it all looks fine. But when I arrived at the conference site, a different staff member asked me, "Did you bring the handouts with you? We never received your tutorial materials."

I was pretty ticked about this. I explained the background and said that I had confirmed their receipt of the handout materials. The staff member looked around on their network and said, "Oh, yes, there's your file. Now I remember. It was in some format we couldn't read."

I replied that the person I had spoken to months earlier had assured me she could open my file just fine. This staff member double-clicked on the file; it opened up and displayed correctly.

"What more do you want from me?" I asked with annoyance. This was highly frustrating, particularly because I had so carefully followed up after my multiple previous problems. Fortunately, they were able to get the handout printed and delivered to my room only a half-hour late. I never delivered a tutorial at that conference again, just a keynote a few years later. They were too unreliable.

DURING THE PRESENTATION

So now you are ready to go. Your abstract is written and distributed; the slides are laid out and fine-tuned to perfection. You've practiced the talk and have a clear mental image of what you want to say for each slide. Even your jokes are ready to launch.

The big day arrives. You go to the presentation room, heart in your throat. There are a lot of people out there, waiting to hear what you have to say. Keep the following tips in mind to calm your nerves before and during your speech.

Presentation Tip #6: No one knows what you're going to say next

Don't worry if the words that come out of your mouth don't exactly match the way you planned, scripted, or practiced them. Just keep going. A presentation is very different from, say, a piano recital of a well-known musical composition, where someone in the audience is sure to notice a B that should have been a C. If you forget to make some point, try to work it in smoothly later on. No one will know.

Presentation Tip #7: You are in control

You're the one with the podium, the microphone, the projector, the laser pointer. You're the one who can ask the audience if they have any questions. You can terminate the discussion and move on whenever you like. You control the pacing. It's your show—enjoy it.

Presentation Tip #8: You probably know more about your topic than anyone else in the room

Otherwise, one of them would be speaking, and you'd be listening. Even if you're not the world's expert on the subject, you're likely to be the local expert for that hour or day.

It can be disconcerting to stand before a conference audience and recognize a well-known authority on your topic in the crowd. Most such authorities will keep a low profile and not ask embarrassing questions or try to take over the presentation. At least, that's what I do when I'm attending a talk in one of my areas of expertise. I don't want to make anyone uncomfortable. I might amplify upon an answer to a question if it seems appropriate or if the speaker invites me to. Otherwise, I just sit, listen, and learn.

Rarely, I have seen a famous person take an inappropriately intrusive role in someone else's presentation. I find that irritating; the speaker probably does as well. So if you're the famous person at someone else's talk, please remember that it's the speaker's show, not yours.

Presentation Tip #9: You rarely face a hostile audience

Attendees are there because they want to hear what you have to say. This isn't necessarily true if you're dealing with a controversial issue or if you're speaking at a political or government meeting of some kind (see Presentation Tip #3). But if you're delivering a factual presentation to a group of people who are attending of their own volition, they usually start out with an open and receptive attitude. After that, it's up to you to hold their interest and persuade them of the merits of your message.

Keynote presentations at conferences might constitute an exception to this tip. A keynote topic sometimes is deliberately provocative, chosen to recalibrate the thinking or trigger the emotions of the audience. In a case like that, you should expect a more energetic reaction than usual from the audience.

I opted for this approach when I delivered my very first keynote address at a software process improvement conference with some 1,800 attendees in 1999. In fact, the man who invited me to do the keynote told me to bring my most stimulating and provocative material. I came up with the title "Read My Lips: No New Models!"

My premise was that the software industry already had plenty of models and methods available for increasing our quality and productivity. What we lacked was the effective and consistent application of those proven techniques. So I was encouraging people not to develop any more new models just then, but rather to work on reducing to practice that which we already knew worked.

This was indeed provocative, especially because the organization that sponsored this large conference had led the creation of many of the models about which I was saying "Enough!" When I reached the podium, I was a bit taken aback to see the man who began this whole improvement-model movement sitting in the very front row of the huge auditorium. I had never met him, although of course I knew his work. He didn't say anything during the presentation (see Presentation Tip #8), but his body language wasn't encouraging.

Years later, I met someone who had sat with that luminary at my presentation. I was relieved to learn that his reaction to my thesis was: "Karl's right." I'm not sure everyone who attended the talk agreed, but my keynote certainly did stimulate discussion that went on for the duration of the conference. That was my goal.

Presentation Tip #10: Avoid saying "on the next slide . . ."

I learned this trick from my PhD thesis advisor in graduate school. Maybe you don't remember just what's on the next slide, or perhaps you changed the sequence from the last time you gave the presentation. When we used actual 35mm slides back in the Stone Age, they might not have been loaded in the slide carousel exactly as you had planned.

If you say "on the next slide" but you're surprised by what then pops up, you might have to backtrack a bit—awkward. Instead, just display the next slide in the sequence and talk about whatever is on it. In other words, it's okay to fake it a little bit. You have to roll with reality even when it doesn't match the plan.

Presentation Tip #11: Don't state how many points you want to make about something

In some of my talks I will reveal a particular bullet point and then say, "There are three things I want to say about this." That can be a bit dangerous, especially for those of us with brains that are, shall we say, slightly older than average. On several occasions, I have conveyed the first two points just fine but forgotten precisely what I intended to say in the third point. So then I either have to mumble some new "third point" on the fly, hope my brain comes through with my original third point before I move on to the next slide, or hope no one remembered how many points I had promised them. It's safer to say, "I want to make several points about this." Then I can offer as many—or as few—comments as come to mind at the time without worrying that someone might ask what my third point was going to be.

Presentation Tip #12: Don't read the slides to the audience

They can all read just fine (assuming you've used a suitably large font—consider the room size when laying out your slides). Don't cram masses of text on your slides. Show concise bullets and images that will help the listener remember what you told him when he reviews the presentation in the future. Reveal elements of the slide, such as bullets or graphics, one at a time, instead of showing an entire complex slide and then walking the audience through it.

To prompt your memory, especially with a new presentation, you can use the notes view in PowerPoint to write the abstract of what you want to say about each slide. If you need the reminders during your talk, you can keep a stack of printed notes pages on the table or podium in front of you and unobtrusively flip the pages while you're speaking. If you need more space for text, put sticky notes on the back of the preceding page with more visual reminders.

I have delivered many webinars, in which I'm speaking on the phone from the comfort of my home office, displaying slides over the internet to attendees all over the world. Because no one can see me during those presentations, I can make the process easy for myself. I write rich notes for each of my slides in a conversational style, based on how I've given the talk live in the past. That way I can just read the notes, with appropriate vocal inflections and additional commentary relevant to that audience. The PowerPoint notes thus serve as a script, enabling me to give a natural-sounding presentation of repeatably high quality.

Presentation Tip #13: It's okay to say "I don't know" in response to a question

If you aren't sure how best to respond, it's better to say "I don't know" than to stand there silently because you can't think of the right answer. It's also better than making up an answer on the fly that might turn out to be wildly erroneous. Even better than a simple "I don't know" is "I don't know, but I'll find out," or "I'm not sure off the top of my head, so let me think about your question and get back to you." Then be sure to follow up later on.

Because you are controlling the presentation (see Presentation Tip #7), you may also choose to defer questions to the end. You might suggest that you follow up off-line with someone who's asking a complex question or one that's of limited interest to the rest of the audience. For reasons of time management, you could even decline to answer questions. But do show respect for serious questioners, even if you can't give them all a perfect answer in real time during your presentation slot.

Presentation Tip #14: Watch the clock

Speakers who run past their allotted time get dinged on their evaluations. This goes double if you're speaking just before a break, prior to lunch, or at the end of the day. Try not to run more than one minute past your scheduled finish time.

If you see that you might run out of time before you cover everything you planned to say, that's your problem, not the audience's problem. Skipping some material is much better than holding captive a fidgeting audience who would like to move on with their lives. With practice, you'll get better at selectively condensing your planned material while underway to bring the talk to a smooth close. Nobody enjoys seeing a speaker whir through 20 slides in the last five minutes.

Similarly, when you're teaching a class, start on time and resume promptly following breaks. I always tell people exactly how long the break will be, and I start right up at the appointed minute. If some people trickle back in late, that's their problem. I've been called a Time Nazi; I took it as a compliment. We have a lot of material to cover and I don't wish to be constrained by the last person to return to the room. Once students appreciate that you are serious about staying on schedule, they'll come back on time.

I plan on spending an average of three minutes discussing each slide. I know one speaker who says he averages just one minute per (information-dense) slide. Particularly toward the end of his overstuffed presentations, he goes so comically fast that I've given up trying to follow him. While it is good to move along briskly, people can only absorb information transmitted at a reasonable rate. Flashing up a slide for only a few seconds is pointless if the audience gets nothing out of it.

Presentation Tip #15: Talk about what you said you were going to talk about

I firmly believe in truth in advertising, so I write abstracts for my presentations that are both inviting and accurate. The audience has a right to know what to expect, and the speaker has a responsibility to deliver. This tip might seem obvious, but I've attended more than one presentation in which the content didn't fulfill the promise from the title and abstract.

Let's say the title is "Conjugating Verbs in Swahili," but the material presented misses the mark. At the end of the talk the speaker invites questions. One attendee asks, "Were you going to say anything about conjugating verbs in Swahili?" The speaker doesn't know how to respond. He thinks that's what he just spent an hour discussing, but he really didn't. That's an embarrassing position for any speaker to be in. I've seen it happen, though fortunately not to me.

Presentation Tip #16: Don't Be Nervous If a Lot of People Attend Your Webinar

My webinars typically draw 800 to 1,200 registrants, although only about 40 percent of them attend. That's a fairly large audience. However, from the speaker's perspective, the experience of delivering a webinar is identical whether there are two attendees or two million. I'm just talking into the phone to whoever happens to be listening on the other end. The only difference might be how many questions I get. But I'm going to have only a certain amount of time for Q&A anyway, so I can answer just a few questions, no matter how many people submit them.

While it can be intimidating to think of your message going out to a lot of people at once, when you're giving a presentation over the web it really doesn't feel like there's a large audience out there. So don't let that faceless crowd daunt you the way it could if you were staring from a podium out over a vast sea of faces.

Presentation Tip #17: Remember that you're wearing a microphone

I have respiratory allergies that make it difficult for me to speak loudly for more than about one hour. Therefore, I always request that the client provide a wireless lavalier microphone when I teach a full or multi-day class, or when I deliver a presentation in a large room. These microphones use a transmitter that clips to my belt. It's important to switch that transmitter off at breaks and at other times when I don't wish the entire audience to hear what I'm saying—or doing.

I once returned to a classroom after a break and noticed that some of the students were snickering quietly. I knew why. I had walked way down the hall to refill my water bottle and visit the toilet (in that order). As I was filling the bottle from the fountain outside the toilet, I noticed that my microphone was still turned on, so I quickly switched it off. Although I was quite some distance from the classroom, the microphone was transmitting just fine. My students heard the water coming into the water bottle and logically misinterpreted the sound. Hence the snickers. I don't know if they believed my explanation. Ever since that experience, I am super careful to check that microphone transmitter switch before I leave the classroom and during class practice sessions.

You might also want to be aware of where you're standing when you switch on the microphone's transmitter. At the very beginning of a class once, I just happened to turn on the mike as I was walking in front of a high-mounted speaker for the PA system. The feedback just about blew my head off. In a room that has speakers mounted in the ceiling, I sometimes have to walk around a bit to find spots to avoid feedback. Being a public speaker presents no end of unexpected learning experiences.

I find these 17 tips help keep me confident, comfortable, and poised when I'm speaking in public. I'll bet they'll help you too.

Next Steps

- List the aspects of public speaking that make you the most uncomfortable. Consider whether any of the tips in this chapter can give you more confidence about giving presentations.
- Review the slides for the various presentations in your portfolio to see if any of them contain excessive or unreadable quantities of text. Can you condense that text or replace any of it with figures or other visual elements? Make sure the fonts used on your slides are easily viewable, even from a distance.
- What aspects of public speaking (or listening) do you find most enjoyable? Try to think of ways to structure or build content and activities into your presentations to yield more of those pleasurable moments.

28

SOME PRESENTATION TRICKS
I HAVE LEARNED

Since I began giving professional presentations in 1991, I've picked up a number of useful techniques. Some of these I figured out on my own; others came from observing other presenters or hearing their suggestions. These tricks might help you deliver more effective presentations too.

OPEN BIG

As soon as the spotlight shines, your immediate challenge is to gain the audience's attention, to get them on your side so they're receptive to your message. Try to think of an opening for your talk that will get the audience smiling and nodding in agreement immediately. Then they're on board for the rest of the show.

I begin several of my talks with a short audience survey. I list 10 typical problem areas that frequently occur in the domain of my presentation, be it on software requirements, process improvement, or something else. I ask the audience members to note which of these issues they've experienced on their projects. Then, by a show of hands, I ask who has experienced none of the problems I described, then one, and so on, up through all 10.

Because these are such ubiquitous problems, I know that most of the audience members can relate to them. That is, they start nodding along with me from the very beginning of my talk. We've created a bond of common experience, forged a bit of rapport. This helps make the audience open to my suggestions for addressing those all-too-common project challenges, which then constitute the rest of the presentation.

COLORFUL FLIP CHARTS

In some presentations, I write items on a flip chart, such as ideas and comments contributed by the audience during a group discussion. I picked up a useful technique from a speaker I saw doing this at a conference. She used two markers, alternating the colors as she wrote each item on the paper. This made the contents of the flip chart easier to read, as the items didn't all blur together visually. I now use this simple but effective technique all the time.

HUMOR DOESN'T HURT

Okay, I admit it: a lot of the material in my courses and short talks is quite dry. It's difficult to make topics like project management, process improvement, and business analysis entertaining. So I try to incorporate a bit of levity, as humor livens up even the dullest material.

Over the years I've accumulated a suite of random one-liners. They just popped out of my mouth at some point and elicited a chuckle from the audience, so I keep them in. For instance, when I'm introducing myself at the beginning of a course, I often say, "I started out in life as a research chemist. Actually, I started out as a small child, but then I quickly became a research chemist." I realize this kind of material is not going to get me on Comedy Central, but audiences find it amusing and it helps us to become comfortable with each other. Smiling people are more receptive to what you have to say.

Everyone can relate to cartoons, but avoid showing overused, trite, potentially offensive, or excessive numbers of cartoons. Also, unless you drew it yourself, someone else likely owns the copyright to your cartoon. Be careful about incorporating copyrighted material of any kind into your presentation without citing the original source, procuring permission to use it, and possibly paying a licensing fee. Respect others' material as you would have them respect yours.

QUIET QUESTIONERS

An audience member once asked a speaker a question from the front row of a large room. The questioner was speaking too quietly for people in the back of the room to hear. I noticed that as the speaker listened to the question, he slowly walked *away* from the questioner.

The speaker's body language indicated that he was listening attentively. Perhaps unconsciously, the questioner began speaking more loudly as the speaker grew more distant. This made it easier for other attendees to hear the question. I'm not sure if the speaker took that little walk deliberately, but it seemed like a good idea to me. Now, whenever I'm in a similar situation, I do the same thing. Most people really do start talking louder as they see you moving away. Subtle, but effective.

Unless you're confident everyone in the room could hear the question, the audience will appreciate it if you repeat or paraphrase it. You usually have voice amplification available; the questioners usually do not. Reiterating the question also gives you a few seconds to think about the answer, or perhaps to reframe the question into one you'd prefer to answer. Politicians are masters of that last technique. I've never yet heard one answer a simple yes-or-no question with a simple yes or no.

LET'S GET MOVING

Listening to a presentation is a passive activity. It's easy for your attention to wander, to drift into a daydream, or even to nod off into slumber. And it's even worse for the audience. (Sorry; see the earlier section called *Humor Doesn't Hurt.*)

One way to combat this syndrome as a speaker is to encourage the audience members to interact from time to time, either with you or with one another. Sometimes, I ask them to spend a few moments talking among themselves about a particular topic and then share each small group's thoughts with the rest of the audience.

I also conduct quick surveys periodically. I might describe a particular technique in a class and then ask, "Have any of you tried this?" Then I follow up with, "How did it work for you?" This gets at least some of them moving their bodies a bit with a show of hands and perhaps a contribution to the discussion.

I have some ulterior motives here as well. These informal and totally un-scientific surveys help me to calibrate the audience's past experience and knowledge. If I describe an unfamiliar technique and a skeptical audience member sees that some other people around her have tried it, maybe my suggestion doesn't seem so strange. It's not just Karl's wacky scheme any-more. She might even ask one of those people who raised his hand to share his experience with the practice at the next break.

Audiences have particular trouble remaining engaged right after lunch. While I schedule breaks in my full-day classes about every 90 minutes, I will often invite the attendees to take a one-minute stretch break halfway through that interval in the first session of the afternoon. They can stand up, loosen up, and wake up just enough to make it through the next chunk of the class until we take a real break.

MAKE EYE CONTACT

I once took a university class in which the professor stared at a single student for the entire semester. I'm glad I wasn't that student. I suspect that professor wasn't very comfortable in front of the audience and had read a suggestion to focus his presentation on a single individual so it feels more like a personal conversation. Maybe that's less intimidating for the speaker, but it can make the rest of the audience feel left out.

During my presentations, I look at all the attendees randomly in turn, making eye contact for a few seconds at a time with each one. I want to make each member of my audience feel as though I am speaking directly to him or her. If the presentation involves some kind of sales pitch ("Hire me! Hire me!"), I don't speak only to the person who I think is the decision maker. Other people in the room might have input into the decision or just want to know what is going on; I want them to buy into my message also.

This eye contact also gives me a bit of feedback as I see people smiling or nodding in reaction to my comments—or not. If anybody appears to be tuned out, turned off, perplexed, or annoyed, I might not be connecting well with everyone. Perhaps I'm going too fast or not being engaging enough. Maybe there's a mismatch between their expectations for the presentation and what they're hearing from me. That unspoken feedback might trigger me to interact with the audience to see if I'm missing something that I can correct on the fly.

TELL ME A STORY

Human beings are storytellers. Passing down history and tradition through stories around the campfire is built into our culture. A litany of facts, tools, charts, and principles gets boring quickly, but stories of true experiences bring the material to life. You became a consultant because you had a wide range of experience to draw from. Incorporate your personal stories and those you've heard from others into your presentation to illustrate the points and show how the techniques can be applied in the real world. This changes your content from theory to practice, from abstract to pragmatic.

True stories also reinforce the validity of your perspectives to the audience. If you've actually been there and done that, they're more willing to accept what you describe as being relevant to them. Frankly, I prefer taking classes and hearing presentations from more seasoned instructors than from young people who are perhaps proficient in the training material but have little personal experience yet to share with the audience.

Audience members also have stories to share. I recently gave a presentation on use cases to a group of 30 business analysts. I began by asking how many of the attendees had some previous experience with use cases. Most people raised their hands. I then invited them to share any of those experiences: how well use cases worked for them, what problems they encountered, or what aspects of use cases confused their teams. Several people did relate such stories. This gave me a chance to connect their real-world experience with the content I planned to present. Hearing a story sometimes also prompts me to mention something I had not originally intended to include, thereby enriching the presentation for all. (See, I just told you a story.)

DOOR PRIZES

When I speak at a conference or a professional society meeting, I will sometimes give away door prizes. These could be copies of some of my books, a CD of one of my e-learning courses, or some other product. Giving away such prizes is a way to advertise my products and services, including the nontechnical books I've written.

Here's a trick I've come up with. If the lucky winner is several rows back in the audience, I hand the item to someone in the front row and ask him to pass it back. This way several people have a chance to touch and look at the item, which might stimulate their interest in it.

Webinars also are good ways to promote any products you sell. I might offer the attendees a special discount code for, say, the Process Impact Goodies Collection. Because you often will draw more attendees at a webinar than at a live presentation, this is a high-leverage marketing technique. I once mentioned such a discount code during a webinar with some 8,000 attendees worldwide. It must have been an appealing offer, as I began getting email messages that my website wasn't responding. Apparently, so many people hit the site at the same time that it was swamped; my hosting server couldn't keep up. I hadn't anticipated that possibility. I guess there are worse problems than having too many customers trying to buy my product simultaneously.

OTHER TIPS FROM THE EXPERTS

Over the years I've heard many ideas from experienced speakers about how to deliver effective presentations or training courses. Following this paragraph, in no particular order and in their own words, are some of the suggestions I've heard from numerous experts, including Richard Bender, Frank Galea, Capers Jones, Howard Podeswa, and Ed Weller.

- Show actual data. The speaker evaluations I have seen as a speaker or program chair were better when presentations included data with sufficient discussion or interpretation.
- I use language and metrics that evoke memorable images in the audience's mind. This is especially important if you are presenting by audio only. For example, recently our Corporate Controller gave an update by audio-only conference call on Dodd-Frank financial reform. To convey the scope and breadth of the legislation, he created some visual imagery around the page count (2,300+) of the legislation and compared that size to past landmark reforms of various lengths.
- Some of the topics I teach are inherently dry, so I use historical analogies to liven them up a bit. For example, when discussing quality assurance strategies I'll mention the QA programs of the Roman Empire and the Danish navy in 1600. I then tie them to what people do today, what works, and what does not. These stories and images help the attendees understand and remember the key points I'm trying to make.
- I begin each training session by asking the attendees what their expectations are for the class or what project issues they've encountered related to the class topic. I solicit this in an open-ended manner so as not to bias what they come up with. I write these down on a flip chart page and keep this list visible for the duration of the class, revisiting it periodically to see how we're doing. This list of expectations allows us to tie the course materials to the issues that most concern the students.

- Exercises can enhance any learning experience. All of the examples and exercises in our courses are taken from real projects, scrubbed to protect the guilty and preserve confidentiality. Real-world examples do not work out as tidily as made-up ones. However, that is what students will run into once they return to their projects. The exercises are a blend of individual and team efforts.
- Look for ways to illustrate concepts with images and video clips, instead of just loads of textual bullet points. Look for the emotional connection to an issue and find an image that conveys that and helps the listener remember.
- Lately I've been trying something revolutionary: ditch the Power-Point. It's amazing how not using slides immediately puts me more in touch with the mood in the room, keeps me and the students more engaged, and allows me to better pace the presentation in tune with the energy and needs of the students. It's like throwing away a crutch.

The next time you attend a presentation that you enjoy, reflect on what aspects of the speaker's style and approach held your attention. Then, look for ways to incorporate those same desirable characteristics into your own presentations. You'll be a more comfortable, confident, and competent speaker in no time.

Next Steps

- List four or five techniques you could use in your next presentation to keep the audience more engaged.
- Before you give your next presentation, come up with several true-experience stories you can relate to illustrate and reinforce your points. They don't even have to be your personal stories, as long as they are relevant. Remember, though, if you have a fixed time block for the presentation, spending time on stories means that you'll have to compress or omit something else to finish on time.
- Reflect on the training instructors, conference speakers, and webinar presenters you've found to be most memorable and influential. Why do you remember things from their presentations and perhaps not from others? What did they do to retain your focus, to make you want to learn more about the topic, or to motivate you to try some new technique when you went back to work? Try to adjust your speaking style to be more effective based on this analysis.

Part VI

Writing Your Way to Success

29

YOU ARE WHAT YOU WRITE

I wrote my first computer magazine article in 1984, not many years after what were then called microcomputers first appeared on the scene. Back then, we early adopters all were just trying to learn how the things worked and to get them to do something interesting, useful, or amusing. I figured out how to use one fairly complex feature of my new computer. It occurred to me that other people also might find my newly gained insight valuable, so I wrote an article. A magazine bought it. I began to write more articles about a wide variety of computing topics, and I haven't stopped yet.

The ability to communicate effectively in writing is an essential skill for consultants, business analysts, and project managers. Much of the consulting work I've done has involved developing process-related materials for clients. I have created all manner of procedures, document templates, checklists, guidance documents, and the like. Other engagements have involved performing a process or document assessment that resulted in a written report of my observations and recommendations.

As you gain experience and wisdom in a particular domain, you might wish to share what you've learned with others through articles, conference papers, blog posts, or books. I've now written about 180 articles on numerous topics in software engineering, quality, and management, in addition to more than 20 articles on chemistry and military history, of all things. Traditional print magazines published most of these articles, although more and more have appeared on websites in recent years. Most magazines will pay for articles; many websites will not.

But as we learned in Chapter 17, everything is negotiable. If you have a good enough story to tell and enough credibility in the industry, you might be able to negotiate some payment from anyone who publishes your work. In very broad terms, you might get between $100 and $1,000 per article.

Chapter 31 provides many recommendations regarding writing for magazines, websites, and blogs.

Eventually, you might decide to write a book. That's a whole different proposition from penning a set of magazine articles or blog posts. Telling a story in a few thousand words on a focused topic isn't terribly hard. Writing 60,000 to 100,000 words in a typical book takes considerable planning, time, and effort. By way of calibration, this book contains about 90,000 words of text, not counting the front and back matter (such as the table of contents and index).

Then there's the whole matter of getting the book published, negotiating contracts, promoting it, and all the rest. It ain't trivial. Chapters 32 and 33 are devoted to suggestions about writing and publishing books. If you decide to go the self-publishing route, you might find the information in Chapter 34 (*Being Your Own Publisher*) helpful.

Many nonfiction books result from collaboration between two or more co-authors. I've tried this a couple of times. The first attempt was a complete failure. I quickly discovered that the man who had invited me to co-author the book with him expected me to do all the writing, based largely on his material, while he would review what I wrote. Unfortunately, he didn't review my drafts expeditiously, which hampered my ability to move the project along. That partnership lasted for just two draft chapters before I bailed out. In contrast, my second co-authoring experience, much later, was a grand success, as I describe in Chapter 35 (*On Co-Authoring a Book*). The insights there about working with a partner apply to a variety of collaborative projects, not just writing books.

CHOOSING A ROLE MODEL

Here's one tidbit of wisdom I've acquired: think about whose writing you find particularly appealing and learn from them. You might have favorite authors whom you find to be especially helpful, interesting, and enjoyable to read. Take the time to study their work and assess just *why* you like their writing. Then you can try to emulate some of those characteristics in your own work.

Many years ago, I realized that Steve McConnell was one of my favorite authors of software books and articles; he's also a good friend now. Steve has written numerous top-selling software books and is esteemed in the industry. When I thought about it, I realized that Steve uses fairly short sentences in much of his writing, and he writes in a direct, conversational style.

I also favor that informal writing style, although I confess to being somewhat long-winded by nature. My sentences can get wordy. I also tend to overuse adverbs, and I say "tend to" a lot. We all have our shortcomings. But Steve's acclaimed writing resonated with me and presented a goal to strive for.

FOCUSING ON CLARITY

Once I recognized what I liked about Steve's writing, I tried to steer my own style in that direction. I use the statistics from Microsoft Word's grammar checker (part of the spell check feature) to provide guidance. I find the grammar-checking feature in Word largely useless overall—I think it was programmed on Opposite Day—but I do like the grammar statistics.

The grammar statistics report the average number of sentences per paragraph in the document, along with the average words per sentence and characters per word. The average number of characters per word should be around five when writing in English. I aim to keep the average words per sentence no higher than 20 and preferably fewer. Shorter words, sentences, and paragraphs all enhance readability.

The statistics report includes several readability measures. The higher the Flesch Reading Ease, the easier the document is to read (duh). I aim for at least 40. The lower the Flesch-Kincaid Grade Level, the easier the document is to read. I keep my technical writing to a grade level of 12. For nontechnical writing, I aim for a grade level of eight to nine. I also like to keep the number of passive sentences low. Sentences written in the active voice, where you can tell what entity is taking an action, are more direct and easier to understand than passive sentences.

If the statistics don't come out like I want, I'll do some revision to simplify the material and increase the readability. By way of example, here are the statistics for this chapter:

- 1823 words
- Average of 4.3 sentences per paragraph (fine)
- Average of 15.6 words per sentence (fine)
- Average of 4.8 characters per word (typical)
- Two percent passive sentences (okay)
- Flesch Reading Ease of 57.0 (great)
- Flesch-Kincaid Grade Level of 9.0 (perfect)

If these statistics are meaningful, you should find this chapter easy to read. I hope that's the case.

ACQUIRING THE INFORMATION

During our professional careers, we each accumulate a store of knowledge and experience in various areas. It takes a certain type of skill to synthesize that accumulated knowledge—particularly from multiple domains—and deliver it to readers in an appealing and accessible way. Technical writing can be as dull as dishwater. It helps to brighten it up with bits of thoughtfully-selected humor and personal experiences.

As with my presentations, my technical publications include many true-life stories. These anecdotes make the content more tangible to the reader. When a reader can relate to an actual experience, pleasant or not, the point you're making comes across as more real and hence more meaningful. Every story in this book is true, whether it is my personal experience or one related by a colleague. I have collected countless stories from my clients, who shared with me their challenges, frustrations, and successes. After relating one unhappy story, a client said, "Gee, I hope that won't end up in your next book."

"Sure it will," I replied. "Where do you think I get all these stories? I don't make them up; I collect them."

Of course, I anonymize all such stories. It's not important how we learn a lesson—from doing something silly, from forgetting to do something important, or from a flash of brilliance—so long as we absorb, apply, and share the insight.

DEVELOPING A STYLE

The whole point of writing is to communicate with your readers. Readers respond to writing they don't have to work hard to understand. They love direct, simple tutorials that teach techniques they can apply immediately. Readers appreciate clearly explained concepts, examples, and opinions.

Some authors write as though they want their readers to know how smart they are, using big words, lengthy paragraphs, and convoluted phrasing. Nobody cares how smart you are. They just care if you're helpful to them; hence, my interest in using a simple and conversational writing style.

Long ago, I wrote a series of tutorials on assembly language programming—not the simplest topic—for a computer magazine. I met a fan who told me, "When I work through your articles, I feel like you're standing there explaining them to me." This is exactly the kind of reaction I hope for. It was delightful to hear that at least one person felt that I was communicating through the written word in just the way I wanted to.

As you develop your writing style, you might consider what kind of compliments from an admiring reader would mean the most to you. Then you can work to develop a style that elicits that sort of feedback. Just this week, a reader commented on one of my blog posts: "I always enjoy your articles, as they provide so much insight and information in a simple and interesting way. I find that your books are also very user-friendly and practical." Words like simple, interesting, user-friendly, and practical are music to my ears. It's one thing to inspire people with ideas, but I'm most interested in giving busy practitioners both useful techniques and the motivation to apply them.

I was educated as a scientist. The first major document I wrote was a PhD thesis in physical organic chemistry titled "Kinetics and Mechanism of Lithium Aluminum Hydride Reductions of Ketones." (What could be more fascinating than that? Actually, it was pretty cool.) Scientists neither write nor speak like normal people. When I began to write on topics other than chemistry, it took me some time to unlearn how scientists write, to revamp my writing style to be more accessible.

One of the best compliments I ever got on my writing was from someone who said, "You don't write like you have a PhD." I was most pleased.

Next Steps

- Write down the names of authors in your field whose writing you enjoy and admire the most. Why do you like their material? Can you identify specific characteristics of their writing that you could build into your own?
- Identify what you see as the biggest weaknesses in the way you write. Create a checklist to remind you of specific writing patterns to search for and correct in your articles.
- Write down several sample compliments you'd love to hear from readers. Can you think of any ways to modify your writing style to better elicit those kinds of reactions?

This book has free material available for download from the
Web Added Value™ resource center at *www.jrosspub.com*

30

FOUR EYES ARE BETTER
THAN TWO

One of the most powerful tools available to help you become a better writer is peer review. I cannot overstate the importance of having selected individuals carefully critique what you write before you inflict it on an unsuspecting world. As I reflected on how I learned to write, I realized that I benefited greatly from a few college professors who took the time to give me detailed critical feedback on papers I had written. By studying that feedback, I learned how to write better papers the next time.

Preparing a piece for publication involves at least four steps: your own review and self-editing, peer review (also called beta reading), outside editing, and proofreading. Additionally, developmental and technical editing are appropriate in some cases. No matter how brilliant a writer you think you are, a good editor will make you look better. Even when I write something that seems clean and focused to my eye, reviewers and editors always find small mistakes and ways to improve the delivery. Here I explain the different types of reviewing and editing activities and their importance.

TAKE A LOOK YOURSELF

The first quality improvement round is your own critical review. After I've written a new article, book chapter, or blog post, I set it aside for a full day before I review it; longer is better. If you re-read something immediately after writing it, you don't really review it—you mentally recite it. I like to let my memory of the piece decay for a while so I can look at it with fresher, less biased eyes. Sometimes, I will then see sentences that make me wonder what in the world I was thinking when I wrote them.

213

When I'm looking over my writing, occasionally I hear a little nagging voice (just one voice, fortunately). It says, "That part doesn't work. Fix it or cut it out."

I used to reply to myself, "Let's see how the reviewers feel about it." The reviewers invariably spotted that bit, and they invariably hated it. I've learned to trust that little voice and to fix the awkward chunk right away. The voice hasn't been wrong yet.

Being naturally wordy, I use a little technique to help me tighten my writing. Each time I make a review or edit pass through an article or a chapter of a few thousand words, I try to remove 100 words. I don't always achieve that goal. Nonetheless, a constant focus on tightening helps me to deliver the maximum value per sentence to the reader. You'd be surprised how much you can take out and still say everything you want.

Use your word processor's tools to help find errors. Run spell check. Search for double periods. Replace any double spaces with single spaces following periods and colons or between words. Globally replace all single and double quotes with themselves to make sure they are all styled as curly ("smart") quotes. Make sure your headings, the body of the text, and references are all styled consistently. Run grammar check and see if any of the potential errors it reports do require correction. Run spell check again after making edits, as it's so easy to introduce a typo when you change something.

ENLISTING OTHER EYES

Once the piece is in good shape to your own eyes, it's time to send it to your peer reviewers. These people are also known as beta readers. The peer review process varies depending on what kind of work you're writing. Even if the piece is informal, I recommend asking at least one person to look it over. I would rather have a trusted colleague point out a typo, garbled sentence, or factual error than to have a website visitor or a prospective customer spot it. It's always a little embarrassing when someone finds a mistake in my work. But when a friendly reviewer detects it early on, I think of that as a *good catch*.

Tough peer reviews are the most useful. They aren't much fun to read, but they sure help improve whatever you write. I've been fortunate in this regard. For each of my technical books, I have had a few—never more than three— very thorough reviewers who didn't let me get away with anything.

Once I learn who those reviewers will be on a particular writing project, I always dread receiving their feedback. I know I'll feel like an idiot, and I'll have to spend a lot of time processing their comments and reworking the piece. However, I also know that their input will make my work far better. Many reviewers just rubber-stamp what I send them as being fine, point out only minor typos, or don't respond at all. While I appreciate my beta readers' time and their glowing feedback, that kind of input isn't of much help.

At the end of the review process, I reward my most helpful beta readers with a small gift, such as a gift card for an on-line retailer. It's a minuscule compensation for the substantial effort they've devoted, but they always appreciate the gesture. And, of course, all reviewers' names appear in the book's acknowledgments section. That is literally the least I can to do thank them.

In my experience, reviewing nonfiction writing typically makes a document longer, whereas editing makes it shorter. Reviewers often suggest that I add more content, tell another story, show another example, or include a figure to illustrate a point. By the time I've addressed all the reviewer input, the piece is perhaps 10 or 20 percent longer than the original version. So then it's time to go back to my remove-100-words philosophy to snug it up again, particularly if I'm writing against a length limit. Good copy editing also will fix wordiness, repetition, redundancies, duplication, and saying the same thing over and over again multiple times.

Peer review is painful. You wrote the best piece you possibly could, you're proud of it, and you're eager to share it with others. It hurts when some of those other people don't respond as positively as you hope or recommend major revisions. You have to learn to accept the critical input in the spirit in which it's intended.

Quite naturally, authors get their egos tied up with their writing. As an author, you need to set your ego aside enough to be receptive to the input. Reviewers also must set their egos aside. A good reviewer will show respect for the effort the author put into the piece and will provide thoughtful, constructive feedback. The broad comment "This sucks," even if true, is not helpful. I've been passionate about peer reviews for a long time, even to the extent of writing a book titled *Peer Reviews in Software: A Practical Guide.*

A colleague I have known for more than ten years recently asked if I would review a short e-book she had written. I agreed, although I'm not a devotee of her topic. I gave her detailed and frank feedback on both the content and the structure of her book, as that's the kind of input I always welcome most from my own reviewers. This was her first book, and I have written eleven, so I thought some of my authoring experience was worth sharing.

Alas, I fear she was offended by my frankness. She referred to it as "harshness." Certainly, I did not set out to offend her, nor did I feel I was being unduly harsh. I was just very direct, which I thought was appropriate with someone whom I knew fairly well. I don't know how many of my suggestions she will take, but quite honestly I don't feel that my review feedback was out of line. I was blunt but not—in my opinion—insulting. I'm sorry she took my input that way, as I never intend to offend. I'll be more careful next time, both in what I agree to review and in how I phrase my comments.

We all want to hear how wonderful our writing is. The sad fact is that sometimes it's not. Different reviewers will approach what you've written from diverse perspectives and with varying expectations. As the author, you're always welcome to disregard any input a reviewer provides. But I suggest you think about the point being made before you dismiss it.

Another colleague has invited me to review several of his book manuscripts over the years. They were in my main technical area and he's a nice man who knows his stuff, so I agreed. I gave him extensive and detailed feedback on the first two books. But then I realized he was making virtually none of the changes I proposed. I concluded that my perspectives didn't align well with his, so I declined his invitations to review subsequent manuscripts; the effort would have been wasted.

There's a certain quid pro quo associated with being a beta reader. If you ask someone to look over your manuscript, don't be surprised if they invite you to reciprocate sometime in the future. It's only fair to help each other out. Although it won't be your top priority, one of the things I like about the peer review mindset—whether for writing or for software development—is that we all get better at our work when we participate in reviews.

DEVELOPMENTAL EDITING

Your publisher might have a developmental editor work with you, particularly if you're not an experienced author. A developmental editor will propose more radical changes than will a copy editor. This is particularly helpful if you have something significant to say but your manuscript is not well structured or well organized, or if the manuscript has technical shortcomings that must be rectified before it's ready to print.

The editors at Dorset House Publishing added enormous value to my first book, *Creating a Software Engineering Culture*. They performed two stages of editing. First, developmental editing helped me transform a poorly structured, flabby manuscript into a much more effective vehicle for telling my story. Second, copy editing greatly cleaned up and tightened my prose and presentation. We cut 20,000 words of text along the way—words I had spent many hours crafting to the best of my ability—but it was a far better book after the surgery. This experience gave me an intimate appreciation of the phrase "cutting-room floor."

Given that the traditional publishing business has changed considerably in recent years, a book publisher might not be so accommodating today. Publishers are looking for manuscripts in near-complete form, ones they don't have to massage much before going to press. You'll have a much better chance of selling your book to a publisher if it's already in very good shape. Therefore, if you are not an experienced author, consider hiring a professional editor on your own to help polish your work before you submit the manuscript to a publisher. That investment might make the difference between a rejection letter and a shiny new book with your name on it.

TECHNICAL EDITING

Logically enough, technical books sometimes go through a process called technical editing. This is most common with less experienced authors and with material written on particularly complex domains. The technical editor will confirm the technical accuracy of the text, the proper use of terminology per standard conventions, and the correctness of any data and analyses presented. He might also help the author present the complex material as clearly as possible. The book project editor at a traditional publishing house will sometimes solicit experienced peers of the author who have deep technical domain knowledge to provide this level of constructive critique.

Only one of my software books went through a technical editing step. When I wrote *Peer Reviews in Software*, the project editor engaged as a technical editor a man who had written a comprehensive book on a major aspect of the same topic. He was a true world-class expert in the field; I was merely an experienced aficionado. Alas, this reviewer stopped providing feedback just halfway through the manuscript for this rather short book. I'm not sure what turned him off. That was disappointing, as I respected and valued his input.

As I described previously, all of my books go through extensive peer review from respected colleagues before I submit the manuscript, so no other publisher has felt that formal technical editing of my work was necessary. Don't be offended if your editor suggests it, though. It can help a lot.

COPY EDITING

If you're writing articles for print or online magazines, you'll be dealing with one or more people who have *editor* in their job title. The copy editor's job is to correct errors in spelling, grammar, and punctuation and to ensure the consistency and clarity of expression of your work. A copy editor probably won't make substantial content adjustments or suggest structural changes, as a developmental editor will. The copy editor will ensure that your piece conforms to the publisher's house style standards for formatting and other conventions. For instance, consider the placement of a comma before the conjunction in an in-line list: "We vacationed in Germany, Belgium, France, and Luxembourg." The comma after France is called the Oxford, or serial, comma. The house style at some magazines decrees use of the Oxford comma; others don't use it. I do like the clarity that final comma provides.

The definitive reference for many copy editors is *The Chicago Manual of Style*. I keep a copy handy and refer to it when I'm not certain how to express something. For example, should a number such as "20" be shown as numerals or be written out? If you're referring to a time in the morning, which abbreviation do you use: AM, A.M., am, or a.m.? Should there be a space before the "a"? *Chicago* will tell you.

With a book, a traditional publisher generally will engage either an in-house or freelance copy editor (possibly along with an artist to redraw your figures, a compositor to lay out the pages, and an indexer, depending on the book). It's a good idea to build a collaborative relationship with your editor. You really have to learn to respect the editing process. Conversely, the editor needs to understand your preferences, respect your style, and deal considerately with your hot buttons. A good editor will preserve your "voice" even as he or she hones your message.

You're not obligated to accept every change the editor suggests. Nonetheless, you should carefully consider each one. Most of them are no-brainers: accept the change. The editors are better at this than you are. Ultimately, though, the author's name, not the editor's, goes on the byline, so you are the final authority on what gets printed (house-style issues excepted).

Good editing makes a big difference as to how a sharp-eyed reader perceives a publication. For some reason, I'm quite good at spotting typographical and word usage errors (which is not to say that my own work is flawless; it rarely is). When I find these mistakes in a published book, they annoy me. When I was writing my first book years ago and starting to think about seeking a publisher, I realized that several software books I had read from one publisher were riddled with errors. The editing looked sloppy to me. Although that publisher did offer me a contract for my book, I declined it for that very reason. Fortunately, the editors with whom I worked at the ultimate publishing house were fantastic. The text is error-free.

One of the most common mistakes I see in books these days is the incorrect use of homophones, words that sound alike but are spelled differently: write, right, rite, wright. The reader doesn't care whether these errors originated with the author or not. A published book riddled with such mistakes indicates inadequate editing and proofreading—and only your name is on the cover.

CHECK IT CAREFULLY

With both articles and books, be sure to read the edited version very carefully to make sure that editing did not introduce inadvertent changes. This happens all the time. I was surprised to see an error in one of my very earliest published articles that wasn't in the submitted manuscript. I had said "flak," but the magazine printed "flack" (another of those pesky homophone errors). These words have very different meanings. Mine was right.

That experience taught me that when you think the author has made a mistake, an editor actually might have introduced it. Making corrections in text can easily generate additional errors. For this reason, I always request to do a quick proofread of the final copy before it goes to press.

My worst editing experience took place with a magazine article of about 4,000 words. The freelance copy editor said he did a light edit. However, his modifications changed the meaning of what I was trying to say in *26 places*! For instance, I was presenting a case study, and I wrote, "We did *A*, and then we did *B*." The editor thought it read more smoothly as, "We did *B*, and then we did *A*." But it was a case study; that wasn't what we did. You have to proofread very carefully to catch those kinds of issues. The editor is not an expert in your domain—you are. It might not be obvious to the editor that a small change can disrupt the meaning of your message.

Rarely, you might find that you and the copy editor just don't click. I experienced that problem on one of my books. The editor was introducing too many errors, changing my voice too much, and generally adding little value. After giving it enough time to be sure I wasn't overreacting, I shared my frustration with the overall project editor. He then took over the copy-editing responsibility himself and did a superb job. Nearly all of the editors I've worked with have been excellent, though, and I'm grateful for the countless improvements they made in my writing. Learn from your editors' input so you can do a better job the next time.

A friend who's a highly experienced editor offered the following wisdom:

> *For new or first-time writers, working with any editor on staff can be touchy. If they don't like the editor and want him removed, they will need to be very tactful with the editor's supervisor. Another tip: be really nice to anyone you work with on the publishing team. Lowly copy editors sometimes become acquisitions editors and project editors, or they move on to bigger publishing houses and websites. Forming a good relationship with your editors can work to your advantage.*

This is first-class advice. When I met this woman, she had just started as a copy editor at a magazine devoted to software development. Within a few years, she had risen to the top position on the masthead, Editor in Chief. We worked together very well and got along well also. That's a nice plus.

A professional book copy editor will typically build a style sheet as he goes along. The style sheet will list items such as names that appear in the work, proper nouns, specialized terms, jargon, and any expressions that might be punctuated or spelled in a specific way. One of my books discusses something called a dialog map. "Dialog" can be spelled this way or as "dialogue." It's important for the editor to know—and remember—which of those alternatives the author wishes to use. Maybe in some places the author used the term "login" and in others she used "log in," "logon," and "sign in." The style sheet helps the copy editor ensure consistency throughout the book.

PROOFREADING

Editing isn't the end of the prepublication process. You still need to proofread the final copy after the pages have been laid out, be it an article or a book. This is a different type of activity than editing. You're not looking to improve the piece further but rather to make sure it's in final form, free from errors, and ready to present to your eager readers.

Ideally, the proofreader and the editor will be different people. I always proofread the final copy myself as well, but of course, I'm already very close to it. The closer you are to the material, the harder it is to spot errors. I encountered an example of this just recently in my novel, *The Reconstruction*. A sharp-eyed reader pointed out a typographical error that I had not seen on the multiple proofreading passes I had made after editing was complete.

If possible, line up an independent proofreader, in addition to scrutinizing the piece yourself. But even that offers no guarantees. Another reader called my attention to a second error in *The Reconstruction* that had been present in the manuscript from the very first draft. I never spotted that mistake on my approximately fifteen passes through that chapter. But I didn't feel too bad, because neither did my 21 beta readers, nor my copy editor, nor my two proofreaders. But it's wrong, and it's my responsibility.

People use a variety of techniques to proofread their own text. As I suggested earlier, setting it aside for a few days helps. You can read the copy line by line, looking just at the words and punctuation instead of their meaning. Some people use a piece of paper to cover all of the text except for the one line they're proofreading. Others read the text aloud, which is far slower but also meticulous. A proofreader might wish to refer to the style sheet the copy editor created to ensure that names and specialized terms appear the same way each time they occur.

Another technique is to read the text backwards sentence-by-sentence or paragraph-by-paragraph. This will help you focus on the words without getting caught up with the story and just flowing along. That's especially valuable if you are proofreading your own writing. You've already gone through it countless times, and your brain tends to recite it back to you, rather than letting you look at it fresh and catch subtle errors. However, don't try to proofread backwards word-by-word; you'll never spot a missing word or a nonsensical sentence at that super-fine level of granularity.

I find that I discover different mistakes if I read the text in various formats. Certain problems will pop out at me if I read it on the computer screen, but I always find other improvements to make if I carefully examine a hard copy. Sometimes I have seen errors when proofreading an e-book on my iPad that I hadn't spotted on either the computer screen or the printed page. Find a proofreading strategy that works for you. You might be surprised at how many errors you detect; I always am.

USING SPEECH-RECOGNITION SOFTWARE

For about 20 years I've done nearly all of my writing by voice, using Dragon NaturallySpeaking speech-recognition software. This software does quite a good job of recognizing what I say and typing it out for me. Once I got the hang of writing verbally I found it to be considerably faster than typing. It's also easier on my wrists and forearms, preventing repetitive strain injuries.

Speech-recognition software will never misspell a word. However, it sometimes misinterprets what I say, which results in text other than what I intended. Therefore, I need to proofread anything written by voice more carefully than usual because spell check doesn't help. It can also make those annoying homophone mistakes that I mentioned earlier.

As I was proofreading this very chapter, I found an error that resulted from exactly this type of speech misinterpretation. The text said "are" instead of my intended "or." Those two words do sound similar, particularly if I'm talking too fast or not enunciating clearly. Dragon NaturallySpeaking does a very good job at choosing the right word based on context, but it will never be perfect. Proofread vigorously!

WHEN IT'S ALL YOUR RESPONSIBILITY

If you elect to self-publish a book or write an e-book, you're on your own for copy editing and proofreading. Don't think you can do this yourself or just hand it over to a friend—professional editors are much better at it than us amateurs. My memoir of life lessons, *Pearls from Sand: How Small Encounters Lead to Powerful Lessons*, was not self-published, but I was responsible for supplying the publisher with the final perfected manuscript, ready to format and print. Therefore, I had to line up a copy editor and a proofreader to make my manuscript as clean as possible.

I began by hiring my old friend Barbara Hanscome. I worked with Barbara on many articles when she was an editor at *Software Development* magazine. Now she does freelance editing. Barbara is the best editor I've ever worked with. As I expected, she did a terrific job on my book manuscript. She saved me from myself more times than I could count. I also hired a local firm in Portland, Oregon, to do some of the copy editing and all of the proofreading. They too did an excellent job, as did an editor I hired recently through another Portland company when I wrote *The Reconstruction*. They were all worth every penny.

Next Steps

- Search for editors in your area that you could hire if you choose to go with a professional. Look for one who has considerable experience editing the kind of material you are writing.

- Make a list of potential beta readers you could invite to review an article or book you might be contemplating.
- If you're thinking about writing an article for a magazine or trade journal, request a copy of their writer's guidelines or look for them on their website. The more closely your manuscript conforms to the editor's expectations, the less work they—and you—will have to do to prepare the piece for publication.

31

WRITING FOR MAGAZINES, WEBSITES, AND BLOGS

A wide variety of software magazines were published during the 1990s and early 2000s. Some of those have since faded away, but there are plenty of websites that post articles on every aspect of software development, business analysis, project management, and every other topic under the sun. If you have something insightful to say about business analysis or project management, there's a place to post your story.

Writing for publication is a powerful way for consultants to gain visibility for their ideas and expertise. It is one of the best investments of time and effort anyone going into consulting can make. I have written articles for more than thirty software magazines, trade journals, and websites. Working with so many different outlets and editors has given me a good feel for how to prepare articles for publication.

KNOWING YOUR AUDIENCE

If rule number one for effective writing is *know your subject*, rule number two certainly is *know your audience*. Before you submit an article, contemplate what kinds of people read that periodical or visit that website. Read previous articles so you have an idea of topics, content, and writing styles that will appeal to the readers and—just as important—to the editor or site manager. Are the articles highly technical in nature, perhaps including code fragments or research data? Are they written in a conversational style or more formally? Are figures, diagrams, or tables commonly used? How are references cited, if at all? Are most of the articles how-to tutorials, opinionated essays, reports of industry trends, or what? Do the authors incorporate much humor in their pieces? How long are the articles on average? Do they ever publish multiple articles in a series? Are most of the authors opinion leaders or practitioners?

It's a good idea to align your article with the content and format that people expect to find in a particular forum. You might be able to get some of this information from the periodical's submission or writer's guidelines. Look for topics that haven't been covered well in that forum recently. Think about whether you could present a different take on a hot topic that would be useful or thought provoking. Perhaps you could build on a theme that runs through several previously published articles and take it to the next step. Alternatively, just ask what kind of material the editor is looking for and propose some topics you could write about.

FITTING IN

I try hard to make my submissions look like a natural fit for a particular destination. For instance, I always ask how many words the editor wants. Magazine articles typically range from 1,500 to 3,000 words in length. Articles intended for website or blog publication are shorter, perhaps 800 to 1,500 words. A figure ordinarily is counted as 200 words for space purposes, although it can be resized to be smaller or larger than that.

If a magazine editor requests 2,000 words, that's what he gets from me. If you submit a manuscript with 3,000 words, it simply won't fit in the space the editor has in mind for it. The most likely outcomes are either outright rejection or substantial editing if he likes your story but needs something shorter. In rare cases, you might persuade the editor to run a long article as a series of shorter pieces, but don't count on it.

Through some amazing good fortune, I've managed to place every piece of writing I have ever submitted for publication. If the first magazine rejected my submission, I would modify it to fit in with the next one I tried. It occasionally took up to four attempts, but each article always found a home.

It's not always necessary to submit a full manuscript. If you have an idea for an article, float it past an editor who you think might find it interesting and see if you get a nibble. If no one is interested, maybe you don't need to spend the time writing and polishing the piece. One year, I outlined a series of nine possible articles for one magazine. After the editor and I agreed on the topics, I began writing them at my convenience. The better you understand the readership the magazine's editorial staff is targeting, the easier it is to get a proposal accepted.

DELIGHTING THE EDITOR

My philosophy is to make the editor's job as easy as possible. I want her to sense immediately that my submission feels right for her periodical and audience. That's why I conform to the periodical's house style. If it's not customary for their articles to have sections titled Introduction or Conclusion, my submission won't contain them either. It's an old dictum that in an article or a presentation you "tell 'em what you're going to tell 'em, tell 'em, then tell 'em what you told 'em." That's not a bad policy, but you can do that without having sections mundanely titled Introduction and Conclusion.

I've always had the impression that the less work an editor has to do to turn a submission into a published piece, the more favorably inclined she will be toward the author in the future. For each of my professional interactions—article, book, presentation, training class, consulting gig—my goal is for the other party to think, "I'd be happy to work with Karl again." Preparing an article that requires as little editing as possible is one step toward this outcome.

If you really want to get on an editor's bad side, missing deadlines will do it. Magazines come out on a fixed schedule, and websites must deliver streams of fresh content; they aren't going to wait for your late article. I take great pride in having never missed a deadline for submitting an article, conference presentation materials, or a book manuscript.

Not everyone is like this though. More than one frantic editor has called me to ask if I could plug a hole in their magazine because some other contributor didn't deliver when promised. Editors will come back to you if they know they can count on you to deliver on time. Emergencies do arise, so if you find that you cannot meet a writing commitment, tell the affected parties as soon as possible so they can adjust. Going dark is the worst thing you can do.

DANGLING THE BAIT

Editors like catchy titles and captivating opening paragraphs. The editor might retitle the article to make it better fit the magazine's style or grab the reader's attention, so don't get overly attached to your initial title. A clever title initiates the connection between author and audience. Concoct a title that both accurately reflects what you're presenting and piques the reader's interest in just a few words. Some of my article titles promise a certain number of tidbits of wisdom: 7 deadly sins, 10 traps to avoid, 21 success tips.

Other titles are intended to make the reader ask, "Interesting, I wonder what this is about?" Some examples:

- "See You in Court" (about an engagement I had as an expert consultant for a party in a lawsuit)
- "When Telepathy Won't Do" (key practices in requirements development)
- "Know Your Enemy" (a tutorial on risk management)
- "Just Too Much to Do" (described a project prioritization spreadsheet tool)
- "Stop Promising Miracles" (about a project estimation technique)

SETTING THE HOOK

You have a very short window in which to get the reader's attention, so work hard on the opening paragraph for each article. If you don't engage readers with that first paragraph, it doesn't matter what you say in the rest of the article—they won't read it. And if the very first sentence doesn't grab them, the rest of that paragraph doesn't matter either. Busy people aren't likely to wade ahead, patiently hoping the article gets interesting at some point. Make your opening catchy enough that a reader can't help but keep going.

I often open with something that will get the reader nodding in agreement with me from the outset, such as an indication that I feel the reader's pain and frustration. Here's an example:

> Software managers sometimes assume that every skilled programmer is also proficient at interviewing customers and writing requirements, without any training, resources, or coaching. This isn't a reasonable assumption. Like testing, estimation, and project management, requirements engineering has its own skill set and body of knowledge.

Once readers get the idea that you understand their challenges and can offer some relief, then you can reel them in and wow them with your wisdom.

CONTRIBUTING TO BLOGS

It seems that everyone and his brother has a blog these days. If you know of some blogs that carry articles in your areas of interest, see if they include posts from guest contributors instead of all being written by the blog's owner. If you have a story to tell that fits in with the theme of the blog, contact the owner and inquire about posting your contribution. I frequently receive solicitations from people I've never heard from before asking if I'm interested in guest contributions. When I was writing my Consulting Tips and Tricks blog a few years ago, I definitely wanted to hear from other consultants who had experiences and ideas to share. In fact, each of the chapters in this book that was written by somebody other than myself began as a guest contribution to that blog.

Look at the websites for tool vendors in your domain, book and magazine publishers, consultancies, professional organizations, and individual thought leaders (or at least people who think they are thought leaders) for possible places to post your contributions. Start a blog of your own if you wish, to begin sharing your wisdom and also to acquire writing experience. Even if you don't get paid for them, you will get some air time, and readers will come to recognize that you have something to say. Your contributions are more likely to be welcomed if they contain genuine content instead of just being thinly veiled marketing pitches for your products or services.

Make sure your blog posts, LinkedIn articles, and the like are substantive, not just fluff or superficial rehashes of common knowledge. I get annoyed when I follow a link to an article with a promising title that turns out to consist of maybe 500 poorly written words, some meaningless stock photos of people at work, and zero bits of useful, unobvious knowledge. Those clickbait authors aren't the kind of people I'm going to follow in search of practical wisdom.

YOU HAVE ARRIVED!

If you establish a reputation for writing high-quality material, delivering on time, and stimulating reader interest, a magazine editor might even offer you a column. I was so excited in 1986 when I was invited to write a tutorial column on assembly language programming for a monthly computer magazine. I could write about anything I wanted, knowing that it would be published. Magazine editors aren't always thrilled about publishing a series of articles by the same author, but with a column I could address larger themes across multiple articles. And I'd have a sustained income stream to boot. That was a lot of fun and a great learning experience for two years.

Next Steps

- List several periodicals that people in your target audience might read, such as trade journals focused on your areas of business expertise.
- Make a list of websites that post articles in your specialty. Popular websites for business analysis include ModernAnalyst.com and BATimes.com.
- Make a list of blogs in your field that you follow. Check to see if those bloggers accept guest posts. They won't pay you, but they might give you some exposure.
- List some possible titles for articles you could write that might be of interest to readers of the magazines, websites, and blogs you identified.
- Select several articles from pertinent websites and magazines that you like. Think about what makes the articles appeal to you. Study the first paragraph of each to see why and how it grabbed your attention. Try to emulate that catchiness in articles that you write.
- Select a topic that you can write up and post on LinkedIn as an article. Then identify several LinkedIn groups whose members might find the article interesting and post announcements about it in those groups.

32

YOU SAY YOU WANT TO WRITE A BOOK?

Consultants are the kind of people who like to share what they know (at a reasonable price), so many consultants get the notion of writing a book. They might already have been speaking at conferences, delivering courses, and writing articles and blogs; a book is the logical next step.

I've met many people who said they were writing a book, planned to write a book, hoped to write a book, or wanted to have written a book. Most of them never do. In 1996, I met a man who told me he was co-authoring a book with another experienced writer. Periodically over the years he has said they were still working on their book. It hasn't appeared yet.

Most of the people I know who never finished a book didn't treat it as a project. At least in my experience, writing a book takes a lot of time. I usually spend about six months of significant effort writing each book, with additional time devoted to editing, revising, and proofreading during the production process. If you're serious about getting it done, you must elevate it to a suitable priority in your work queue. This might mean turning down paying work to free up time for the book. That's a tough trade-off for many consultants. Technical books often are time sensitive. If the world of technology or business evolves too rapidly, you might miss the window of opportunity if you dawdle on the writing.

You also need to instill discipline into your writing approach. One author I know sets aside several hours to write every morning, starting about 5 a.m. I've never taken that approach, but when the urge comes to write a book, I do carve out the necessary time to get it done. Other projects and amusements are put on hold for the duration. If you don't dedicate the hours, it won't happen.

A seasoned author once told me, "It's an exciting day when you hold the first copy of your first book in your hand." He was absolutely right. It really was a thrill. And it never gets old, matter how many books I write.

WHY WRITE A BOOK?

If you envision a book in your future, think carefully about why you want to write it. Having books to your credit certainly looks good on a resume. They give you both visibility and credibility in your field. It's fun and exciting to be able to tell people about "my book." I get a lot of personal fulfillment and pride from having written multiple books—eleven now, including this one. It's always a treat to hear people say they find my books useful and interesting. Whatever your reasons, keep them in focus as you structure the book and consider publishing alternatives, just as you would manage the vision and scope of a software project.

It wasn't obvious to me initially just how much a well-received book could help me build my business. When prospective clients contact me to discuss a training class or consulting engagement, I always ask how they found out about me. The most frequent answer is, "From your book." Authoring respected, solid-selling books in the areas in which you plan to consult or train can launch you and your business into a strong and lasting position. It's one of the best ways to become recognized as a leading expert in your field and to create demand for your services.

People who have read your book already know quite a bit about you. They understand your breadth and depth of knowledge in a particular area, the issues you believe to be important, and how clearly you can communicate to them. They have a sense whether the techniques you espouse can help solve their problems. Readers feel a comfortable connection to you that is only strengthened if they later communicate with you directly. Readers—including myself—often are rather excited to speak personally to an author whose work they know. I'm flattered, and a bit amused, when someone who calls my company says they are honored to talk to me. I always tell them, "My wife has to talk to me every day. She doesn't seem to feel honored at all. But thank you for your kind comments."

Having a book to your name provides you with a competitive advantage over other consultants that a potential client is considering for a particular engagement. You can include the book with classes you teach or give it away as a marketing tool to promote your company's services. Plus, you can almost certainly charge more than you could as an unpublished consultant.

Sometimes, you feel that you just *have* to write a book to tell a story you're driven to share. That was the case with both my first software book and my first nontechnical book, a memoir of life lessons titled *Pearls from Sand*. I described this feeling to another aspiring author as, "There was a book inside of me that had to get out." He stared at me as though I came from another planet. I guess he hadn't experienced that same emotion, although he professed a desire to write a book himself. I never learned what his motivation was.

I knew early in my adult life that I wanted to write a book one day, but I wasn't sure what to write about. A little book-writing safety tip: having a clear topic in mind is a valuable starting point. Two events converged to lead to my first book, *Creating a Software Engineering Culture*, which appeared in 1996. First, I had written an article by that same title in 1994 for *Software Development* magazine. More emails poured in after that one article than for all the other articles I've ever written before or since—combined. "Hmmm," I thought, "perhaps there's something there."

Second, at about the same time, I happened to win a prize at a conference presentation, a copy of the speaker's book on software management. As I was reading the book on the flight home, I said to myself, "I think I could write a better book than this." So I did. But it wasn't easy.

After I decided to try to write a book, I set myself five, somewhat fanciful, goals:

1. Write a book.
2. Write enough books that a reviewer might say, "In his latest book . . ."
3. Get well-known people to write cover blurbs (also called testimonials or early praise) for my book.
4. Become well-enough known as an author and consultant that people invite me to write cover blurbs for *their* books.
5. Have my name appear on the cover in larger letters than the title.

I have now accomplished all but the last of those goals. Close enough! Let me share some insights I've acquired along the way.

HOW DO YOU LEARN?

Where do you learn how to write books? Nothing I studied in high school or college prepared me for that. Consequently, I really had no idea what I was doing when I embarked on Book #1. My inexperience showed in the original manuscript. I'm writing these chapters to help you avoid struggling as much as I did.

At a meeting of the Editorial Board for the journal *IEEE Software* one year, I sat down with two other experienced authors and compared notes. Among the three of us, we had published around eleven well-regarded books by that time. We discovered that we all took different approaches to writing. Hearing how some other authors approach a book was illuminating.

I work best from a detailed outline that ensures I will meet my objectives for the project. In contrast, one of those other authors said, "When I conceived <*Book X*>, I didn't know exactly where I was going with it, so I just started writing and watched what happened." That free-form approach wouldn't work for me, but it served this respected author well on the innovative topic he was trailblazing. You'll need to figure out what writing method will work best for each of your own book projects. I'm still an outline guy.

My first draft of *Creating a Software Engineering Culture* left much to be desired. I began with a laughably skimpy outline, less than three pages for what turned into a nearly 400-page book. The result was a poorly structured manuscript that had 13 chapters of wildly varying length, countless long bullet lists, a lack of continuity and focus, and many other problems.

Thanks to much valuable feedback from my very tolerant publisher, who saw some potential there, I was able to greatly improve the manuscript. Fixing it took a lot of effort that added little value to the content but a great deal to the presentation. I am forever indebted to Wendy Eakin and her colleagues at Dorset House Publishing for their patient and meticulous editing and guidance. The result was a nicely focused, cohesive book with a distinctive visual presentation and a well-received conversational tone that I've tried to maintain ever since.

So in my case, I learned a lot about writing books by drafting a poor one and adopting many fine suggestions about how to write a better one. Perhaps that's the way most of us learn, but it wasn't much fun at the time.

SOME BOOK-WRITING RECOMMENDATIONS

Writing my first book was a painful experience. As with so many painful experiences, it also afforded a powerful learning opportunity. Countless books on how to write books are available. You might check out *Weinberg on Writing: The Fieldstone Method* by Gerald M. Weinberg, a prolific and respected IT author. The following are some things I've learned about book writing. Perhaps not all of these will apply to every opus in your future, but they're all worth contemplating.

Structure

Many books are organized into several parts, each containing groups of chapters on a common theme. At my editor's recommendation, I restructured the 13 chapters in my initial draft of *Creating a Software Engineering Culture* into 20 chapters of more uniform length, grouped into six parts. This restructuring required a month of tedious drag-and-drop editing.

I learned my lesson though. On my next book, the first edition of *Software Requirements*, I began with a far more carefully thought-out, 17-page outline that described nineteen chapters grouped into three parts. Consequently, I had to do almost no restructuring along the way. This is analogous to designing your software before writing the code. I'm a big believer in working hard on your book's architecture. It's a lot faster, and far less painful, to revise and iterate on an outline than on fully-written text. Trust me on this: I've done both.

Themes

It's important to have some threads of continuity—recurrent themes—running through the book. Tie all sections of the book back to those themes, both to make sure the content you include is on-message and to constantly reinforce those themes to the reader. You might be tempted to incorporate certain material that intrigues you, but if it doesn't align with one of your book's themes, perhaps it doesn't belong there.

I read the draft manuscript for one colleague's proposed first book and told her, "There are two and a half books in here. Figure out which one you're writing this time, and save everything else for later." She condensed it down and then wrote an excellent book. Subsequently, she put out others. Focus, focus, focus.

Sometimes, when I've read manuscripts by other authors, it seems that they've thrown in every thought, idea, and experience they're excited about, regardless of whether it fits with the chapter or even with the book's mission. To help avoid this tempting trap, I place a few bullet points at the top of each chapter before I begin drafting it. These bullets remind me of the key messages I wish to impart in that section. As I write, I refer back to that short list periodically to ensure I'm not including extraneous stuff just because I think it's interesting. I might adjust the chapter's focus if it becomes clear that my initial intent wasn't quite right. When the chapter is all drafted, I remove those temporary bullets, because they've served their purpose of keeping me on track.

Hooks

Consider devising some "hooks," structured devices that give your book some memorable presentation patterns. You might study other books that you find appealing and see what distinctive characteristics they have that stick in your mind or make the content more accessible. The following are some hooks I've used or seen:

- Begin each chapter with a pithy quotation or a concise focal statement, like the "pearl of wisdom" that opens each chapter of *Pearls from Sand*.
- Begin each chapter with a short vignette, a little story—true or imagined—that illustrates the point of the chapter.
- Place icons in the margin to identify elements such as "culture builders" and "culture killers," cross-references to other chapters, traps to avoid, and true experience stories.
- Summarize key points at the end of each chapter.
- Place an annotated bibliography at the end of each chapter.
- Append a list of next steps, practice activities, or worksheets to each chapter to help the reader begin applying the material immediately. You might have noticed the *Next Steps* that close out each chapter of this book.
- Embed true-life anecdotes in boxes or sidebars that both reinforce your points and visually break up endless pages of dense text.
- Incorporate original cartoons to illustrate important points, possibly in a humorous fashion.
- Sprinkle pull quotes of key sentences throughout the text.
- Include a repeating or evolving visual element, such as a tab printed on the outside edge of each page that provides a "you are here" navigational aid.

Thinking about such design elements early on and getting a clear focus on the scope, objectives, and themes for my book helps me write much more efficiently. One big benefit is needing far less rework than my first book demanded. There's no single correct way to write a book, of course, but I find this approach effective.

Supplemental Materials

Technical and professional books often describe materials that can be useful to the reader on the job, such as document templates, spreadsheet tools, checklists, and forms. Consider making these sorts of items available to readers by downloading from a companion web page that's accessible from your own website where you describe the book. Some publishers provide such download mechanisms on their website page for your book, as well. The companion page for this book is at the Web Added Value™ Download Resource Center at www.jrosspub.com.

Making supplemental materials available like this provides numerous benefits for readers, authors, and publishers:

- The book is perceived as providing more value than that contained in just the words on the page, which might encourage a wavering potential customer to make the purchase.
- Readers can quickly access the supplemental materials and take advantage of them. This reduces the barrier for a busy professional to try new ways of working.
- Providing them in editable electronic forms (such as Word rather than PDF) allows each user to customize the materials to best suit his needs.
- Academic professors and other trainers who wish to use your book as a textbook can access the materials and modify them for their purposes.
- If the set of tools is substantial and significantly extends the book's value, you can sell them as a standalone product, rather than just giving them away to anyone who visits the companion website.
- Drawing book buyers to your publisher's website to access the downloads, regardless of where they purchased the book, makes it easy for them to learn about other books from your publisher.
- Links from the publisher's companion website back to your own website can help drive traffic so you can make the reader aware of your other books, consulting services, and products.
- Asking readers to provide their contact information to enable the download helps both you and your publisher build a database of people to whom you can market other books, products, and services. Be aware that not everybody appreciates having to provide their contact information to download items from a book for which they've already paid money.

Textbook Opportunities

Consider whether your book might be suitable for use as a university text. My *Software Requirements* book is used in many universities, although I didn't do anything special to prepare it for that purpose. Academic professors have expectations for textbooks that go beyond what a practitioner is looking for. I receive several inquiries each year from professors worldwide asking if I have slides to accompany the book, which could save them a lot of preparation time. I do have slides from my own training courses based on the book, though they don't cover all the topics, and I'm frankly reluctant to just give that valuable intellectual property away. I have licensed the slides at a modest fee to several professors, but academic budgets often don't permit this.

If you want to make your opus appealing as a textbook, do consider developing a supporting set of slides. It's easiest, of course, if you already have those available from your own training materials; developing high-quality courseware is a lot of work. You might also incorporate exercises for students to do (with answers in the back of the book, perhaps) and provide sample exams. The time you invest in developing such materials might lead to a higher price for the book, but you can ring up a lot of sales if it becomes a popular university text. Getting your material taught in universities also amplifies your reputation and gets your ideas into broader distribution in your field. After all, that's why we write books.

ARE YOU READY TO TAKE THE STEP?

Writing a book is not easy. It takes dedication, persistence, and time. When I was working on my first book, while concurrently working full-time at Kodak, periodically I would call out to my wife. "Chris," I'd say, "would you come shoot me, please?" One day she replied, "I'm about ready to." Not being totally stupid, I stopped asking.

As with everything else, writing books gets easier with practice. When I completed the manuscript for my second book three years later, I said to Chris, "That didn't go too badly."

"No," she said, "you didn't ask me to shoot you even once."

I guess that's progress.

Next Steps

- If you see a book in your future, carefully think through why you want to write it. Write down your motivations and objectives. What would you consider to be a successful outcome from a book-writing project (besides getting to "The End," of course)? What benefits do you think having a book under your belt might present for your career?
- If you're working on a book project now, write down four or five ideas for possible hooks to give it a distinctive look and feel or to engage the readers and hold their interest.
- If you have a book in mind or are working on one now, write down three to five themes of the book—the key messages you want to deliver to the reader—and continually reinforce them with the contents. If you've already begun writing, review what you've created so far and ensure that it all aligns with one or another of those themes.
- Think about how many hours per week you could realistically expect to spend working on a book and approximately how many weeks you think it would take to write it. (Safety tip: it will take you longer than that.) What might you have to give up in your daily life, both professionally and personally, to free up the necessary time? Are you willing to do that? Is your family? Can you afford to?
- Imagine you have written the book of your dreams and it has been shipped to the world. Write a review from the perspective of a reader who loves the book and found it to be just what he was looking for. Imagining a delighted reader's review might help you to steer the book toward that desirable outcome.

33

GETTING YOUR BOOK INTO PRINT

Writing a book is one thing; making it available to the world is an entirely separate proposition. The world of book publishing has changed in recent years, as self-publishing and electronic books have skewed the economic value proposition for both authors and publishers. While today's author has other alternatives available, there are still numerous traditional publishers who seek high-quality, marketable manuscripts.

Once you've established a reputation as someone who can write books that sell, publishers are always happy to hear from you. Getting your foot in the door can be challenging though. For this reason, and many others, I'm deeply grateful to Wendy Eakin of Dorset House Publishing, who took a chance on a first-time author in 1995 and helped him learn the craft.

This chapter describes much of what I've learned about publishing books. No doubt other authors have had different experiences. I don't claim that this is the only way—or even necessarily the best way—to go about creating a book. It's just the approach I have taken for seven books on software development and management, as well as a memoir of life lessons and a novel. Oh, and this book too.

My friend Scott Meyers created an extensive web page that's an excellent resource for the aspiring book author. It can be accessed at www.aristeia.com/authorAdvice.html. Scott is a talented and prolific writer who is renowned for his expertise in the C++ programming language. He combined his own publishing experiences with input from numerous other book authors into that web page. If you're thinking of writing a technical book, carefully read what Scott has to say, recognizing that the publishing industry is evolving as we speak.

Even if you're able to get a book written and published, you shouldn't expect financial miracles. Don't quit your job and buy that beach house, expecting book royalties to keep you in margaritas for the rest of your life. I don't have any firm figures about industry sales, but here are my own heuristics. If your technical or professional book sells five to ten thousand copies, you should be pleased that you created something your peers find useful. If you sell 25,000 copies, you should be delighted. And if you exceed 100,000 copies with any book, you're in a small group of highly-regarded (and very happy) authors.

TARGETING A NICHE

I once knew a consultant who envisioned publishing a large set of books on a particular subdomain of software engineering. He had already drafted numerous volumes in the series, which he distributed in his training courses. However, it's not easy to find a publisher willing to release such an extensive series of books by a single author in any specific niche.

As far as I know, this consultant never did get any of his books published. It's a shame, because he had a lot of great knowledge and communicated it well. I think he would have been better off to distill his vast quantity of material down into perhaps two focused, practical, and distinctive books in that area and then approach a publisher.

My writing approach often has been to identify some area of software engineering that I felt was lacking an appropriate book and then attempt to plug that gap. At the time I wrote the first edition of *Software Requirements* in 1999, few recent and practical texts on requirements engineering were available. None covered the breadth of topics that I thought were important, so I took a stab at it. The result was a book of 90,000 words that sold about 45,000 copies.

A few years later, I realized that I had accumulated considerable additional material, much of it in response to questions that people had asked me about requirements. That extra material, along with many other enhancements, eventually led to the second edition—what publishers call a 2E—of *Software Requirements* in 2003. (A second edition is not the same as a second printing. A new edition contains significant revisions and considerably more content, whereas a new printing will—at most—correct minor errors.) This edition was 60,000 words longer than the first; I guess I did have more to say on the topic. The 2E also sold well. I released a third, much longer edition in 2013, as described in Chapter 35 (*On Co-Authoring a Book*).

As another example of plugging a hole in the literature, I've long been a strong proponent of software peer reviews and inspections (a type of well-structured, formal peer review). My own software work was greatly improved by getting a little help from my friends through peer reviews. Some years ago there were several books in that niche already, but they were all hefty—350 to 450 pages—and they focused on the inspection technique, giving little attention to other possible ways to perform reviews.

I didn't think the topic was complicated enough to require such imposing texts. So in 2002, I wrote *Peer Reviews in Software: A Practical Guide*. It was just 230 pages long, covered several review techniques besides inspection, and added some fresh content on review metrics and how to install a review program into a software organization. I targeted this book at practitioners who were serious about software quality but might be daunted by a massive tome on inspection alone.

My recommendation is that you aim your book at a niche that isn't already well covered in the existing literature for your domain. You can drill down into a specialized area, synthesize related topics into a comprehensive overview, improve on the existing books in a particular field, hybridize multiple disciplines, or invent something entirely new.

A prospective publisher will assess how your proposal fits into the marketplace. Something that's going head-to-head against numerous similar titles could be a tougher commercial prospect than a book that stands alone or offers something distinctive. Publishers don't simply print interesting or well-written books; they need to publish books that sell. Otherwise, they go out of business.

THE ELEVATOR PITCH

You step into an elevator in a big hotel and press the button for the 24th floor. During the ride, you chat idly with the elevator's other occupant, who is attending the same conference you are and is heading for the 19th floor. You just happen to casually mention that you're writing a book. "Cool," she says. "What's it about?" You have perhaps 20 seconds to tell this prospective customer just enough so she says as she departs, "Sounds interesting. I'll look for it when it comes out. Good luck."

This condensed summary of your book is called the elevator pitch or elevator story. The first time someone asked me what my book was about, I confess I was stumped. How do I distill a 400-page book into 15 or 20 seconds?

This puzzlement was constructive though. It forced me to carefully think through just what my book *was* about and how I could quickly explain that to even a normal (i.e., non-software) person.

With practice, your elevator pitch will roll right off your tongue whenever you encounter a possible reader. For instance, here's the official pitch for my first novel, a mystery titled *The Reconstruction*:

> *When Jessica, a forensic sculptor, completes a facial reconstruction on unidentified remains found in a forest grave, she discovers that she has a shocking personal connection to the victim. Jessica is then driven to identify the victim, confirm their relationship, and deliver justice for her death.*

Devise your elevator pitch early in the writing process. It will help keep your overriding objective and book themes in the front of your mind as you develop the contents. If you have an initial conversation or email exchange with a prospective publisher or literary agent, the elevator pitch is your first shot at piquing his interest.

CHOOSING A PUBLISHER

Scan the spines of the books in your office; you'll see many publishers represented. As an author, you need to identify publishers who might be interested in your work and will do a good job of both producing the book and marketing it. Look for publishers that release titles you like for their content, visual presentation, and production quality.

Speaking of titles, don't get too emotionally committed to yours. The publisher might prefer an alternative title for marketing purposes or to position it relative to other titles in their catalog. That's happened to me several times, not always to my liking. But they do get the final say.

Try to identify a publisher who might find your book to be a good addition to its portfolio. Large publishers often have several book series on various themes, so you might target your book for inclusion in a particular series. Several of my books are in the Microsoft Press Best Practices series. My book on software peer reviews is in Addison-Wesley's Information Technology series. If you can pitch your book as a logical fit for a particular series, the series editor might receive your proposal warmly.

Some of the biggest publishers in software are Addison-Wesley (an imprint of Pearson Education), McGraw-Hill, Microsoft Press, O'Reilly, Prentice

Hall, and Wiley. There are many others. J. Ross (publisher of this book) has a catalog with numerous books on business analysis, project management, and many other topics. Dorset House has a long-standing reputation as a publisher of high-quality IT books. The Pragmatic Bookshelf is a relatively new publisher that has established an impressive portfolio of titles, mostly on programming topics.

There are pluses and minuses with both large and small publishers. If you're just starting out as an author, you might get more personal coaching and guidance from a smaller publisher, as I did. Then again, a small publisher has fewer resources available to devote to individual projects. A large publisher might work harder to get your book into physical bookstores, instead of just making it available on-line. You'll want to talk with your contacts at prospective publishers to understand what they can—and cannot—offer you and your masterpiece.

To help you select a candidate publisher, ask some authors you know who have published with a particular company about their experiences. Even if you don't know the authors except by reputation, go ahead and write to them. The book authors I know are all nice people who are happy to help an aspiring writer.

I have always dealt with publishers directly, not through a literary agent. This is common with professional and technical books, far less common for fiction. Referrals from colleagues can help get you in the door. People sometimes approach me with book ideas and questions about publishers. If their project seems to have merit, I'm happy to introduce them to the publishers I've worked with.

I did seek an agent when I was trying to publish my memoir of life lessons, *Pearls from Sand*, because I had no contacts in the self-help publishing world. I didn't end up with an agent after all, although one I queried did point me toward the publisher who ultimately accepted the book.

If you're dealing with a small publisher, your initial point of contact might be one of the principals of the company. When dealing with a large publishing house, you'll usually work first with an acquisitions editor (AE). The AE is responsible for evaluating ideas and proposals and landing promising projects. Publishers need authors as much as authors need publishers, so don't be shy about approaching them with your idea, proposal, outline, or manuscript.

Opinions vary as to whether it's appropriate to submit the same manuscript or proposal to multiple publishers concurrently. I think it's fine, so long as you don't get carried away. That is, I think it's reasonable to submit your book concurrently to a few candidate publishers for whom you think it would be a good fit. However, I wouldn't broadcast it to every publisher of software books in the universe, hoping for at least one hit.

THE PROPOSAL

You begin with an idea, a title, and maybe an elevator pitch. If you want a publisher to give your idea due consideration, you'll need to submit a full proposal. Once you've identified candidate publishers, peruse their websites for templates or suggested outlines for their preferred proposal format. If you've already spoken to an AE or other contact person, they can describe what they want to see in a proposal. Whether dealing with an agent or a publisher, follow their requested submission form and content carefully. They're all different.

If all else fails, there's some standard information you should include in your proposal, which I will describe in this section. You can see the proposals I submitted for several of my books at the Web Added Value™ (WAV) Download Resource Center at www.jrosspub.com. I'm not saying they're the best proposals ever, but each did lead to a contract and ultimately to a published book.

Once you've identified yourself and your position in the proposal, present a concise overview of the proposed book. Explain why the world needs it. Describe its major characteristics and the value proposition for the reader. Include a synopsis of the topics you intend to cover, either in narrative form or as a high-level outline. The publisher doesn't necessarily need to see the full outline that you might have developed to guide your writing, but he wants to know your topics and how you anticipate organizing them.

Estimate the final word count for the book and the approximate number of figures and tables you expect to include. By way of calibration, a 200-page technical book probably contains around 60,000 words. My *Software Requirements, 3rd Edition* book with co-author Joy Beatty contains 245,000 words that fill nearly 650 pages. Word counts are more meaningful than page count estimates, as fonts and formatting have a huge impact on how many words will fit on a page. Publishers also are concerned about page count, though, because that influences such practical matters as pricing, perceived value, manufacturing and shipping costs, and even how many copies they can pack into a box. Books that are either far thinner or far thicker than typical can be a tough sell. Maybe you've packed your life's work into a thousand-page tome, but the publisher knows that busy readers have patience for only about 300 pages. That's a problem.

Another section might itemize the outstanding features of the book, including any hooks you've chosen that would give the book a distinctive look and feel. If you plan to set up a website with supplemental downloadable materials, describe that too. The point of these sections is to convince the publisher that you have a uniquely valuable contribution to offer, and that you can deliver the content in a compelling way that readers will find accessible.

Publishers aren't in business just because they love books—they need to be able to sell whatever books they acquire, preferably many copies. Therefore, include a section on marketing information to help convince the publisher that this is a good business proposition. Describe your ideas for marketing strategies, ways the publisher can position the book to appeal to potential buyers. List the benefits readers would get from it.

Summarize your understanding of the audience profile—the kind of people who would find this book irresistible—and estimate how many of them there are. Don't say, "Every software developer, business analyst, and project manager will want a copy of this book, so the potential market is at least two million copies." First, that isn't going to happen. Second, that doesn't help the publisher position the book in the marketplace.

A key section of the proposal identifies the competitive titles that are already on the market, as well as any that you know are in preparation. For each competitive book, provide the title, author(s), publisher, copyright date, ISBN (International Standard Book Number, a unique identifier for each version of a book), page count, price, and a brief abstract. Describe how your book will complement, supplement, and outshine the competition.

My book proposals include a section on the status of the work ("the Work" is how the publisher's contract will refer to your book-in-progress). The publisher needs to trust that you'll actually be able to deliver a usable manuscript on schedule. I know some people who write the entire book before approaching a publisher. I have never done that with my software books, although I did for my nontechnical books. Instead, I outline the book, and then I write a chapter or two to see how it feels and to get a sense for how the whole project might go. At that point, I can approach a publisher with confidence that I know what I'm talking about. In this section, I let the publisher know how much I've already written and my estimated schedule for completing the remainder.

Include a section of author information with your full name, contact information, degrees and certifications, company affiliation, and professional biography. If you've published books previously, list their titles, publishers, years of publication, number of pages, ISBNs, approximate sales, and any awards they received. Provide references to articles, handbooks, or e-books you have published. Even if this is your first full-length book, publishers need to know that you can string sentences together.

Along that line, publishers want to see samples of your writing. The general guideline is to submit two chapters that you've drafted, neither of which is Chapter 1. This will give the publisher a sense of your writing style, how effectively you present material, and how much work it will take to massage your manuscript into publishable form. If you haven't written any chapters yet, at least make sure the publisher has ready access to some of your articles. But if you haven't written any chapters yet, how confident are you that you can write the entire book?

It's no longer the case that you can just write a book and leave everything else to the publisher, cashing the royalty checks as they pour in. Publishers these days are very interested in an author's *platform*. Your platform refers to your marketing reach: social media; blogs; discussion groups; conferences and other forums where you can sell books; professional connections; and endorsements from people even more famous than yourself. So a section of your proposal should address what *you* will do to publicize, promote, and sell your books. See *Self-Promotion* on page 266 for some ideas.

The better known you already are, the happier a publisher will be to see you come along, because you—and your reputation—will help sell books. If you're not well known yet but have a good idea for a book, you can only hope to find a publisher who's willing to take a risk, so you can then become better known and sell lots of copies of your next book.

It's a vicious cycle that's hard to break into when you don't already have a foot in the door. I have a pretty good platform in the software industry, but I have none at all in the self-help or fiction worlds. This has made it extremely difficult for my nontechnical books in those areas to attract agents, publishers, and buyers—even though they're really good books (trust me). Just be aware of how much promotional work the publisher will want you to do.

THE CONTRACT

If you succeed in convincing a publisher that your manuscript would be a valuable addition to their catalog, congratulations! You've passed the first hurdle. The publisher will then present you with a lengthy contract that itemizes every aspect of the publishing agreement, more details than you ever imagined. Naturally, publishers write these contracts in their own best interest, but you can negotiate some of the terms that might be uncomfortable for you.

I've read—and signed—a number of book contracts, but I am no expert on them, and I am not a lawyer. I again refer you to Scott Meyers's *Advice to Prospective Book Authors* web page, www.aristeia.com/authorAdvice.html, for some insights on contracting. If you haven't wrestled with book contracts before, have an intellectual-property attorney, literary agent, or other expert review yours for anything you might want to adjust. Here I'll address some of the points I always examine in my contracts.

Author Copies

The first change I always request is in the number of free copies of the book that I'm going to get. The publisher might offer you 10 or so copies. But you might need 25 or 30 copies for your beta readers and testimonial contributors, to send out for post-publication reviews, and to have a few on hand to give away or sell yourself (your mother will want at least one). Don't be shy about asking for more copies. In the scheme of things, that's a tiny expense for the publisher, as they will provide them at their cost, not list price. You can usually buy additional copies for your own use directly from the publisher at a hefty discount from list price—perhaps 40 to 50 percent. You won't receive royalties for free copies or any that you buy at your author's discount.

Royalties

This is the part you're *really* interested in, right? A contract often expresses royalty rates in two or more tiers. Each tier states the royalty as a percentage of net proceeds received by the publisher—which is far less per copy than the book's retail price—on a certain number of copies sold, less any copies returned by retailers. So you might be offered a three-tier structure something like the following (these numbers are for illustration only):

- Ten percent on the first 5,000 copies
- Thirteen percent on copies 5,001 through 20,000
- Fifteen percent on additional copies sold beyond 20,000

The better your track record of selling previous books, the more leverage you'll have when negotiating royalty rates. Unless you are mega-famous in your field, any royalty percentage above the upper-teens is unusual for print books. You might be able to go higher on e-books.

The contract will specify royalty rates for many types of sales: domestic U.S., outside the U.S., electronic books, direct sales by the publisher, discount sales, third-party publication (such as licensing the English version to a publisher in another country), translations, site licenses, and so forth. If your book is translated into other languages, you might receive a one-time payment amounting to half the licensing fee for the translation, but then you might not receive subsequent per-copy royalties. The contract will spell out all those possibilities, as well as the frequency of royalty payments (usually quarterly or semiannually).

You can negotiate on all of these various royalty percentages and the royalty tier breakpoints if you wish. Just remember that you won't win every negotiation. Win-win negotiation means that everybody feels like they got at least part of what they wanted and can live with the compromises they made.

People usually are shocked to learn how little money an author makes per copy of the book. Publishers discount books by as much as 55 percent for distribution to large retailers. So if your book has a list price of $40, a retailer might pay as little as $18 per copy. Your royalties will be based on the smaller amount, what the publisher actually receives.

By way of example, my most popular software book has sold well for 19 years. The average list price for the three different editions of the paperback over that time was about $39. My royalties average less than $3.00 per copy, counting both paperbacks and e-books sold in all formats and markets. Are you surprised? That's just how the traditional publishing business works.

Advances

You can also negotiate on the advance payment, if you are offered one; not all publishers pay an advance to all authors. An advance is a prepayment against future royalties. Let's say you agree to an advance of $10,000. The publisher might pay you $5,000 upon executing the contract and another $5,000 when you submit the final manuscript. As royalties accrue following publication, the publisher will retain those royalties instead of paying them to you, subtracting the royalties due from the amount you received as an advance. The publisher will begin paying you additional royalties only after they have accrued beyond the amount of the advance.

Don't feel bad if you are not able to negotiate an advance with your publisher. Some publishers simply don't pay them, and publishers don't want to pay more in an advance than they are likely to earn back fairly quickly through sales. I know of one highly respected author of numerous books who has chosen not to accept any advances from his publisher, although they would be happy to pay him one. That's certainly your option. Personally, I take the advance if one is offered.

A friend recently told me about an unusual contract offer she received on a software book proposal from a major publisher. Not only did the publisher not offer her an advance, but the contract required that she purchase all of the copies in a print run herself, presumably to resell or give away on her own. This publisher wanted to transfer much of the financial risk associated with this book to the author, to ensure that the publisher wouldn't be stuck with a mountain of unsold copies. That contract clause would have required an upfront investment of several thousand dollars by the author. My friend wisely rejected this skewed contract and was able to place the book with another mainstream publisher, who offered much more reasonable terms.

Reserves

Another point that often requires discussion is the language regarding reserves withheld against returns. Retailers do not always sell all the copies they purchase from a distributor, although royalties from those purchases already were credited to the author. When sellers return unsold copies to the publisher for a refund, those paid royalties must be subtracted from the author's royalty tally.

The publisher might hold back a certain percentage or an absolute dollar amount of royalties that are due to the author as a protection against having to claw back royalties previously paid (as just happened to a fellow author I know). In most cases the royalties you will accrue from ongoing sales will more than cover the amount lost from returns. However, publishers create this reserve of withheld royalties as a cushion against excessive refunded royalties because of book returns.

Nearly every book contract I've read has included such a reserve clause; it's not unreasonable. However, the contract often does *not* explicitly state the mechanisms and timing by which the author ultimately will receive the balance of the withheld reserve. Make sure to work out a resolution to the return issue with the publisher during contracting so they can't hang onto your withheld royalties forever or until the book goes out of print, whichever comes first. Once the publisher sees that sales are rolling along at a reasonable clip and returns are modest, you might be able to request to have any remaining reserve amount released to you. I've done this successfully several times.

Copyright

The contract will state who will own the copyright on the book. I like to get the copyright in my own name, not the publisher's name. Maybe this isn't important, but it makes me happy.

Future Books

Some of the contracts I've seen contained a clause that gave the publisher the right of first refusal on my next book. I always ask to remove that clause, as I don't want any restrictions on where I submit future proposals. Who knows what I might write next or where I'll want to send it?

One publisher was especially egregious on this point. They wanted the first option on my next book, but then even if they rejected it and I then placed it with another publisher, they wanted to be able to match the offer and get the book. Because the contract does not *require* the publisher to publish the book, they could essentially quash it for a period of time, until we worked out having the rights revert to me so I could try again someplace else. That's all highly unlikely, but there's no way I would agree to those terms.

Responsibilities

The contract will make clear who is responsible for doing what parts of the work on the project, including artwork, index, and other elements. Some publishers will create the final artwork from your drafts at their expense. Others expect you to provide the final, camera-ready art, and still others will redraw the figures you provide if necessary, but then will subtract the cost from your royalties.

Incidentally, be sure to proofread the final artwork to make sure all of the elements have been included from your drafts, arrows are all going in the right direction on figures, text is spelled and positioned properly, and the like. If the publisher's staff will be redrawing your figures, try to arrange to work directly with the artist rather than having to go through one or more intermediaries on the editorial team.

I've had problems on some books when the artist zigged when he should have zagged, and it took a lot of communication effort to align his work with my intent. The time and aggravation were greatly compounded when my project editor did not permit me to communicate directly with the artist. In one case, it took five tries for the artist to get one not-that-complicated figure correct (that is, to create simply a cleaned-up version of my original). To add insult to injury, the first printing of the book contained the fourth incorrect version of the figure, not the proper fifth version. That was mighty frustrating.

The publisher will generally hire someone to create the index, although they might deduct the indexing costs from your royalties. I know one author who always generates his own indexes and has even persuaded his publisher to pay him for the effort. I typically provide my indexer with a list of suggested index terms, which is usually ignored. This irks me to no end. I've never yet been permitted to communicate directly with the indexer for one of my books, which is an ineffective, inefficient, and annoying way to collaborate.

Frankly, some of my invisible indexers did quite a poor job initially, requiring considerable time on my end to get the problems fixed. Examine the index carefully to make sure it contains the terms that will help the interested reader find all the goodies contained in the book. This is especially a challenge if you're writing highly technical material that even an experienced indexer might not grasp. If the index—or any other aspect of the book—isn't useful or contains errors, the reader is going to blame only you.

MAKING COMMITMENTS

Be careful not to commit to a contract until you have a clear idea of where you're going with the book and are confident you can deliver it without killing yourself. One consultant who began writing his opus soon realized he simply didn't have the time and energy to devote to the book along with his other responsibilities and family life. He was exhausting himself with the effort. Wisely, he decided that the book was a lower priority for him, and he abandoned it, at least for the time being.

Another established author once told me that he was way behind deadline for delivering not just one, but two book manuscripts. It wasn't clear that he expected to complete either one, although he had happily cashed the advance checks. If you conclude that you aren't going to deliver the manuscript on time, let the publisher know as soon as possible so they can take appropriate corrective action. This might involve adjusting the schedule, having someone else finish the book, or abandoning the project entirely. The contract should specify what happens under these conditions. And plan to return the advance if you can't finish the book. It's the right thing to do.

A publisher takes a gamble when he offers a contract. Unless they have worked together before, the publisher has to trust that the author will deliver as promised. Here's what one publisher told me:

> *I met with an author prospect a couple of times recently to discuss planned content and so forth of a book she was writing. I was interested enough to send her a contract, but first I sent her my author questionnaire to complete. She said she would have it back to me within a week or two. It has now been two months. She has sent me a few emails providing reasons for the delay, but new dates have come and gone. If I were to receive her questionnaire tomorrow, I would not offer her a contract. If she can't complete a well-written proposal within the time frames promised and has one excuse after another, that tells me that delivery of the book per plan isn't likely.*

This is not the kind of story you want a publisher telling about you. I have a personal life philosophy to under-commit and over-deliver, which helps me to avoid making iffy schedule commitments. This attitude serves me well when I'm working on a book project, and it delights publishers and editors.

Honest and timely communication with your editor and publisher regarding your project's status is vital. A publisher's production, sales, and marketing plans and schedules for books are time-sensitive; they must meet numerous external deadlines over which they have no control. Delivering on time—or even early—is never bad. However, early delivery without the publisher knowing what's going on can result in missing opportunities that are tied to specific calendar periods. Late delivery is never good, but if the publisher knows it's a possibility and can adjust their plans to mitigate the negative effects, they might not be too upset. I guarantee you that the publisher *will* be upset if you deliver late without warning and advertising dollars are wasted, book retailers are upset and cancel their orders, potential purchasers lose interest, and the publisher's reputation takes a hit.

Publishing is a business very much based on relationships and trust. Be sure to hold up your end of the deal.

STAYING ON TRACK

It will take longer than you expect to write the book, perhaps much longer. Be sure to build in schedule buffers to allow for lost time due to issues that can arise in anyone's unpredictable life. And remember, simply writing it is just the beginning. I always line up about 15 friends and colleagues to review the manuscript, chapter by chapter, before the publisher ever sees it. These are my beta readers, as described in Chapter 30 (*Four Eyes Are Better Than Two*). This adds more time to the process but results in a far better work. Besides keeping an eye on the schedule, I'm usually aiming for a book of a particular length, so I have to track the size of the book, as well as the status of each chapter as I'm writing. There's a lot to monitor.

To help me stay on top of all this, I set up a status tracking spreadsheet at the beginning of each book project. You can see a sample of one of my book status tracking spreadsheets at the WAV web page for this book at www.jrosspub.com. I admit it: I like data. This level of tracking is comfortable for me; it might not make sense for you at all. My spreadsheet contains three sections in separate Excel worksheets: chapter status, review status, and size tracking.

Chapter Status

I list all the book elements I need to create, including chapters, dedication, acknowledgments, foreword, preface, introduction, introductions to individual parts of the book, epilogue, appendices, glossary, references, bibliography, author biography, and index. (You won't necessarily have all of these components.) For each element, I record the following dates:

- Drafted
- Sent out to beta readers
- Review comments received
- Baselined as complete
- Submitted to the publisher
- Received after copy editing
- Revised copy returned to the publisher
- Page proofs received
- My page proof comments returned to the publisher
- Comments on final pages returned to the publisher

I establish target dates for major milestones, such as sending out chapters for review and submitting them to the publisher, so I can quickly see whether or not I'm on schedule.

Review Status

For each of my reviewers, I record the date that I received their comments on each chapter. I note how helpful their feedback was, on a scale from 0 to +++. The pattern that results lets me identify the most helpful, reliable, and prompt reviewers. I'll keep them in mind for the next book.

Even though I don't have any trouble getting reviewers to volunteer, I'm surprised at how many of them fail to return any feedback at all. They don't even explain why they aren't commenting on what I send them. They disappear as though they were abducted by space aliens. Weird. If you sign up to be a beta reader but then cannot participate for some reason, please let the author know as early as possible. He's counting on you, and time is of the essence.

Size Tracking

I generally target my books for a particular approximate length, based on the story I'm trying to tell and what I think will best fit the market. If you're not doing this, you can skip this section. I estimate the length of each chapter in words, based on my outline. Then I record the actual number of words in the draft version that goes out for review and the final version of each chapter. My spreadsheet calculates the cumulative number of words to date and charts the actual versus expected word count so I can see what the deviation is. Some books have wound up as much as 20 percent longer than I estimated, although I'm getting better at projecting lengths and writing to those targets. The publisher might provide you with a formula to estimate page count from the word count, based on some formatting assumptions.

I agree, this is all rather high-resolution, but it helps me get the book done in the way that I'm aiming for. Being a research scientist by background, I'm a data kind of guy, so this is actually fun for me. Peculiar, I know.

Alternatively, you could just start writing your book and stop when you reach the end; whatever works for you.

Next Steps

- Assuming that you have a book in mind, write the elevator pitch for it. Try this out on some of your friends and colleagues to see if it grabs them and reveals what the book is about. Adjust it until it does. Then practice it until it rolls off the tongue smoothly.

- Make a list of competitive titles that you know about for the book you're thinking of writing. How could you and the publisher position your book to compete effectively against those others? In other words, why would a reader want to buy your book instead of one of the others? You'll want to have a good answer to that question.
- Examine the books in your professional library, and then list a few publishers who produced books that you like and who might be candidates to whom you could submit a proposal. Do you see any existing book series into which your title would logically fit?
- If you have not yet submitted your book to a publisher, download the sample proposals from the Web Added Value™ Download Resource Center at www.jrosspub.com and use those as a starting point to craft an outline for your proposal.

34

BEING YOUR OWN PUBLISHER

Writers who wish to publish books on their own today have numerous options available. You might opt for self-publication for several reasons. Perhaps you haven't been able to attract an agent or publisher. Maybe your technical book is targeted at a small niche market, or your nontechnical book is a family keepsake, not a commercial endeavor. Or perhaps you just don't want to wait the years it can take to submit queries to potential agents and publishers and suffer through countless rejections in hope of eventually getting a hit.

You might have heard about authors who self-published and scored big, selling tens of thousands of copies of their books and maybe ultimately attracting a traditional publisher that way. Yes, it happens; no, it's not common. According to Statista (www.statista.com), 1,009,188 books were self-published in the United States in 2017. That's a lot of books, far more than traditional publishers released. But a friend who has been in the publishing business for decades told me that the average book published in English in the United States sells fewer than four copies per year. You're not going to retire early on those royalties.

I've gone the self-publishing route myself a few times. Let me tell you what I've learned.

SELF-PUBLISHING: CHEAP

It used to be that self-publishing a book was essentially an admission of defeat, acknowledging your inability to entice a real publisher. Today, however, self-publishing is a viable option for many authors. Some authors turn to vanity presses, companies that charge you money to publish your book. They may or may not effectively promote it, distribute, it, sell it, or pay you reasonable royalties. Self-publishing and vanity presses aren't the same thing these days.

259

Self-publishing probably still means that your book didn't attract a traditional publisher. However, many tools and options are available, and it is possible—although not a certainty—to achieve commercial success doing it yourself.

I have self-published two books. The first was a special situation. When I was a child, my family lived in Europe for three years because my father was in the U.S. Air Force. We did extensive sightseeing throughout Europe. My parents wrote up notebooks about our adventures—half memoir and half travelogue, complete with photographs—which became treasured family keepsakes. For my mother's 85th birthday in 2011, my siblings and I decided to publish all of these notebooks together as an actual book titled *You Can't Get There from Here.* Our family often used that catchphrase as we drove around Europe trying to figure out how to get to some interesting-looking castle or other attraction.

You should have seen the expression on Mom's face when we gave her the book. How often does someone present you with a book with your name as the author, yet you didn't see it coming?

For this self-publishing experience, I used CreateSpace, which at the time was Amazon's self-publishing platform for paperbacks. In 2018, Amazon merged CreateSpace into Kindle Direct Publishing (KDP), their platform for publishing e-books for the Kindle reader. I'll refer to the combined platform as KDP from here on.

The process went surprisingly smoothly and was a valuable learning experience for me, in many respects. We did not attempt to sell this book. Of course, with KDP you can have your book listed for sale on Amazon.com—and optionally in other places—almost immediately. Just set the price in various currencies, choose the distribution channels you have in mind, and click a button to release your masterpiece to the whole world.

These books are printed on demand, so the author need not pay for, stockpile, and perhaps ultimately discard hundreds or thousands of copies from a big press run. With print on demand (POD), when someone orders a copy, the printer manufactures a copy and ships it to the customer. They look like regular books, although you can sometimes spot self-published books because of the minimalist cover design, low page count, and amateurish interior layout from some do-it-yourselfers. Many brick-and-mortar bookstores will not stock POD books.

KDP offers a wide range of publishing options. I took the simplest path for my mother's book. I did a light copy edit on my parents' original text, and then I tackled the cover design (full cover wrap = front cover + spine + back cover) and interior design—both new experiences for me. After laying out the pages, I simply uploaded the interior and cover PDF files to my account at kdp.amazon.com. KDP staff reviewed my files and concluded they would print satisfactorily, so I ordered a paperback proof copy. I made a couple of small corrections in the cover layout, and my sharp-eyed sister spotted several content errors during a final proofread. A second proof copy verified the changes in the corrected files, and we were done. The entire process cost just $63.34:

- $10.00 for an ISBN, so the book could be published using my own publishing imprint: Agent Q Bookworks. Alternatively, you can publish a paperback using a free ISBN from KDP, in which case it is shown as being "Independently published."
- $39.00 as an account upgrade fee that cut the cost of books we purchased approximately in half (this option is no longer available at KDP)
- $3.58 plus $3.59 shipping for each of the two proof copies
- My mother's reaction: *priceless*

This seemed pretty cheap to me. We could purchase all the additional copies we wanted from KDP for just $3.58 each plus the cost of shipping. Of course, we bought Mom some extra copies to give away to friends and family.

So that is one self-publishing extreme—doing everything yourself. It was a lot of work, but this was a labor of love and, as I said, a great learning experience. I never imagined I would be scanning and retouching 83 photographs taken a half-century earlier.

SELF-PUBLISHING: LESS CHEAP

At the other end of the spectrum, the self-publishing author who wants to create a professional-looking product will hire experts to provide essential services such as copy editing, cover design, interior design, page composition, proofreading, and conversion to e-book formats. That's what I chose to do when I wrote my first novel, *The Reconstruction*, in 2017. One of my goals for this project was to never have someone pick up a copy of the book and say, "This looks like it was self-published." Achieving this—and I think we did—required a team effort.

Having never written fiction before, I knew that I had much to learn about writing style. So after I had drafted the manuscript, I hired a copy editor who gave me exactly the sort of feedback I was looking for. She helped me correct tenses, suggested when I should replace narrative text with dialogue and vice versa, prompted me to add more descriptive information about certain characters and scenes, corrected some formatting issues, and the like. Laura was very helpful in guiding me to be a better fiction writer.

I also knew I wanted an eye-catching cover that would make people eager to learn what this book was about. I mocked up one cover concept as a starting point, but then I hired a professional to take it from there. Vinnie's website displayed a number of appealing covers he had designed for both fiction and nonfiction books. He provided me with several cover concepts, some of which I liked and some of which I did not. It took a number of iterations, with us both contributing ideas and modifications, but eventually we came up with a cover design I really liked. You can see it at www.TheReconstructionBook.com. Hiring a professional also ensured that he could create high-quality graphics and properly size the full cover wrap so it would be accepted by the self-publishing printers I selected.

The price I was quoted for the book's interior design seemed high to me. I decided to give it a shot myself, having had a little bit of experience with that on my mother's book. Her book contained many photos that had to be positioned just right, some maps, and other graphics. My novel was just plain text; how hard could it be?

It turned out not to be terribly difficult to come up with a basic interior design. I went to the library and studied the layout of numerous novels that were published in the trade paperback format (as opposed to mass-market paperback or hardcover). I measured margins, took notes on running headers, looked at fonts and their size and spacing, and examined how the first pages of chapters were styled.

Beyond the text of the novel itself, I had to lay out all the front matter and back matter: title and copyright pages, dedication (to my wife, of course!), acknowledgments, and author biography. Some self-publishing platforms will let you download templates for the interior layout and full cover wrap once you've selected a trim size (the dimensions of the printed book).

Interior book design includes the following activities:

- Set the margins all around each page, mirroring the left (verso) and right (recto) pages and recognizing that the inside margin needs to be larger on each page to account for the binding.
- Choose the typeface (font), its point size, and leading (pronounced "ledding," the vertical white space between lines) for the body text.

- Define the typeface, style, and formatting for any special types of text, such as block quotations and chapter titles.
- Define and format running headers and footers, which could vary from chapter to chapter and might be different on the left and right pages and on the first page of each chapter.
- Make the first page of each chapter distinctive somehow.
- Define indentation standards that you'll follow. Typically the first paragraph in a chapter and paragraphs immediately following a heading or a scene break within a chapter are flush left, but all other paragraphs are indented. Normal body text is fully justified using a proportionally-spaced font.
- Select any highlighting patterns you wish to follow. For instance, I highlighted the first three words of each chapter in *The Reconstruction* using a different typeface in **BOLD SMALL CAPITALS**, just to provide a bit of distinction.
- Lay out the table of contents and index, if you have them. The novel did not, of course, but nonfiction books do.

The novel's interior design was not very complicated, once I decided what I wanted it to look like. However, flowing 88,000 words of text into that template opened my eyes to a whole new world of hyphenation rules and layout conventions. Following these rules can help ensure that your printed book doesn't look like it was self-published.

As an example, the bottommost lines on facing pairs of left–right pages should align. If you created your manuscript in Microsoft Word, you might have turned on widow and orphan control. This prevents having the first line of a paragraph alone at the bottom of a page (an orphan) or the final line of a paragraph alone at the top of the page (a widow). But this can leave you with different numbers of lines on some pairs of facing pages. You need to turn off widow and orphan control, then fix any widows and orphans manually so those final lines on facing pages align.

And the hyphenation rules! Do not have an end-of-line hyphen in the first line of a paragraph, the next-to-last line of a paragraph, the last or next-to-last line of a page, or the first line of a new page. Do not have end-of-line hyphenation in an already hyphenated word, a URL, or a word that contains other punctuation, such as an apostrophe. Have at least two or three characters before and after the hyphen in a word that's hyphenated at the end of a line. I also discovered that Word's automatic hyphenation did not always split words correctly, so I had to fix a few such errors manually.

Correcting all of these layout issues required numerous passes through the book and a lot of manual tweaking. To follow all the hyphenation rules, I needed to squeeze characters in certain lines closer together so a hyphenated word at the end of the line would wrap upward. In other spots I had to insert manual line breaks to force a hyphenated word down to the next line. Even then, some pages that looked fine in Microsoft Word did not look fine in PDF, for unknown reasons. Very tedious work. I mean, seriously tedious. Tedious to the max. On the plus side, I did discover some formatting functions in Word that I had never encountered before.

Word is not the ideal tool for such manipulations. Professional book designers use tools like Adobe InDesign—true desktop publishing software—but I didn't have that available. My book interior came out fine, but it took considerable manual effort.

A valuable resource that helped me make my interior layout look as professional as possible was *80 Common Layout Errors to Flag When Proofreading Book Interiors* by Lynette M. Smith. Fortunately, not all 80 of those rules applied to my novel, although they would be relevant to technical and other nonfiction books.

The good news is that, if you only plan to publish in e-book form, you don't need to worry about all those layout minutiae. The user of an e-reader can change the font, text size, line spacing, and page width so the words do not flow in a predictable way on the page. Such text is in fact called *reflowable*. Issues like hyphenation, widows and orphans, and the fine-tuning of spacing within a line disappear.

Getting people who really know what they're doing to contribute to the project adds to the cost. You need to decide what your budget will bear and how much of the creative work you can do yourself instead of hiring experts. Consider whether the investment is likely to pay off in higher sales, might help to get the book picked up eventually by an agent or a traditional publisher, or will just give you the personal satisfaction of a job well done. Note that if you're self-employed and you pay a contract editor or designer more than $600 in a calendar year to help with a book that you're self-publishing for your business, you must issue each such contractor a 1099-MISC tax form and report the payment to the IRS.

Here's approximately how the costs broke down for the 300 pages of *The Reconstruction*:

- Copy editing: $2,640
- Cover design and consulting on self-publishing: $1,275
- Proofreading: $1,050

- Conversions into two e-book formats, MOBI for Kindle devices and readers, and EPUB for most other readers: $750
- A package of ten ISBNs plus a barcode with price to put on the back cover of the paperback: $320 (Each book format—paperback, various e-books, audiobook, large print—needs a unique ISBN, although Kindle e-books published through KDP do not. You can buy ISBNs individually or in packages from Bowker Identifier Services at www.myidentifiers.com.)
- Licensing images for the cover from Shutterstock.com: $29
- Registering the copyright with the U.S. Copyright Office: $35

Throw in a couple of proof copies and some other odds and ends, and the total price to turn the manuscript for my exciting forensic mystery novel into an actual, high-quality book was about $6,300. That's nearly 100 times what it cost to self-publish my mother's book, for which I did all the work myself. Not cheap.

Was it worth it? I'll have to sell a lot of copies of *The Reconstruction* to earn back my investment, and that probably won't ever happen. But, hey, I wrote a novel! It was the most fun I've ever had writing. So it was worth it to me to do it right. And it's actually a good read—just check out all the five-star reviews.

Many self-publishing companies offer a range of other services if you're not willing or able to do all these things yourself or to locate and hire professionals who can. You can pay those companies to help with cover and interior design, editing, marketing, promotion, and distribution, in just about any combination, for prices ranging from a few hundred dollars up to several thousand dollars.

I'm not pushing KDP over other self-publishing alternatives; it's simply the one with which I've had the most personal experience. Other self-publishing companies include IngramSpark (which I also used as a printer and distributor for *The Reconstruction*), Lulu, AuthorHouse, Dog Ear, Booklocker, and many more. Smashwords specializes in e-books; I used them for another project. IngramSpark offers the advantage of providing both printed and e-book distribution to many retailers—including brick-and-mortar bookstores—that might not stock books published through KDP, or POD books in general.

It can be confusing to try to navigate all the complexities of self-publishing: setting up distribution channels, getting books into all the right formats, choosing prices in various currencies, setting up payment mechanisms, and on and on. I did encounter a few problems during my self-pub journeys. Fortunately, the customer support from both KDP and Smashwords was first rate, so we solved the problems.

Self-publishing your professional or technical book might seem to be an appealing option. The fact is that you will sell far fewer copies if you self-publish than if you work with a traditional publisher. They have a marketing reach that individuals do not. I have seen some professional-looking technical books that were self-published, so quality is certainly achievable. Nonetheless, if you are just starting out on your consulting and writing career and have not yet developed a following in your field, don't expect smashing sales from your self-published book.

Whatever you do, don't calculate how many dollars per hour you're earning from royalties—you would be horrified. You're going to put in more effort to self-publish than if you go with a traditional publisher, for a lower monetary yield. Money should not be your primary motivation for self-publishing a technical book. As we saw earlier, there are numerous other reasons why you might wish to write and publish your treatise.

Of course, even having a lovely new paperback available through major book distribution channels is no guarantee that a particular store will elect to stock your book or that customers will buy it. You need to tell the world about it first.

SELF-PROMOTION

No, not telling everyone what a fine human being you are, but rather telling prospective buyers what a great book you've written and why they need to buy it. Regardless of which self-publishing route you choose, there's one thing that everyone who has published their own books agrees on: you must be prepared to promote, promote, promote your book. Some people seem to believe that "If you print it, they will come." It's more accurate to say, "If you print it and tell them about it over and over, they might come." Even if you go with a traditional publisher, plan to spend a lot of your own time and energy on promotion and marketing.

Many websites present tips for marketing your self-published book; you can pursue those on your own when you're ready. The approach you take for marketing depends somewhat on the genre in which you are writing. The following are just a few suggestions about possible marketing and promotion techniques. Some may work for you; others may not.

- Post announcements on all of your social media outlets, early and periodically. (A caution: I've learned that garnering many "likes" and nice comments on social media does not translate into sales.)

- Join relevant LinkedIn groups before the book appears and begin contributing to discussions to let other visitors know you have something useful to say.
- Post short, but substantive, articles adapted from the book on LinkedIn, and post pointers to it in relevant groups.
- Contact local newspapers to see if anyone is interested in doing a story about you and your book. I've done this successfully more than once.
- Ditto for local television and radio stations.
- Set up an Amazon Author page.
- Ask some people with name recognition in your field to write early-praise testimonials. You can put those on the back cover, on pages just inside the front cover, on your own web page for the book, and in your book description for online retailers, such as the Editorial Reviews section of your book's Amazon.com page.
- Ask anyone to whom you have sent complimentary copies or announcements about the book to mention it through their social media channels and to post reviews at online retailers and any other forums they frequent. They might need to be reminded a few times.
- Contact libraries and bookstores that might want to stock it. If they can buy it from a large distributor, such as Ingram, that might be more appealing for them than if it's distributed only by KDP or available just from you.
- Contact websites or magazines about publishing articles you adapted from the book and possibly having them review it.
- If you follow any blogs in your field, see if they accept guest posts that you could write based on the contents of your book. Blog writers often reject contributions that are too flagrantly promotional, though.
- Contact anyone you know who writes book reviews to see if they will post a review of it. There are websites that will write reviews for money, such as Kirkus (www.kirkusreviews.com/indie-reviews); I've never tried any of them, so I don't know if they're worth the cost. If you want to pursue that, start early, as some such sites will only review books that have not yet been released.

The list could go on and on. Basically, you are trying to override the sad truth I shared way back in Chapter 2 about being an independent anything, including consultant or author: "It doesn't matter how good you are if nobody knows you're there." I encourage you to search for the numerous websites that offer recommendations for promoting books. Choose the mechanisms that look like they would be the most effective for your title and the most comfortable for the amount of time and money you wish to invest in promotion.

Here's one final promotion tip. After I self-published *The Reconstruction*, my wife bought me a sweatshirt emblazoned with the message: "Ask me about my book." It has been an effective conversation starter at wine tasting events, when volunteering at my local public library, and at parties. That sweatshirt has long since paid for itself.

You can read glowing testimonials from people who sold vast numbers of their self-published book and made a lot of money. The reality, I'm afraid, is that this is highly unlikely to happen with your books—or mine. Sorry. But I wish you the best of luck, and I hope you have fun along the way. I have.

Next Steps

- If you are thinking about self-publishing a book, ask yourself why you wish to go that route rather than with a traditional publisher. Do you perceive barriers to traditional publishing that you could try to overcome if you wished?
- Think about which of the tasks associated with self-publishing you're willing and able to undertake yourself, and which ones you're better off hiring someone else to do.
- Estimate the costs associated with self-publishing your book, so you can see if it fits into your budget. Those costs should be tax-deductible as a business expense, but remember that the IRS expects your company to show a profit at least two years out of five.
- Write down six or eight actions you would be willing and able to take to promote your self-published book. Which actions would you launch while the book is still in preparation, and which ones would you take after it's released?

35

ON CO-AUTHORING A BOOK

Several years ago I did something I had never done before: I co-authored a book. It worked out remarkably well. I had written several magazine articles with other people, which went fine, but nothing like the scale of a book. If you've ever thought about writing something collaboratively—or even working together long-distance on a different type of project—you might find the story of how we approached this project informative.

In August of 2012, Joy Beatty, vice president of research and development at a software requirements consulting company called Seilevel, asked me if I had thought about writing a third edition of my popular book *Software Requirements*. The first edition was published in 1999 and the second in 2003, both by Microsoft Press.

I had indeed, from time to time, considered writing a third edition. Everything in the second edition was still valid nine years later and the book still sold well, but I knew it would benefit from an update. Some significant changes had taken place in the software world in the intervening years. Portions of the content definitely were ripe for beefing up, and others could use an improved presentation.

Frankly, though, the prospect of revising a 500-page book was daunting. It would be a massive amount of work. I hadn't been following the software requirements literature closely since I had largely retired from consulting and training a few years earlier. The hammock, my guitars, and volunteer work were more appealing to me than spending hundreds of hours at a keyboard yet again. I recognized the need, but I wasn't super-motivated.

Joy's question got me thinking, though. What if she and I were to write the third edition of the book together? Joy was well respected in the business analysis field, up-to-date on current happenings, and the co-author herself of a nice book called *Visual Models for Software Requirements*. We began kicking this possibility around. It quickly became clear that there might be value in this collaboration. We agreed to give it a try.

REQUIREMENTS FOR REQUIREMENTS

Our first task was to create an outline. We began with the outline for the second edition, or 2E. We identified chapters that would benefit from major enhancements, chapters that just needed a tune-up, and new topics we could add. We each went through a copy of the 2E and noted specific changes to make. I came up with more than 150 sticky notes with ideas, strategically placed at the relevant spots in the 2E. My email archives contained dozens of email exchanges that I had with readers over the years (including several with Joy herself from 2004 and 2008), replying to questions they had asked me. Those messages were a rich source of improvement ideas and stories to share.

Working from the 2E as a starting point, Joy and I soon settled on the overall chapter structure and our preliminary first- and second-level headings. Then we enhanced this outline, both of us adding bullets under each chapter with our thoughts about possible changes. This annotated outline became our primary working tool for exchanging ideas. In essence, that outline and all the associated notes established the requirements for our book on software requirements.

We incorporated the high-level outline into the proposal we submitted to Microsoft Press. Joy and I were pleased when Microsoft accepted our proposal, as they had done a nice job for us on our previous books.

ACROSS THE MILES

I live in Portland, Oregon. Joy lives in Austin, Texas. We had only met in person one time—a year earlier at a conference—before we kicked off this project. We needed to determine the best way to exchange and manage materials throughout this many-month project.

Joy established a Microsoft SharePoint repository for us to use as a configuration management tool. We also set up an issues list to track the myriad questions we knew would arise. We created the following folders in the repository for managing several types of files:

- The final chapter files from the 2E, which served as a great starting point for much of the new book

- Draft chapters we would be iterating on during initial writing, while making our own revisions, and during peer review
- The dozens of figures and other images, organized into subfolders for each chapter
- The submitted chapters that went off to the publisher for copy editing and the edited versions the publisher returned to us
- PDFs of the formatted chapter pages we received from the publisher for final proofreading
- Our status tracking spreadsheet, chapter checklist, collaboration process, reviewer's guide for our beta readers, and the issues list—the infrastructure of our project

Whenever one of us uploaded a modified version of a chapter or other document to one of these folders, it was added to the collection so we could retain the history of previous versions. We used check-out and check-in procedures to ensure that only one of us at a time could alter a particular file. This basic configuration management discipline kept us from overwriting each other's work and losing changes one of us had made. Retaining the earlier versions of each chapter allowed us to go back and see how we had handled some topic before and to repair an error if we accidentally lost some material. It would be a real challenge to execute a project like this without a shared file repository.

PLANNING THE COLLABORATION

I have long suspected that many teams of people who work together on a project don't spend much time thinking about exactly *how* they're going to work together. They can do fine for a while, but when deadlines loom, there's too much going on, and the stress level ramps up, the lack of a process begins to show. Joy and I invested considerable time working out the process we would follow for our collaboration on the different aspects of this book.

Each of us took primary authorship responsibility for certain chapters. We adjusted that allocation as we went along to balance the workload equitably. We crafted a detailed process that described how we would hand materials off from one to the other, address feedback received from our beta readers, and interact with the publisher's editorial team.

We also agreed on some writing style and formatting issues. A key goal was to give the book a consistent feel and style. We did not want it to be apparent to a reader which of us had drafted a particular chapter. This was perhaps easier when we began with chapters from the 2E, which I had written alone. Even on new chapters, though, the numerous passes we made back and forth smoothed out the final presentation into a consistent voice.

Joy and I even discussed how we would resolve conflicts if we held different opinions about a particular issue. My experience has been that in business collaborations it is far better to agree on how to resolve these matters *before* you confront the first conflict, not in the heat of the moment when the parties are emotionally defending their entrenched positions. It was well worth the time we spent working out all these details of our collaboration process.

TRACKING STATUS

When writing a large book, there is a vast amount of information to keep track of. At any given time, each of our chapters was in one of many possible states:

- Not yet begun
- Initial draft written
- Initial draft being reviewed by the other author
- Reviewed draft being revised by the lead author
- Out to beta readers for peer review
- Being revised following peer review
- Being edited by our own internal editor (one of Joy's colleagues)
- Submitted to publisher for copy editing
- Being revised following copy editing
- Final manuscript version submitted to publisher
- Formatted PDF pages and artwork received from publisher
- Formatted pages being proofread and corrected
- Corrected pages being proofread yet again
- Final final final pages submitted to publisher (unless, of course, we spot any more errors after that)

Our book contained more than 40 components, including 32 chapters, front matter (dedications, introduction, acknowledgments), and back matter (epilogue, three appendices, glossary, references, index). There were also more than 100 image files for figures. We worked on many elements simultaneously in these various states. Sometimes I felt as though I was juggling a dozen flaming chainsaws. We set up a spreadsheet to track the date each chapter transitioned from one of these states to another. Each of us had to maintain our own set of pending revisions to the shared tracking spreadsheet so we wouldn't step on each other's changes when we updated it periodically.

We also established a tracking spreadsheet for review status. We recorded when each chapter went out for peer review, the target date for receiving review feedback, the actual date we received feedback from each reviewer, and a rating of how useful each reviewer's input was. Frequently updating this status tracking file was a bit of a nuisance, but it was part of the necessary process overhead associated with remote collaboration. Any time multiple people work on an activity there's a certain amount of inefficiency, along with a need for coordination that you simply have to expect and accommodate.

Tracking status like this was imperative in order to make sure that we always knew what each of us should be working on. It helped to guarantee that we could achieve our target dates for getting chapters where they needed to be.

Joy and I carefully scheduled those target dates for critical chapter milestones, and then we rescheduled them as we saw how the work progressed. We had a lot of schedule flexibility until the publisher's editorial team was put into place. At that point, they needed firm commitments regarding when they could expect to receive chapters. They also needed predictable turnaround on our review of copy-edited chapters and final page proofs. Once the editorial team was assembled, the project switched from being rather open-ended to being time-boxed with firm constraints. I'm pleased to report that we met all of our deadlines.

THE RESULT

Writing the third edition of *Software Requirements* was an interesting and fun experience, as well as being a huge amount of work. Joy was, well, a joy to work with. She closed significant gaps in my own knowledge and brought a wealth of personal experiences and stories to share. Fortunately, our fundamental philosophies and perspectives were quite similar. Those minor disagreements that we had were easily worked out through the flurry of emails we exchanged daily and an occasional phone discussion. Neither of us ever got too annoyed with the other or had to exercise a veto.

It was great to have someone to bounce ideas off, to clarify my thinking, to help me choose between possible approaches, to judge whether or not to include a particular topic, and to straighten me out when I was off in the weeds.

Joy also obtained some input periodically from her colleagues at Seilevel, running small chunks of text past them to test their reaction. This quick, real-world input saved us from ourselves more than once.

You might think that working with a co-author who has responsibility for many of the chapters would save time. That was not my experience. If anything, this book took more effort than if I had done it all myself. That's mainly because each chapter went through more iterations than if only one author had been involved, as Joy and I both revised and polished each chapter.

On the plus side, there were many important benefits from the collaboration. First, I simply couldn't have done it all myself. Joy had expertise that allowed her to write content that I could not. She also took certain chapters that I had written years ago for the second edition and greatly enhanced and updated them. In some ways, it's easier for an outsider to step back and see these improvement opportunities.

One of my fellow book authors asked me at the beginning of this project, "How are you going to feel about someone messing with your baby?" I did have to set my ego aside whenever Joy shredded my work on an old chapter from the 2E. That was easy to do when I saw how much she could improve it.

In addition, working with a co-author made the material each of us wrote far better. On my previous books, I just did the best job I could on each draft chapter and sent it out to a dozen or so beta readers for peer review. This time, Joy and I carefully went over each other's work before anyone else saw it. We committed acts of unspeakable editorial brutality on each other's writing—respectfully, of course—all toward a positive objective. We were each other's toughest critic.

As a consequence, our ultimate presentation of each topic was far clearer and more thorough than it would have been otherwise. We learned a lot from each other. The quality of the work shows the benefit: *Software Requirements, 3rd Edition* won an Excellence Award from the Society for Technical Communication.

SHOULD YOU TRY CO-AUTHORING?

Would I work with a co-author on a book again? It would depend entirely on who the co-author was and what value I thought he or she could bring to complement my own knowledge and experience. A few years ago, I met a woman who has written a standard textbook on human sexuality, now in its thirteenth edition. She told me that she and her co-author prepare an updated version every three years. I couldn't imagine having such a long-term partnership, spanning decades and writing the same book over and over again. Admittedly, her topic is more interesting than mine.

If you're considering a co-authoring arrangement, assess your motivations and expectations, as there are a lot of ways for any partnership to go wrong. Perhaps you are seeking someone who can share the workload and time needed to put the book together. Or maybe you lack the in-depth knowledge of some topic you think your book should address. One person who invited me to co-write a book was an expert on the topic, but he frankly acknowledged that I was a much better writer than him. He was looking more for a ghostwriter than a co-author. (That project didn't work out, for several reasons.) If your native language is different from the language in which the book will be published, you might want to partner with someone who can write well in the required language. Partnership also makes sense for marketing and sales purposes, as two (or more) of you can reach out to your own networks of professional colleagues to promote the work.

Even if all the stars align and the prospects look positive, the work ethic of the potential co-author is critical. Can you trust your co-author(s) to hold up their end of the bargain? Can they trust you, as well? Some authors have been unable to complete their project because they depended on a co-author who possessed necessary knowledge, but the co-author dropped the ball. That happened to me once; I cut my losses and bailed out early. Talk to anyone else you know who has worked with your potential co-authors, in any capacity, to learn what you can about their reliability before you approach them.

Unless you already know the other person well, consider finding a way to test their commitment to the objectives and their responsiveness. You could schedule a few phone meetings for initial discussions, and then devise a specific activity related to the book to be completed—in writing—before one of those meetings as a check of how things might go. If your candidate doesn't finish that assignment on time and makes excuses early on, you could wind up writing a lot more of the book than you planned. Your reputation as a trustable author is on the line, so you don't want the manuscript delivery to be seriously delayed because you are dependent on an unreliable collaborator.

It's not unreasonable to reallocate work during the course of the project, as Joy and I did, but too large an adjustment could have financial implications. What if you had agreed to split royalties equally with your co-author, but you ended up doing 90 percent of the work instead of roughly half of it? You don't want to have to renegotiate the royalty split late in the game. Of course, make sure you are fully committed to the project yourself and deliver on your own responsibilities on time. There's a certain symmetry to these partnering relationships.

Fortunately, none of those bad things happened when Joy Beatty and I worked together. After this experience, I now have a far better appreciation of how to partner successfully with a co-author. The lessons I learned working with Joy on *Software Requirements, 3rd Edition* would be extremely valuable on a future such project. In fact, that knowledge would help with *any* type of project partnership. I wouldn't change much about the way we collaborated, as the results show the value of our process and we are still good friends.

That said, I think I will let Joy write the fourth edition herself in another few years. My hammock awaits.

Next Steps

- Who in your profession would you most want to co-author a book with? Why? What do you expect they could bring to the project?
- If you do consider co-authorship, make a list of the topics you would want to discuss with your co-author to lay a solid foundation for an effective and enjoyable partnership.
- Identify the risks you envision for your anticipated co-authorship project. State the possible negative consequences of each such risk. What signs might you look for as an early warning that each risk could be raising its ugly head? Envision ways to mitigate both the likelihood of each risk materializing into a real problem and the possible impact if it does.

BIBLIOGRAPHY

Block, Peter. 2011. *Flawless Consulting: A Guide to Getting Your Expertise Used, 3rd Edition*. San Francisco: Pfeiffer.

Fisher, Roger, William Ury, and Bruce Patton. 2011. *Getting to Yes: Negotiating Agreement Without Giving In*. New York: Penguin Books.

Fishman, Stephen. 2017. *The Copyright Handbook: What Every Writer Needs to Know, 13th Edition*. Berkeley, CA: Nolo.

International Institute of Business Analysis. 2015. *A Guide to the Business Analysis Body of Knowledge (BABOK® Guide), 3rd Edition*. Oakville, ON, Canada: International Institute of Business Analysis.

Meadows, Donella H. 2008. *Thinking in Systems: A Primer*. White River Junction, VT: Chelsea Green Publishing Company.

Project Management Institute. 2015. *Business Analysis for Practitioners: A Practice Guide*. Newtown Square, PA: Project Management Institute.

———. 2017. *A Guide to the Project Management Body of Knowledge (PMBOK® Guide), 6th Edition*. Newtown Square, PA: Project Management Institute.

———. 2018. *The PMI Guide to Business Analysis*. Newtown Square, PA: Project Management Institute.

Smith, Lynette M. 2015. *80 Common Layout Errors to Flag When Proofreading Book Interiors*. Yorba Linda, CA: All My Best.

The Chicago Manual of Style, 17th Edition. 2017. Chicago, IL: University of Chicago Press.

Weinberg, Gerald M. 1985. *The Secrets of Consulting: A Guide to Giving & Getting Advice Successfully*. New York: Dorset House Publishing.

———. 2002. *More Secrets of Consulting: The Consultant's Tool Kit*. New York: Dorset House Publishing.

————. 2006. *Weinberg on Writing: The Fieldstone Method*. New York: Dorset House Publishing.

Weiss, Alan. 1998. *Money Talks: How to Make a Million as a Speaker*. New York: McGraw-Hill.

————. 2016. *Million Dollar Consulting: The Professional's Guide to Growing a Practice, 5th Edition*. New York: McGraw-Hill Education.

Wiegers, Karl, and Joy Beatty. 2013. *Software Requirements, 3rd Edition*. Redmond, WA: Microsoft Press.

INDEX